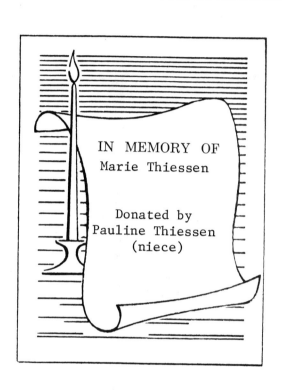

Religion and
the Rise
of the
American City

THE NEW YORK CITY
MISSION MOVEMENT,
1812–1870

Carroll Smith Rosenberg

RELIGION AND
THE RISE
OF THE
AMERICAN CITY

THE NEW YORK CITY
MISSION MOVEMENT,
1812–1870

*Cornell
University
Press* | ITHACA AND LONDON

First published 1971 by Cornell University Press.
Published in the United Kingdom by Cornell University Press Ltd.,
2–4 Brook Street, London W1Y 1AA.

International Standard Book Number 0-8014-0659-5
Library of Congress Catalog Card Number 76-164640

Printed in the United States of America
by Vail-Ballou Press, Inc.

TO LEAH AND

HER FATHER

✦✦✦✦✦✦✦✦✦✦

Contents

++++++++++

Acknowledgments

I have accumulated many debts in the writing of this book. Robert Cross, now President of Swarthmore College, directed my research through its early stages at Columbia University and gave generously of his historical insight. Dr. Robert Handy of Union Theological Seminary advised me at length, and to him I owe the circumvention of several treacherous theological sloughs. Richard Hofstadter, as well, gave generously of his time. To him I owe not only interpretive and stylistic assistance, but the inspiration of a great historian and of a warm, unaffected, and humane person. I and indeed all historians are the less for his early death.

Many librarians and archivists rendered invaluable assistance. Nils Sonne of General Theological Seminary was particularly helpful, as was the library staff of the New-York Historical Society, in particular the now retired Miss Geraldine Beard and Miss E. Marie Becker (whom whole generations of historians will remember). The librarians of Union Theological Seminary and of the Presbyterian Historical Society were also most patient. Without the cooperation and assistance of the directors and archivists of New York's city missions this study would not have been possible. Mrs. Elva Harstedt of the Five Points House of Industry, Mr. Douglass Merrill and his excellent staff at the Woodycrest Youth Service, the directors and staff of the New York Protestant Episcopal City Mission Society and the Community Service Society allowed me access to manuscripts and generously pointed out additional sources.

I should like to thank Karl De Schweintz, who befriended a young historian at the beginning of what was to be a long and at times arduous task.

My thanks also to the *New-York Historical Society Quarterly*, for permission to reprint the chapter on the Five Points House of Industry, and to the Social Science Research Council, whose award of a predoctoral traineeship, 1961–1962, began me on my research.

A word about my husband, Charles Rosenberg. Husbands rarely assist in such traditional duties of the academic spouse as typing and footnote checking, and so, unlike many historians, I cannot thank my spouse for such efforts. But he did aid me at all times with his brilliant insights, his own deep knowledge of nineteenth-century America, his penetrating (and often painful) criticism, and, when writing was most difficult, with his characteristic and valuable gift—wit.

My thanks as well to my parents, who first, now many years ago, inspired me with that perhaps perverse ambition —to become a lady historian.

Finally, to my daughter, to whom this book is dedicated. One always works best when one wishes the approval of those one most esteems. Perhaps then my greatest debt is to Leah, who I trust will in twenty years still be pleased with this dedication.

C. S. R.

Philadelphia, Pennsylvania

*Religion and
the Rise
of the
American City*

THE NEW YORK CITY
MISSION MOVEMENT,
1812–1870

Introduction

By the closing decades of the nineteenth century, thoughtful Americans had become aware of the problems which urbanization, industrialization, and immigration had brought to their country. Few historians today would question this, and indeed the study of urban reform and philanthropy in post-bellum America has become a well-established field.

The roots of concern for the urban poor extend, however, well back into the decades before the Civil War. Societies to feed, clothe, and employ the urban poor antedate the nineteenth century. By the late 1820's and early 1830's the problems of slums and chronic underemployment had markedly increased, as immigrants in large numbers began to settle in America's eastern cities. By the 1840's, responsible, churchgoing Americans had founded a host of industrial training schools, orphanages, free medical dispensaries, and city missions. The public health movement dates, in essence, from this decade, as do the first plans for model tenements. To understand urban poverty and American responses to this need, one must begin one's studies well before the Civil War.

[1]

The term "city missions" may be vague and unfamiliar, suggesting perhaps the memory of skid-row visits and the sound of Salvation Army tambourines; city missions seem perhaps amusingly wistful attempts to convert that dubious object of salvation, the Bowery derelict. Yet the alcoholic drifter was the "client" of a later and highly specialized form of city mission. Throughout the nineteenth century, urban missions played a far more central role, clarifying the understanding and sharpening the conscience of Americans with respect to urban poverty.

What precisely was a city mission? In the nineteenth century, it was an organized effort to disseminate the truths of revealed religion and the hope of eternal salvation among the city's unchurched and deprived. As this book will demonstrate, however, the scope and methods of these pious associations changed significantly during the first half of the century. By mid-century, the city mission had become the principal instrument of the respectable New Yorker for dealing with the social problems of his city.

New York's charitable efforts, as indeed its poverty, antedated the city mission. New Yorkers had studied urban problems and experimented with methods of amelioration for thirty to forty years before they founded their first city mission. Though, as I shall argue, the city mission was a peculiarly "Jacksonian" institution, it must also be seen against this evolving background of philanthropic activity.

Beginning in the late 1780's and 1790's, concerned New Yorkers had founded a number of public and private institutions to care for the dependent and the indigent. The New York Society for the Relief of Poor Widows with Small Children, for example, the Humane Society to aid imprisoned debtors, and the New York Dispensary were all established during these years. Other societies provided education and outdoor relief for the poor.

These organizations were—essentially—a product of the

enlightenment and the social consensus of the eighteenth century. Respectable Americans assumed that society was inevitably graded: that the better sort—the wealthy, the cultured and educated—would automatically be regarded with appropriate deference and be granted social and political power. The poorly educated and politically disfranchised laboring classes, they assumed, would seldom rise socially and economically, but would remain the base upon which the better sort built their world. Essentially, conservative New Yorkers founded their philanthropic organizations to make the depressed condition of the poor more palatable, to feed and clothe the destitute, and to reform the criminal. They expected no change in the structure of society or even in the numbers of the poor to result from their labors. The poor they would have always with them.

One is tempted to think of such late eighteenth- and early nineteenth-century charities, and the period that produced them, in secular terms. But the founders of these organizations—Isabella Graham, Thomas Eddy, John Griscom, John Stanford, among the more prominent—were, Quaker or Calvinist, pious Christians who also saw the world in deeply religious terms. They founded their charities, nursed the sick, and educated the ignorant in part at least because Christ had admonished all true Christians to care for their less fortunate brothers. And when they distributed food and clothing or attended the ill, they attempted to inculcate Christian truths—even to the most hardened unbelievers. Nevertheless, their goals were more purely melioristic, their rhetoric more secular, and their attitude toward the poor more explicitly a product of traditional class assumptions than the charities founded by New York's next generation of urban philanthropists.

Many of the philanthropic organizations founded in America's first decades continued to care for the urban poor far into the nineteenth century. Few, however, continued to attract broad-based support. Despite some overlap in leadership it is not really to these societies that we can trace the far more active and long-lived city missions founded in the late teens, the 1820's, and the 1830's. A factor other than awareness of urban poverty and traditional pietism spurred the formation of the first city missions—this was the evangelical movement often referred to as the Second Great Awakening. In New York, and in many parts of the north and west, this revival of religion was associated with the name and work of Charles Grandison Finney, whose career in the late 1820's and 1830's seemed to crystallize and intensify a growing pietism.

New York's earliest true city missions were a product of this religious enthusiasm. The New York City Tract Society, for example, New York's first city mission, was founded as an auxiliary of the American Tract Society, its goals being to distribute religious tracts and to transmit the word of God to all New Yorkers. The American Female Guardian Society, another early city mission, was founded by a group of Finney's closest disciples in order to convert New York's prostitutes to evangelical Protestantism and to elevate the morality of all Americans—rural as well as urban. Both organizations anticipated the imminent arrival of Christ and the commencement of the millennial age—a culmination made possible, in part, by their missionary efforts. Organically related to this religious enthusiasm was the redefining of social and economic expectations so characteristic of Jacksonian America.

Gradually, however, the general cooling of pietistic enthusiasm within American Protestantism, growing stress within the city missions themselves, and the pressure of an implacable urban environment narrowed the perspective and goals of these mission organizations; by the 1840's and 1850's, they had largely reformulated their objectives. By mid-century, missions worked almost exclusively among the urban poor. The decision to limit their religious labors to one particular class in society soon involved the city missions in an increasingly pragmatic—and in this sense perhaps materialistic —program of social meliorism among the city's slum population.

The city, as well as religion, had clearly helped to shape this evolution. American cities had changed drastically between the presidencies of John Adams and Abraham Lincoln. It was in large part as a direct response to the problems of urban growth, and because their missionary labors had already made them familiar with slum conditions, that mission leaders adopted increasingly melioristic programs. New York's city missions constructed America's first model tenements, operated lodging houses for vagrants, initiated a fresh-air program of summer camps for slum children, and restructured the city's medical charities. They became pioneers in the formation of industrial training schools, job placement, and systematic outdoor relief.

City missions thus inevitably came to serve also as a source of ideas and career options in the gradual professionalization of social work. By the mid-1840's, the New York City Tract Society and the American Female Guardian Society had developed professional staffs of visitors, teachers, and missionaries. In the 1850's the larger city missions and related religious philanthropies began as well to depend upon full-time salaried general managers to direct their day-to-day operations, a function originally performed by the organization's voluntary board of managers. Robert M. Hartley of the New York Association for Improving the Condition of the Poor,

Louis M. Pease of the Five Points House of Industry, Charles Loring Brace of the Children's Aid Society are three prominent examples. These men were quick to formulate programmatic statements outlining the correct goals and procedures for managing urban philanthropies—formulations which then became blueprints for new organizations and new men entering the field. By the 1850's the city missionary had in many ways become a distinct professional role—a blend of the religious missionary, public health expert, and relief administrator—filled by men recognized by society generally as experts in the problems of the city, the slum, and the factory.

The city missionaries were recruited from two quite different groups—clergymen who felt a particular vocation for work among the city poor (or who could not obtain a satisfactory pulpit) and urban middle-class women, partially released by growing affluence from the pressures of domestic labor. The clergymen were for the most part salaried and tended increasingly to see the position of city missionary as a permanent career—or at least as a legitimate stage in the development of a more traditional career. Women served as volunteers but regularly devoted long hours to the supervision of asylums and the investigation of applicants for outdoor relief, or to finding homes for vagrant children. Others became salaried employees of the city missions, teaching in industrial schools, serving as nurses and custodians of homes for vagrant children, visiting the poor in their homes. They broke the ground for later and better-known pioneers in social work—for Josephine Lowell of the Charity Organization Society, and for the scores of young women who followed Jane Addams, Alice Hamilton, and Lillian Wald into the settlement houses of the Progressive movement.

There can be no question of the central role of evangelical pietism in creating New York's ante-bellum city missions;

both formal rhetoric and day-to-day policy make such motivations clear enough. There remains, nevertheless, a central
problem in defining the precise role and function of such
overt religious sentiment. This is the necessity for evaluating
the role played by a desire for social control in the consciously pietistic motivational framework of mission leaders.[1]
Historians examining the objectives and rhetoric of ante-
bellum reformers have frequently concluded that their under-
lying purpose was indeed social control. Institutions such as
the Children's Aid Society, the Association for Improving the
Condition of the Poor, the city missions, Bible and tract societies, historians have argued, sought essentially to muffle
social protest and to preserve traditional social forms and
practices. And one can find much evidence to support such
an interpretation. The well-to-do church-going sponsors of
urban charities during the first half of the nineteenth century
clearly revered private property and found distasteful the
violence, the filth, the latent anarchy of the poor and the immigrant. But to discount the depth of their religious commitment and to interpret this commitment as a rationale for
the imposition of social control is to distort the mid-Victorian
mind.[2] The active intervention into the urban environment

[1] I use the term "social control" to describe policies intended to
insure the continuity of a stable, graded society based upon universal
acceptance of traditional patterns of deference and morality. Another
logical objection that might be raised to my interpretation is that it
does not consider the role of secular institutional alternatives in the
discovery of urban poverty. For a discussion of this problem, see the
Appendix.

[2] No thoughtful American in these decades would have consciously
defended the formal proposition that the possession of wealth implied moral health. Yet the connection between right living and prosperity seemed to them so natural that it was rarely questioned. When
pre-bellum Americans referred to the "respectable" classes in society,
the phrase served as a convenient shorthand to express the convic-

which the city missions, the industrial schools, and the juvenile asylums of the middle period exemplified did not develop solely or even primarily because of the alarming growth of urban problems as such. As I shall hope to demonstrate, such works were the product of an optimistic, truly "Jacksonian" belief in the perfectibility of man. Finney and other leaders of the Second Great Awakening had argued that all mankind could be saved and society itself perfected. This millennial hope they combined with their own sincere religious faith and their belief that eternal life was the greatest gift they could give to the poor. More mundane benefits would be garnered inevitably; it was inconceivable that a consciousness of grace would not bring more responsible citizenship.

These middle-class New Yorkers simply assumed that without religion one could not rise in the world. By converting a poor child, they secured not only his eternal happiness but his worldly success as well. Moral virtues were economic virtues, and men deeply committed to the need for universal salvation could not but assume that a secular by-product of this spiritual change would be universal thriftiness, temperance, prudence —and hence social stability. These reformers desired both to save souls and to control social stress—but saw the two goals as essentially the same. Emphasis by historians on the religious benevolence of the period as a form of social control thus

---

tion that an assured economic position implied a particular and appropriate life-style. Indeed, the term "respectable" was used perhaps most frequently in these decades as a necessary qualifier in describing those elements in the working and lower-middle classes regarded as morally laudable by the wealthy and pious. The *Oxford English Dictionary* precisely defines this particular usage of respectable in regard to persons: "Of good or fair social standing, and having the moral qualities naturally appropriate to this. Hence, in later use, honest and decent in character and conduct, without reference to social position, or in spite of being in humble circumstances."

creates an artificial distinction, a misinterpretation of the Jack-sonian world view, by assuming a nonexistent distinction be-tween the realms of the secular and the spiritual, and thus, by a kind of necessary extension, seeing as conspiratorial design a common vision of the good society.

[2]

The history of New York's missions is divisible into three relatively distinct phases. First, there was a period preceding the actual formation of the city missions when pious New Yorkers attempted to aid the indigent and the disadvantaged of the city in essentially traditional and material ways. Sec-ond, a period of millennial revivalism occurred in the late 1820's and 1830's in which the first true city missions were founded, and in which zealous New Yorkers sought the con-version of all their fellow citizens—the poor among them. A third period in the mission's history followed the Panic of 1837; increasing and finally exclusive emphasis was now placed upon work with one class alone, the poor.[3] In a similar fashion, increasing emphasis came to be placed upon prag-matic meliorism, decreasing emphasis upon the means of con-version, the tracts, visiting, and prayer meetings that had so characterized the work of the missions in their revivalistic period.

Since much of the evolution of the city missions will be seen in terms of responses to growing urban problems, I have chosen to devote the opening chapters to a discussion of New York: its size, something of its class structure, its slums and their inhabitants, and its social dilemmas. But although such

---

[3] Though its role is difficult to define precisely, the 1837–1843 de-pression was crucial in reshaping the mission leaders' attitude toward the city and poverty. It must be remembered that the depression of the 1840's was comparable in severity to that of the 1930's.

social problems were central in the establishment of the city missions, it was the ideas and assumptions of their founders that shaped the specific form assumed by particular missions and that determined their special aims and methods. I have, therefore, followed my description of New York with an analysis of what seemed to be the controlling ideas motivating the mission's founders, especially in the areas of religion and theology, class relations, and what the mid-nineteenth century called "political economy." When did conservative Calvinists espouse the evangelical and increasingly millennial zeal of the Second Great Awakening? When did the "cleanliness" of public health begin to find an unquestioned place beside the traditionally pietistic "godliness" in the values of the middle class?

I have divided this book into two sections corresponding to demonstrably different phases in the growth of the nineteenth-century city. The first section covers the years between the War of 1812 and the mid-1830's, the second from the Panic of 1837 through the Civil War. Each section contains a sketch of the city, of particular city missions, and of the evolving patterns of thought and action adopted by their workers and supporters.

Since the success of such an analysis rests necessarily upon depth and unity of focus, I have limited the study to one city. Institutional change and interaction with other aspects of society are often quiet, and subtle shifts can be detected only by studying a few institutions in detail. Though there were a great many missions or comparable institutions in pre-bellum New York, I have chosen to describe only the largest and most influential and those for which the fullest records are available.

New York was, moreover, America's largest and most important city. The receiving point for so much of the country's immigration, New York was naturally the city with the most dramatic social problems: slums, crime, unemployment, and high mortality rates. Here the problems of other urban communities were intensified and magnified. This, at least, was the opinion of contemporaries. New York, even in the third and fourth decades of the century, had already become a symbol of wealth and elegance, but also of poverty, crime, and sin. Philadelphians, Bostonians, and residents of the newer western cities looked to and copied New York's social experiments— with city missions as with other institutions.

PART ONE

New York, Her Pious
and Her Poor,
1812-1837

CHAPTER I

The City

Today's visitor to New York City frequently arrives by air, descending into the noisy confusion of the city's major airports, or by automobile, on a complex of superhighways which increasingly invades the city's confines and imposes itself upon streets and avenues. Avoiding New York's waterfront of dilapidated warehouses and menacing slums, the mid-twentieth-century visitor settles into a routine of shopping or business at the island's center. Seldom does he even see the city's two great rivers or realize that he is visiting one of the world's greatest ports and North America's finest harbor.

The city deceives its visitors. Over the centuries its merchants, artisans, mechanics, and shopkeepers have moved away from the waterfront and created an inner-city—seemingly divorced from the ships, independent of the harbor. New York today seems a city of advertising agencies, office skyscrapers, and apartment houses.

[1] New York: 1815

The visitor of 150 years ago encountered a far different city, a city of wharves and packet ships, of wood and brick houses crowded into a spit of land which divided New York harbor in two. He saw New York as a provincial port, a city comparable perhaps to Bristol, not London.

The early-nineteen-century traveler came almost always by ship—if from New England, past the rocks and whirlpools of Hell's Gate, if from the south or Europe, along the sand spits of New Jersey and Long Island, past the Narrows, and into the broad basin of the upper bay. In either case, New York appeared to float toward him, surrounded by the masts and rigging of the scores of ships which filled its harbor and crowded its twin rivers. Behind this shield of sails and wood a small red-brick and wooden city crowded toward the shore line, held in and softened by the nearby woodlands and farms of New Jersey and by the heavily forested upper reaches of Manhattan Island.[1]

Commerce was New York's *raison d'être*. Save for its magnificent harbor, the city possessed few natural resources. Its soil, sandy and thin, had never encouraged farming. Nor at first did manufacturing thrive, for the island boasted few streams, and its broad rivers provided no readily harnessable energy.[2] But its rivers connected the city with New York

[1] There are a number of accounts of travel to New York City covering roughly the period 1790–1820. Many of them present the visitor's first view of New York. These include, among others: Frances D'Arusmont [Wright], *Views of Society and Manners in America* (New York, 1821), pp. 7–11; Timothy Dwight, *Travels: in New England and New-York* (4 vols.; New Haven, 1821–1822), III, 449, 481, 483; John Duncan, *Travels through Part of the United States and Canada in 1818 and 1819* (2 vols.; New York, 1823), I, 26–27; John Melish, *Travels in the United States of America in the Years 1806 and 1807, and 1809, 1810, and 1811* (Philadelphia, 1818), pp. 57–61; John Palmer, *Journal of Travels in the United States of North America and in Lower Canada* (London, 1818), pp. 3, 174, 293. Fortunately many descriptive prints of New York dating from these years have been preserved. The most striking are reprinted in I. N. Phelps Stokes, *Iconography of Manhattan Island* (6 vols.; New York, 1915–1928). Cf. III, plates 84, 89, 92, 93, and 117.

[2] Horatio Gates Spafford, *A Gazetteer of the State of New York*

States' vast interior and with the protected shore line of lower New England. Its bay was deep and wide, freed from ice by powerful tides, and sheltered by the Narrows from ocean storms.[3]

If our visitor arrived at New York harbor immediately after the peace of 1815, he witnessed a period of remarkable commercial activity. No sooner had peace been announced, the cold night of February 11, 1815, than the merchantmen lying in drydock were cleaned and refitted, crews reassembled, and new ships scheduled for construction. By the time the news of Waterloo and a secure European peace reached the city in August, New York merchants had already sent a dozen ships to Europe and had re-established their trade with India, China, and the West Indies. New York shipowners and jobbers dominated the coastal trade as well, drawing lower Connecticut and Long Island into the city's commercial orbit. At the same time, the city's merchants increased their role in the marketing of southern cotton and tobacco. As New Yorkers sought to regain prewar commercial prosperity and to open new trade routes, British merchants independently decided to use New York as the principal port for dumping their accumulated stocks of textiles on the American market. By the end of the decade, with construction of the Erie Canal well under way and regular packet

---

(Albany, 1824), p. 85; Edwin Williams, *New-York as It Is in 1833* (New York, 1833), pp. 11, 159, 248–249; Edmund M. Blunt, *The Stranger's Guide to the City of New-York* (London, 1818), pp. 161–162; Benson J. Lossing, *A History of New York City* (2 vols.; New York, 1884), I, 224.

[3] Undoubtedly the best modern discussion of New York harbor and New York's commercial development are still those by Robert Greenhalgh Albion: *The Rise of New York Port* (New York, 1939), and *Square-Riggers on Schedule* (Princeton, 1938).

service established between New York and Liverpool, New York had become the *entrepôt* of North America, the nation's unchallenged commercial center.[4]

To her visitors in the years that followed 1815, New York seemed a picture of unbounded energy and growth. Her warehouses were full, her auction rooms crowded. Tall brick buildings rapidly replaced the clapboard houses of colonial times, and the Battery, Greenwich Street, Park Place, and Hudson Square, where Rensselaers and Schermerhorns lived, reminded many of the fashionable streets of London's West End. Yet everywhere, it seemed to both natives and visitors, noise and confusion reigned. Rubble, bricks, and lumber—of old houses just demolished, for houses being constructed— blocked streets and sidewalks. Dust and dirt filled the air.[5]

Most New Yorkers simply accepted this congestion, indeed pointed to it with pride, as token of their city's growing commercial eminence. But nuisances existed which few New Yorkers could excuse. The carcasses of dead animals, cattle and horse manure, littered the streets, mingled with the ashes and dirt which householders casually threw in front of their homes. Notoriously inefficient private companies collected this filth, assisted by the countless hogs and dogs which sub-

[4] Albion, *Rise of New York*, Chaps. I–IX; David M. Ellis *et al.*, *A Short History of New York State* (Ithaca, New York, 1957), pp. 174–179, 258–259, 269–270. It is interesting as well to look at contemporary discussions of New York commerce, if only to get a sense of the mercantile community's buoyant optimism and its aggressive nationalism. A good example is [John A. Dix], *A Sketch of the Resources of New York City* (New York, 1827).

[5] Dwight, *Travels*, III, 470. Melish, *Travels*, I, 57; W. Winterbotham, *An Historical, Geographical, Commercial, and Philosophical View of the American United States* (2 vols.; London, 1795), II, 314; Duncan, *Travels*, pp. 27–28; Spafford, *Gazetteer*, p. 347; Palmer, *Journal*, pp. 6, 175, 293–334.

sisted on the city's offal and garbage. Sewage disposal and water supply received equally casual treatment.[6]

But these were merely the problems of any town faced with sudden growth and prosperity. As late as 1819, Greenwich Village was a hamlet nearly a mile north of the city limits, a place of rural shelter in times of epidemic. Wooden farm buildings clustered around what would come to be the crowded intersection of Hester and Division Streets, and a stream ran where the city's planners envisioned Canal Street. Until that year, indeed, undrained ponds and swamplands lay north and west of City Hall, cutting off population movement and real-estate development.[7]

The city's government reflected the modest size of this provincial port and the comparative simplicity of its business

[6] European visitors were acid in their criticism of the filth in New York streets. Many were amazed as well at the city's practice of permitting hogs to run loose, rooting in garbage. See, for example, William N. Blaine, *An Excursion through the United States and Canada during the Years 1822-23* (London, 1824), pp. 11-12. For a modern discussion of New York City's water problem, see Nelson Blake, *Water for the Cities* (Syracuse, New York, 1956), Chaps. III, VI, and VIII. For official recognition of the problem, see New York City Common Council, *Minutes of the Common Council, 1784-1831* (19 vols.; New York, 1917), XII, 309-311 (hereinafter referred to as *M.C.C., 1784-1831*). For a thorough discussion of public health in New York, see John Duffy, *A History of Public Health in New York City*, 1625-1866 (New York, 1968).

[7] [A. T. Goodrich], *The Picture of New-York, and Stranger's Guide to the Commercial Metropolis of the United States* (New York, 1828), pp. 155-156, reported that as late as the opening years of the nineteenth century, nearly four hundred acres south of Canal Street had been swampland or "covered with water, which in some places was of very considerable depth." See also Robert Sutcliff, *Travels in Some Parts of North America in the Years 1804, 1805, 1806* (Philadelphia, 1812), p. 212; William A. Duer, *Reminiscences of an Old New Yorker* (New York, 1867), p. 13.

arrangements. Public officials were few, their activities many. The average citizen had frequent contact with them, for the city's government was small and intimate. Far into the century, New York had no police, fire, sanitation, or sewage departments; part-time, underpaid, and poorly supervised "watchmen" provided the bulk of the city's protection against crime, disorder, and fire. Until 1849 the common council divided itself into committees to deal with such basic administrative and social matters as poor relief, sanitation, and public health. A private charitable organization ran the city's common schools. New York possessed one hospital, and her almshouse cared for the insane, imprisoned debtors, and the senile, as well as the city's unemployables and vagrants.[8]

The simplicity of these arrangements, however, implied neither political democracy nor social egalitarianism. Although the daily rounds of even the poorest New Yorkers might bring them frequently in contact with the mayor,

[8] Unfortunately, no modern detailed study of New York's municipal government during the early years of the nineteenth century exists. Useful material can be found in: Sidney I. Pomerantz, *New York, An American City, 1783–1803, A Study of Urban Life* (New York, 1938), Chaps. II, V, VI; Stokes, *Iconography*, III, Chap. V; Lossing, *History of New York City*, I, 235, 238–242. A reading of the city's charters is indispensable; they can be found in James Kent, *The Charter of the City of New York with Notes Thereon, Also a Treatise on the Powers and Duties of the Mayor, Aldermen, and Assistant Aldermen, and the Journal of the City Convention* (New York, 1836). For discussions of the public and charitable institutions of early New York, cf. Abram C. Dayton, *Last Days of Knickerbocker Life in New York* (New York, 1882); William G. Bourne, *A History of the Public School Society of the City of New York* (New York, 1870); David M. Schneider, *A History of Public Welfare in New York State* (2 vols.; Chicago, 1938), esp. Vol. I, Chaps. VIII and IX; Lowell M. Limpus, *History of the New York Fire Department* (New York, 1940); Samuel L. Knapp, *The Life of Thomas Eddy* (New York, 1834); John H. Griscom, *Memoir of John Griscom, LL.D.* (New York, 1859).

recorder, or the clerk of the common council, these august officials always demanded an appropriate deference. Until 1821, the government of New York City was essentially a coalition of urban merchants and lawyers allied with the state's wealthy landowners. All executive officers—the mayor, recorder, and common clerk—were appointed by the highly conservative council of appointment, on the nomination of the governor; only the common council was elected. Property qualifications existed; plural voting was permitted.[9]

Yet while most New Yorkers assumed that political power should rest with men of wealth and learning, by European standards extremes of poverty and wealth were lacking. Access to economic and political powers was not closed to those of humble origin. New York's economy was highly fluid. New business conditions constantly called for new men, and the mercantile elite took on an increasingly *nouveau* appearance, as young men from New England villages and Hudson Valley farms, from England or the continent made their fortunes as shipowners, auctioneers, or jobbers. Even the possession of substantial, means, moreover, rarely carried with it the prerogative of leisure. Merchants supervised their own offices, worked side by side with their clerks, even shopped at dawn for their families' food in the city's markets. Some of New York's wealthier citizens still lived near or above their places of business. Artisans and mechanics, on the other hand, demanded civil treatment from their social and economic supe-

[9] Ellis, *Short History*, p. 121, estimates that in 1790 fewer than one out of every ten male inhabitants of New York City could vote; Stokes concurs. *Iconography*, I, 369. In 1821, the state constitutional convention, despite bitter protests from political conservatives, did much to modify the undemocratic aspects of the corporation government, but it was not until the 1830's and 1840's that the city's government began to assume modern form, with universal manhood suffrage and elective officers.

riors and in general seemed better fed, better educated, more ambitious and optimistic than their European counterparts. Their homes although situated in the city's older sections, impressed foreign visitors with their neatness and apparent comfort. Even servants demanded a dignity and civility of treatment amazing to Europeans.[10]

To contemporary Americans and Europeans alike, New York in 1812, and the years immediately following, seemed to hold out opportunity in abundance for all who would work and save. Though deference was still paid in small as in large things to the wealthy and the well-born, Europeans could discover no American counterpart to the immense and stylized distances which separated occupants of the several social classes in every large European city at the beginning of the nineteenth century.

Still New York had always had her poor. The annual budget of the almshouse and the city's hospital, the existence of orphanages, charity schools, and philanthropic societies indicated that each year many New Yorkers could not provide for themselves. In the early years of the century, however, this did not seem to indicate the existence of a permanently depressed or pauper class or to imply a basic criticism of America's social and economic institutions. Residents and foreign visitors alike agreed that while there was poverty in

[10] Abram Dayton in his reminiscences, *Last Days*, gives a detailed but somewhat romanticized and not always accurate picture of New York's early and informal business ways. See also Frank W. Norcross, *A History of the New York Swamp* (New York, 1901); Albion, *Rise of New York*, Chap. XII; [J. A. Scoville], *The Old Merchants of New York* (5 vols.; New York, 1863–1866), *passim;* William Cobbett, *A Year's Residence in the United States of America* . . . (London, 1818–1819), pp. iii, 342–346, 377–379. Wright, *Views of Society*, pp. 11, 34; Henry Bradshaw Fearon, *Sketches of America* (London, 1819), pp. 4–6.

New York, it was limited largely to two sources, first, to the temporary and general unemployment of winter and other crises—especially depressions and epidemics—and second, to the permanent poverty of the dependent and infirm, the widow and orphan, the crippled and aged. In either case, it was the duty of society and of the active Christian to succor such unfortunates.[11]

The cold and the storms of winter were a constant and understandable cause of poverty in the city; eighteenth- and nineteenth-century seaports were exposed to their vicissitudes in a way impossible for the mid-twentieth-century city dweller to appreciate. Few ships, except the aristocratic packets, would dare the North Atlantic between November and March, and throughout these months the city's merchantmen, their crews discharged, lined the Hudson and East River piers. Stevedores and cartmen could now find little employment. The East River shipyards, which employed thousands during the busy summer months, cut their working force to a handful of men. Country shopkeepers and jobbers returned to their homes to await the spring and new business trips to the city. Retail stores and auctioneers trimmed their staffs. Scores of construc-

[11] In 1801, Edward Livingston, Republican mayor of New York, asserted that the city's poor could be categorized into four main groupings: newly arrived immigrants, sick and unemployed workers, widows and orphans incapable of labor, and discharged convicts. There was no reason why these groups should become a permanent pauper class, Livingston asserted; they could easily be transformed into productive members of society. Charles H. Hunt, *Life of Edward Livingston* (New York, 1864), pp. 93–97; Pomerantz, *New York*, p. 337; Cadwallader D. Colden to Charles G. Haines, New York City, December 1, 1819, reprinted by the Society for the Prevention of Pauperism in the City of New York, *Second Annual Report* (New York, 1820), p. 66. See also John Pintard, *Letters from John Pintard to His Daughter, Eliza Noel Pintard Davidson, 1816–1833*, ed. by Dorothy C. Barck (4 vols.; New York, 1940), I, 17; Knapp, *Thomas Eddy, passim*; John H. Griscom, *Memoir of John Griscom, passim*.

tion workers joined the unemployed, for little building was possible until spring. Even road construction, leveling, and paving, resorted to by the municipal government in an effort to make work for the jobless, came to a halt during the depth of the winter.[12]

Winter brought want every year. But certain years saw even greater need. Living in a city dependent upon foreign trade, New York's workers were inevitably the victims of cyclical fluctuations within international commerce. During the years preceding and following the War of 1812, New York was particularly vulnerable to financial panics and depressions. In 1808, Jefferson's embargo plunged the city into a depression which lasted until the peace of 1815, a depression marked by intense suffering among the laboring classes. And peace did not bring immediate prosperity for all. Commercial and financial conditions remained unstable for some time after 1815; 1817 and 1819 were years of particular hardship for the city's workers.[13]

Almost as frequent as financial panics were the epidemics and threats of epidemic which emptied the city and curtailed its business. Flight was the normal response to such threats. Insurance companies, banks, and merchants moved their offices to the healthier air of Greenwich Village. Houses were boarded up; markets closed; and the ferries ceased to run. Yet only those with some resources could flee. Day laborers, artisans, widows, the sick, and the free blacks remained, often

[12] Pintard, *Letters*, I, 93, III, 64; Thomas N. Stanford, *Concise Description of the City of New York* (New York, 1814), p. 49; New York *Evening Post*, February 18, 1817, and January 25, 1821; Philip Hone, *The Diary of Philip Hone, 1828–1851*, ed. by Bayard Tuckerman (2 vols.; New York, 1889), I, 35.

[13] *M.C.C., 1783-1831*, IV, 702–703, 713–715, 728–729, 751–752, VIII, 765–769; New York *Evening Post*, February and March, 1817, *passim;* Pintard, *Letters*, I, 201.

without food, certainly without work. And such epidemics were frequent visitors in these early years. Yellow fever struck seven times between 1793 and 1822. Cholera took thousands of lives in 1832, returning again in 1833 and 1834. "Fevers" came each summer.[14]

The inclemency of winter, the fluctuations of business, the misfortunes of disease were constantly recurring, unrelated seemingly to individual capabilities. Each demanded the exertions of the charitable. To deal with seasonal or sporadic unemployment, with financial panics and epidemics, the charitable resorted to temporary methods of feeding and employing the poor: soup kitchens, fuel societies, public works. They held public meetings to raise emergency funds, and established *ad hoc* committees of merchants to canvass the several wards, seeking out the destitute and raising funds from their well-to-do neighbors.[15]

Equally fortuitous, yet more lasting and personal, was the poverty of widows, the orphaned, or the chronically ill. (And

[14] William Vaux, *Memorable Days in America* (London, 1823), pp. 155–156; Blaine, *Excursion*, pp. 11–12; New York *Evening Post*, September 6, 7, and 18, 1819, and July 23, 1832; Pintard, *Letters*, I, 220–224, 227–228, II, 83, IV, 66, 69, 72–78; John H. Griscom, *A History, Chronological and Circumstantial, of the Visitations of Yellow Fever at New York* (New York, 1858). For two modern discussions of the impact of an epidemic on a city, see John Powell, *Bring Out Your Dead. The Great Plague of Yellow Fever in Philadelphia in 1793* (Philadelphia, 1949), and Charles Rosenberg, *The Cholera Years* (Chicago, 1962).

[15] Stanford, *Concise Description*, p. 49; Pintard, *Letters*, I, 93, II, 330, III, 216, IV, 82, 91; Hone, *Diary* (ed., Tuckerman), I, 35; New York *Evening Post*, January 25 and 27, 1821; M.C.C., *1784-1831*, XI, 452; letter, Isabella Graham, New York, to Dr. H. M., Rothsay, Bute, Scotland, November 11, 1799, in Isabella Graham, *Power of Faith: Exemplified in the Life and Writings of the Late Mrs. Isabella Graham of New York*, ed. by Divie Bethune (New York, 1816), pp. 382–383, also p. 53.

in nineteeenth-century America, marked as it was by a high morality rate and primitive medical knowledge, the sick, the widow, and the orphan were familiar and sympathy-provoking members of society.) For the needs of such poor, New Yorkers evolved more permanent institutional solutions, establishing hospitals, charity schools, and orphan asylums. As early as 1797, for example, a group of wealthy matrons led by Isabella Graham, herself once a poor widow, organized the Society for the Relief of Poor Widows with Small Children. Through this organization, these women sought jobs for respectable yet impecunious women, provided them with food, fuel, and clothing, taught improving lessons in cleanliness, frugality, and household management. The benevolent ladies also distributed Bibles and religious tracts to the widows, questioned them as to their religious state and hoped that, though destitute, these unfortunates might still be among the saved and their children achieve greater economic security. Though this connection between external salvation and temporal improvement was not strictly theological, it was obviously appealing.[16] Such missionary and religious work was not the primary objective of the society. The ladies, being themselves sincerely devout, and sympathizing with the poor, were unable to create a program of temporal aid which would not be spiritual as well.

The experience of these pious matrons in caring for indi-

[16] New York Society for the Relief of Poor Widows with Small Children (hereinafter referred to as N.Y.S.R.P.W.S.C.), *Constitution* [*with Act of Incorporation*] (New York, 1800); N.Y.S.R.P.W.S.C., *An Act to Incorporate the Society for the Relief of Poor Widows with Small Children, Passed April 2, 1802* (New York, 1802); and *The By-laws and Regulations* (New York, 1802). See also Divie Bethune, "Life of Mrs. Isabella Graham," in Graham, *Power of Faith*, pp. 9-72, and Stanford, "Mrs. Sarah Hoffman," in *Heavenly Sisters*, ed. by T. Sharp (Philadelphia, 1822), for contemporary accounts of the Society.

gent women and children led a number of them to found and support other, similar organizations. Mrs. Isabella Graham, for example, and her daughter Joanna, the wife of the merchant and philanthropist, Divie Bethune, led a number of New York women in organizing the New York Orphan Asylum, and later in establishing the infant's and girl's departments of the free school system. Others worked through their churches and denominations to establish the local charity schools which soon came to dot the city. Inspired by the efforts of Mrs. Graham, New Yorkers organized the Free School Society, the city's first public school system, in 1806. Many, viewing free blacks in the same light as widows and orphans, helped establish African churches and charity schools for New York's freedmen. The sick, too, were considered. New Yorkers could boast of some of America's most advanced institutions for the treatment of the insane and the physically handicapped: the New York Dispensary, the New York Hospital, the Bloomingdale Asylum for the Insane, the New York Institution for the Instruction of the Deaf and Dumb. The Humane Society fed and clothed imprisoned debtors.[17]

But perhaps the most characteristic of New York's private efforts to aid the poor in the nineteenth century's opening years was the Society for the Prevention of Pauperism in the City of New York. Organized in 1814 by leaders of New York's mercantile and philanthropic community, by Thomas Eddy, Divie Bethune, John Pintard, and John Griscom, the Society hoped after a "systematic" and "scientific" study of New York's economy and the character of the poor to pro-

[17] Stanford, "Mrs. Sarah Hoffman"; Bethune, "Life," *passim;* Bourne, *Public School Society;* Charles C. Andrews, *The History of the New-York African Free Schools* (New York, 1830); William Ludlum, *Dispensaries. Their Origin, Progress and Efficiency* (New York, 1876); J. F. Richmond, *New York and Its Institutions, 1609–1872* (New York, 1872).

pose solutions to much of the poverty they found in their city. Society members undertook to study such presumed causes of poverty, as gambling, intemperance, winter unemployment, and the debtor's prison. They established two banks for savings (an important charitable innovation in the years before 1820), encouraged education and libraries for the working classes, attempted to suppress lotteries and other forms of gambling, and advocated sweeping reforms in the city's prisons and almshouses.[18]

From reading the annual reports of such early American philanthropies, the letters of their principal supporters, even fictional accounts of poverty and the poor, a significant aspect of American social thought during the opening years of the nineteenth century becomes evident. Poverty and social gradations neither surprised nor threatened these respectable New Yorkers. In 1812, in 1815, they simply assumed a clearly structured society inhabited by wealthy and respectable Christians, by the self-sufficient middle orders, and by the needy poor. (And of course, by a numerically small pauper and criminal class, essentially outside society.) These Americans even accepted, in some instances appeared to approve, street begging, that anathema of later urban philanthropists. If the beggar seemed truly needy, was sober, "possessed an openness of countenance which spoke the veracity of [his] assertions," the passerby was well justified in giving alms. "I have often

[18] New York Society for the Prevention of Pauperism (hereinafter referred to as N.Y.S.P.P.), *Second Annual Report for the Year 1819–1820* (New York, 1820); N.Y.S.P.P., *Third Annual Report for the Year 1820–1821* (New York, 1821); *Fourth Annual Report for the Year 1821–1822* (New York, 1822). See also discussions of the Society in B. K. Peirce, *A Half Century with Juvenile Delinquents; or, the New York House of Refuge and Its Times* (New York, 1869), esp. Chap. II; Griscom, *Memoir*, esp. Chap. V; Pintard, *Letters, passim*.

been pleased," one author wrote, "to see a maimed and disabled soldier, begging through our streets, when the liberal hand of charity has been opened to assist him; a smile of approbation, or something (I know not what) has flashed in my face, to see a very miser relent at his piteous tale, and with a half formed resolution, contribute his farthing." [19] Begging indicated no moral blot on the pauper's character—merely his lower socioeconomic status.

The giving of alms in the opening years of the nineteenth century was both a social and a religious obligation. There was no thought that society might ever be so rearranged that charity would become unnecessary. Nor did this generation of urban Americans expect that their charity could eliminate poverty or social classes. Most would have questioned the propriety, indeed the possibility, of a classless society. And so the tone of their writings, while more class conscious than the writings of the next generation of philanthropists, retains a relatively detached and pragmatic quality—one which their Jacksonian successors so characteristically lacked. Charitable New Yorkers in the first two decades of the nineteenth century supplied immediate needs when hunger and harsh desperation demanded it; they fed the unemployed, aided the widowed and orphaned, cared for the sick and the insane. Such activities were a part of one's spiritual life as well as a response to external human needs.

As poverty, a commitment to political egalitarianism, and millennial anticipation increased during the 1820's and 1830's, however, the expectations and desires, the very quality and tone of philanthropy were to change drastically. And with these changes came basic innovations in the form and methods of urban charity.

[19] *Juvenile Port-Folio and Literary Miscellany*, I, No. 1 (October 17, 1812), 2.

[2] New York: 1830

In 1815, New York, despite the optimism which pervaded her business community, was only a provincial town on the perimeter of a still remote continent. By 1835 she had attained the size, wealth, and commercial importance of a major world port.

In these twenty years New York had tripled in size, pushing far north of the fields and farmlands which marked her outer limits during the War of 1812. The Collect had been filled, Lispenard's Meadows drained and converted into commercial and residential districts.[20] Canal Street, no longer a meeting place for the city's amateur fishermen, was one of New York's more fashionable shopping districts. Even suburban Greenwich Village had been overtaken and absorbed by the ever-growing city. Six-story buildings began to line the city's streets. Commerce and business demanded ever more land, and real-estate values, accordingly, spiraled. New Yorkers, taking advantage of these high prices, deserted longtime residences and moved north. In 1824 alone, 1,624 new buildings were constructed. By 1831, Philip Hone could comment with a combination of civic pride and practiced resignation:

The city is now undergoing its usual metamorphosis; many stores and houses are getting pulled down, and others altered, to make every inch of ground productive to its utmost extent. Pearl Street and Broadway in particular are rendered almost impassable by the quantity of rubbish with which they are obstructed, and by the dust which is blown about by a keen northwest wind.[21]

[20] M.C.C., 1784-1831, X, 523-524, XI, 129.
[21] Hone, Diary (ed., Tuckerman), I, 41, 350. New York's newspapers regularly carried articles commenting rapturously on the city's growth. Cf. New York Commercial Advertiser, August 8, 1818; New York Evening Post, January 8, 1824, and February 10, 1825; New York Mirror, January 20, 1836, and November 30, 1833.

With growth came geographic segregation and specialization. Centers of population, and residential and commercial areas had shifted drastically; no longer did the city's commercial leaders live above their places of business, or mechanics, merchants, and clerks reside near each other. In a city as large and important as New York had become by the 1830's such simplicity was no longer possible. New Yorkers could no longer conveniently walk the length and breadth of their town. By 1832 omnibuses were common. A railroad ran from Prince Street to 14th Street. The common council gradually adopted gas lighting for the city's streets, and by 1833 over twenty-six miles of piping had been laid. Country women no longer served laborer and merchant alike from their crude stalls in the city's markets. Fine meats and vegetables were carried to the kitchen doors of the wealthy, while the poor shopped for their necessities in groceries and grog shops located in the dark cellars of newly developing tenements.[22]

Living conditions tended to deteriorate with the rise of real-estate prices and consequent increases in tenement rentals. Visitors began routinely to comment on New York's high rents. A suitable house for a "respectable tradesman or shopkeeper," one visiting Englishman commented in the early 1820's, brought from £100 to £120 a year. A mechanic, if fortunate enough to manage £15 a year for rent, could no longer secure a modest house on a side street for his family but had to settle into a bare room or two in one of the city's newly rising tenements. Day laborers, seamstresses, domestics, and the unemployed did not fare as well. Several such families might share a single room; others roamed the streets by day,

---

[22] New York *Evening Post*, January 8, 1824; Dayton, *Last Days*, pp. 35–36, 78, 83–84, 140–141; [Goodrich], *Picture of New-York*, p. 460; Stanford, *Concise Description*, pp. 7–10, 16–17. Dayton, *Last Days*, pp. 125–126; M.C.C., *1784-1831*, IX, 718–719.

paying a few pennies a night for a bed in a crowded basement room, where the dispossessed of all ages and both sexes crowded together in fitful sleep.[23]

Perhaps the principal human problem created by the city's growth was a new and greatly changed population. Many prospective New Yorkers came from the farms and villages of New England and New York State. With the mid-1820's, New York became, as well, the destination of an ever-growing number of European immigrants. Between 1820 and 1830, 92,884 immigrants landed at the port of New York; the following decade, over 400,000. Some, coming from the middle echelons of European commercial houses, had some small resources to fall back upon. But others did not, for the poor of Europe had discovered America's great port of entry. And for every Tappan or Bethune, New York made room for a thousand jobless, poorly educated Irishmen, Germans, or Englishmen. Many of these, driven by poverty or enticed by unrealistic expectations, came without funds or with numbers of dependents. Others, defrauded in passage, weakened by the long voyage, arrived in the city sick, destitute, without friends or the prospect of employment.[24] Unable in many

[23] Isaac Holmes, *An Account of the United States of America* (London, [1823]), pp. 268–269; New York *Evening Post*, February 10, 1825; Robert Ernst, *Immigrant Life in New York City, 1825–1863* (New York, 1949), Chap. V.

[24] Demographers have recently begun to question the true rate of population growth in the eastern seaboard cities, but New York's growth was clearly far more rapid than that of the rival ports. One factor in this growth was immigration. Everett S. Lee and Michael Lalli, "Population," in *The Growth of Seaboard Cities, 1790–1825*, ed. by David T. Gilchrist (Charlottesville, Va., 1967), pp. 25–37. Actual statistics for the number of immigrants who remained in New York City are difficult to obtain. Kate Claghorn, "The Foreign Immigrant in New York City," *United States Industrial Commission Reports* (Washington, D.C., 1901), XV, 464, deduces from available statistics that the immigrant population of New York City was large and in-

cases to push further inland, these penniless new arrivals settled into the city, greatly altering its physical appearance, its social and class relationships, its economy—and its philanthropic activities.

Able to afford only the cheapest accomodations and needing to live near their jobs, these newcomers had no choice but to seek homes in the most crowded and unhealthy sections of the city. At first such new Americans rented rooms in the cheap boardinghouses which in the 1820's had sprung up along the Hudson River piers. Once familiar with the city, they sought out compatriots and filtered into the city's developing slum neighborhoods. Few immigrant families could afford to rent more than one or at most two rooms; ten or twelve families would crowd into what had once been a private dwelling, filling its basement and attic, overburdening primitive sanitary facilities. These were the sometime homes of the well-to-do, situated near the Battery, along the lower

creased steadily from the early 1820's on. Between 1820 and 1830, 92,884 immigrants arrived at the Port of New York, and the city's population increased by 78,883 during this decade. During the next decade, 407,716 immigrants landed at the Port of New York, and the city's population increased by 110,121. Between 1820 and 1830, 81,827 immigrants arrived in New York City from Great Britain and Ireland, 7,729 from Germany. Between 1831 and 1840, 283,191 arrived from Great Britain and Ireland, 152,454 from Germany. These statistics but confirm the contemporary impression. Holmes, *Account*, pp. 370–371. See also N.Y.S.P.P., *Second Annual Report, 1819–1820*, pp. 18–25; "Report of the Committee on the Almshouse and the Penitentiary to the Common Council," *M.C.C., 1784–1831*, XIII, 89–95. To understand the problem in adjustment which New York's government, economy, and philanthropic institutions faced, one should compare these figures for the mid-1820's with those a decade later: during the year ending September 30, 1824, 4,889 persons arrived at New York Port; for the year ending December 31, 1835, 32,715 passengers entered the port. *Arrivals of Alien Passengers and Immigrants*, table 7, p. 64, cited in Stokes, *Iconography*, V, 1642, 1736.

west side, or in the narrow streets east of Broadway. Here the poor hoped to find jobs as stevedores, day laborers, or cartmen. But as the numbers of immigrants steadily increased, investors and real-estate speculators began to build clapboard tenements specifically to house numbers of immigrant families. Located in newer sections of the city, on cheap land bordering the waterfront, these tenements rapidly degenerated into immigrant slums.[25]

By the 1830's New York encompassed at least three major areas of substandard, multifamily dwellings: Corlear's Hook, the black ghetto around Bancker Street, and the Five Points. All shared characteristics typical of the slum: an unhealthy physical setting, overcrowding, poor sanitation, high crime and mortality rates. During the yellow-fever epidemic of 1820, for example, the first cases appeared among the Bancker Street blacks, and of 299 fever deaths that year, 138 were among blacks. The even more serious cholera epidemic of 1832 and 1849 first broke out among the Irish immigrant population in the Five Points vicinity, while the annual city health inspector's reports and other public health investigations all pointed to the unhealthy condition of such slums.[26]

[25] Ernst, *Immigrant,* Chaps. IV and V; New York *Mirror,* February 2, 1828; Garrett Forbes, "The City Inspector's Report for the Year, 1834," cited, Claghorn, "Foreign Immigrant," p. 452; Dwight, *Travels,* III, 450; Griscom, *Sanitary Condition,* p. 15.

[26] New York City Board of Health, *A Statement of Facts Relative to the Late Fever which Appeared in Bancker-Street and its Vicinity* (New York, 1821); John H. Griscom, *History, Chronological and and Circumstantial.* For recent discussions, cf. Lloyd G. Stevenson, "Putting Disease on the Map: the Early Use of Spot Maps in the Study of Yellow Fever," *Journal of the History of Medicine and Allied Sciences,* XX (1965), 226–261; John Duffy, "An Account of the Epidemic Fevers that Prevailed in the City of New York from 1791–1822,"*New-York Historical Society Quarterly,* L (October, 1966), 333–364. See also references in Rosenberg, *Cholera Years,*

The Five Points was certainly the best known of these shabby areas. Located at the center of the city, a few blocks north of City Hall, within sight of the elegant shops of Broadway, the Five Points was to remain an eyesore, a reservoir of disease, crime, and prostitution far into the century.[27] As such it came to symbolize for contemporaries all the dangers inherent in the growth of urban poverty. The Five Points was located on the site of the Fresh Water Pond, in the early years of the nineteenth century a bucolic resort for fishing and strolling. With the end of the War of 1812 and the city's expansion northward, blacks and immigrants built shanties around the pond and tanners polluted its water with the carcasses of dead animals. By 1821 the area had become a public nuisance, and the corporation ordered the pond filled and the adjacent hills leveled. This made-land, however, remained damp and, it was feared, pestilential. Despite the pleas of Robert Fulton and Eli Whitney for intelligent "urban planning" in the area, the well-to-do shunned it. By the mid-thirties it had become known as the "Five Points," fully developed as the American paradigm of urban crime and poverty.[28]

Prosperous New Yorkers avoided the Five Points and the city's other pockets of poverty and filth. No business offices

---

Part I. These areas were, significantly, the neighborhoods where New York's first city missionaries labored.

[27] The Five Points derived its name from the peculiar intersection of five streets to form a star-shaped square (ironically known as Paradise Square) at its center. These streets were: Mulberry, Orange (now Baxter), Anthony (now Worth), Cross (now Park) and Little Water (no longer in existence).

[28] For plans for the development of the area, see *M.C.C., 1784-1831*, VII, 168–169, and also VIII, 257–258. For contemporary descriptions of the Five Points, see New York *Mirror*, January 1, 1831, May 18, 1833; New York *Evening Post*, March 19, 1829, June 22, 23, 24, 25, 1835; Stokes, *Iconography*, III, 522.

or fashionable shops beckoned in these enclaves; no friends' homes or fashionable churches were to be found in such locales. Thus, these slums developed apart from the mainsteam of New York life, constantly fed by immigration and the addition of free blacks and unskilled native laborers. During the 1830's, New Yorkers awoke to find sections of their city through which no respectable person could walk and to realize that some among their fellow citizens seemed no different from the denizens of England's worst almshouses and prisons.

Indeed, it took rioting, disease, and epidemics to arouse prosperous and articulate New Yorkers to conditions in their city. Cholera, as we have noticed for instance, struck first among the poor, and New Yorkers learned suddenly and with horror of houses such as that at 31 Renwick Street, which consisted of a basement and two rooms, the home of twenty men, women, and children. "In the yard of this place," the *Commercial Advertiser* reported, "the principal occupant keeps forty to fifty hogs, four cows, and two horses. The place is so filthy that the first physician called . . . refused to enter the house." Equally notorious was a pie-shaped building between Christopher and Grove streets, in the suburban ninth ward. This structure, 120 feet in length, was thirty-nine feet wide at one end and only four feet wide at the other. It housed forty-one families who shared one public privy in the crowded and filthy front yard.[29]

---

[29] New York City, Board of Aldermen, *Documents*, II (New York, 1836), 145–152; New York *Commercial Advertiser*, July 25, 1832; William Caruthers, *A Kentuckian in New York, Or, The Adventures of Three Southrons by a Virginian* (2 vols.; New York, 1834), I, 54. The effectiveness of epidemics and disease in awakening New Yorkers to the social problems of their city can be seen in the comment of one New York matron at the height of the 1832 cholera epidemic. "No one notices the poor ordinarily. Those who frequently are to be found lying in the streets, are now picked up and taken to the

Some New Yorkers, having read accounts of the Five Points, of Renwick and Christopher streets, could no longer think of poverty in traditional terms, of the poor being an inherently limited group composed of widows, orphans, the infirm, the temporarily unemployed, and a scattering of unworthy laggards or drunkards. This poverty had always been assumed; it posed no awkward questions in regard to the nature of American society—or to the social responsibility of its individual members. But the new poor of the Five Points and similar areas were an alien, a threatening force. Existing outside respectable society, they seemed to embody the antitheses of all those virtues cherished by that society—Protestantism, cleanliness, moderation, sobriety, hard work, and self-denial. They nullified, by their sheer numbers and desperate need, traditional methods of charitable support and, indeed, posed in the minds of many concerned New Yorkers a real threat to social order and tranquility.

Thoughtful New Yorkers began naturally to seek new explanations for these changed conditions. Two factors seemed to provide the basis for a convenient and seemingly realistic framework within which poverty could be understood and, hopefully, dealt with. Intemperance and immigration were the two causes which seemed to contemporaries the essential roots of New York's poverty. Both removed the responsibility for the existence of poverty from American society, in the one case placing it upon individual vice, in the other, upon the inequities and oppression of European gov-

---

hospitals—only on occasions such as this is the true extent of the misery of the City known." Mrs. P. Roosevelt to S. R. Johnson, July 13, 1832, Roosevelt Papers, General Theological Seminary, New York City. In addition to the well-known Astor Place Riots, violence between immigrants and native born workers, and between fire company volunteers, were frequent occurrences in the city's slums.

ernments. Both implied no questioning of fundamental social relationships. Both explanations coalesced—and thus reinforced each other—in the emotion-laden image of the drunken Irish or German pauper.

Such an attitude could be seen in John Pintard's disdainful reflections upon "the multitude of newcomers amongst whom are a large portion of the lower offscourings of Europe, who live in low damp dwellings crowded to excess . . . improvident, careless, and filthy." [30] Mark Beaufoy, a visitor to the city, in 1827, remarked that "the lowest stations of the hardworking classes are generally filled by Irishmen, who are as much vilified here, whether justly or not I cannot tell, as in England or Scotland." "They have brought the cholera this year," Philip Hone warned dourly in the summer of 1832, "and they will always bring wretchedness and want." And as Samuel F. B. Morse and others warned, these new immigrants, predominantly Roman Catholic as well as poor, posed an increasing danger to the nation's political institutions. "How is it possible," Morse wrote, "that foreign turbulence imported by ship-loads, that the ignorance in hundreds of thousands of human priest-controlled machines, should suddenly be thrown into our society, and not produce here turbulence and excess? Can one throw mud into pure water and not disturb its clearness? [31]

While most New Yorkers maintained their faith in immi-

[30] Pintard, *Letters*, I, 217.

[31] Mark Beaufoy, *Tour Through Parts of the United States and Canada* (London, 1828), pp. 15–16; Philip Hone, *Diary*, September 20, 1832, Manuscript Division, New York Historical Society; An American [S. F. B. Morse], *Imminent Dangers to the Free Institutions of the United States through Immigration, and the Present State of the Naturalization Laws. A Series of Numbers Originally Published in the New York Journal of Commerce* (New York, 1835), p. iv.

gration as adding to the country's work force and greatly enriching America, by the late 1830's they had come increasingly to urge new arrivals to move on immediately to the vast opportunities awaiting them in rural America. Only the exceptional immigrant, common wisdom had come to agree, could prosper in an urban environment. The majority would sink into pauperism and crime.

Immigration had brought European poverty to America. Intemperance created it here. Or so at least it seemed to many Americans. The first half of the nineteenth century was a period of evangelical fervor and, in the terminology of the day, active benevolence. The most universal of the era's aggressively philanthropic reforms was the crusade against alcohol. It was against this background of widespread temperance agitation that New Yorkers attempted to ascertain the cause of poverty. Clearly the poor were intemperate; and the conclusion that alcohol caused their poverty seemed all too obvious. Certainly it was a factor understandable and appealing to a morally committed generation, a generation perhaps overly fond of emotional and moralistic resolutions to social dilemmas. As early as 1817, a meeting of citizens in New York "to inquire into the situation of the poor and the cause of mendicity" resolved that intemperance among workers was a major cause of poverty in the city. Two years later, the Society for the Prevention of Pauperism concurred, calling intemperance "the most productive source of human wretchedness in all its complicated forms." The Society that year began a drive to prohibit groceries from selling liquor, for it felt that most workers were trapped into the drinking habit while buying groceries in stores which sold both liquor and food. In 1819 Mayor Cadwallader Colden attempted to reduce drastically the number of liquor licenses issued by the city government. John Pintard urged that the city place a prohibitive tax on whiskey and encourage laborers to turn instead to malt beverages. By the 1830's, most philanthropic groups were urging temperance upon workers, and an organization such as the New York City Tract Society was actively distributing temperance tracts to the city's poor.[32]

Not all New Yorkers, however, were willing to attribute the city's new poverty exclusively to immigration and intemperance. Some, even among those of the well-to-do who found personal contacts with the poor distasteful, insisted that economic organization played an important role in the creation of poverty and urged fellow citizens to help the poor and sympathize with them. These men pointed to low wages, to unhealthy and degraded living conditions as causes of vice, immorality, and drunkenness. In 1829, for example, economist and publisher Mathew Carey issued his *Plea for the Poor*. Although Carey's book was written about working conditions in Philadelphia, it was widely read and commented on by New York's newspapers and philanthropists. Carey had made a study of the wages paid urban workers, especially women. He reported that an industrious seamstress in any northern city could simply not support herself on prevailing piece-work scales. Prostitution and crime were inevitable by-products of such inadequate wages.[33]

[32] *M.C.C.*, *1784-1831*, IX, 38–39; N.Y.S.P.P., *Fourth Annual Report*, p. 6; Letter, Cadwallader D. Colden to Charles G. Haines, Manager, N.Y.S.P.P., December 1, 1819, quoted, N.Y.S.P.P., *Second Annual Report*; Duncan, *Travels*, II, 322–323. In March, 1829, the New York City Tract Society (hereinafter referred to as N.Y.C.T.S.) distributed 30,000 copies of *Kittredge's Address* and the following year 30,000 copies of *Dickenson's Appeal to American Youth*, both temperance pamphlets; New York City Temperance Society, *First Annual Report* (New York, 1830), pp. 7–8.

[33] Mathew Carey, *A Plea for the Poor. An Enquiry How Far the Charges Against Them of Improvidence, Idleness and Dissipation Are Founded in Truth. By a Citizen of Philadelphia* (Philadelphia, 1831).

Ezra Stiles Ely, one of New York's first city missionaries, vigorously supported Carey's position. In the years between 1811 and 1813, when Ely served as chaplain to New York City's almshouse, he had protested against the life of poverty which low wages forced upon widows and spinsters. Women were paid only twelve cents for making "common shirts" or pantaloons, yet, he complained, they had to pay twenty-five dollar a year for the rent of one tiny slum room. Southern slaves, he wrote bitterly, fared better than northern seamstresses.[34]

And, of course, even the strongest belief in the evils of immigration, in the temptations of alcohol, did not preclude a simultaneous belief in the significance of economic abuse and exploitation as a collateral cause of poverty. Ely, Carey, and the readers to whom they addressed their protests saw the solution to urban misery in the moral awakening of the respectable and religious.

One question remains, however: Was there a secular—even radical—alternative to the religious charity and social perspective of the well-to-do? There were of course Americans in the 1820's and 1830's who rejected religious philanthropy as a solution to the new economic and social dilemmas. Yet a careful reading of such political radicals of the 1820's and 1830's as Robert Dale Owen and Fanny Wright, editors of the *Free Enquirer*, or of George Evans, editor of the *Workingman's Advocate*, fails to indicate that this group of social dissidents offered any realistic secular alternative to the charitable efforts of the Christian activist—or even that they had much interest in or knowledge about the new urban poor. They sought to

[34] Ezra Stiles Ely, *Visits of Mercy; or, The journals of the Rev. Ezra Stiles Ely, D.D., written while he was stated preacher to the hospital and alms-house, in the city of New York* (Philadelphia, 1829).

remove social inequalities through educational reform, through a war against banks, by thwarting a feared theocratic overthrow of American republicanism. Only occasionally did they discuss the pressing needs of the urban poor—and then ironically they often derived their information from the published reports and accounts of the despised city missionary.[35] In the discovery of urban poverty and the formation of patterns of philanthropic response there was seemingly no truly secular road.

It was against this social and intellectual background that New York's first three city missions, the New York City Tract Society, the American Female Guardian Society, and the New York Protestant Episcopal City Mission Society were established. The city missions were not simply relief or welfare organizations; they were religious societies with religious aims. Why were they founded? Why did New Yorkers turn to religious organizations to distribute outdoor relief, employ the unemployed, educate and clothe neglected children? To begin to understand the city missions we must look beyond the physical city and its social needs, to other influences upon the minds of respectable New Yorkers. And in the first third of the nineteenth century, perhaps the single most important influence upon pious and philanthropic Americans was the religious and social phenomenon known as the Second Great Awakening. This was a deeply pietistic religious awakening which swept through America from the early 1790's

---

[35] This conclusion is based upon a careful reading of complete runs of the *Free Enquirer* (published by Francis Wright and Robert Dale Owen) and the *Workingman's Advocate* (edited by George Evans). For a general discussion of the workingman's movement in New York see Walter Hugins, *Jacksonian Democracy and the Working Class* (Stanford, Calif., 1960), and Edward Pessen, "The Workingmen's Movement of the Jacksonian Era," *Mississippi Valley Historical Review*, XLIII (Dec., 1956), 428–43.

through the 1830's. In a very real sense, as we shall see, the city missions were—like many other voluntaristic reform societies—a direct consequence and legacy of this evangelistic impulse.

It would be at best an oversimplification to argue that urban philanthropy was essentially secular before the advent of this converting influence—yet it would have an essential validity. Though New York's philanthropists before 1820 were themselves, whether Quaker or Calvinist, men and women of great personal piety, and though this piety motivated their benevolence and informed their attitude toward its objects, their efforts were, as we have argued, essentially limited and pragmatic. The millennial enthusiasm of the next generation provided a motivation and world view quite different in character. Coinciding with an increasing commitment to egalitarian social arrangements, this new pietism led Americans to declare a religious war upon the poverty of their cities. The victory they expected would bring both the conversion of the urban poor and, they believed, of necessity, an end to poverty itself.

CHAPTER 2

The Revivals

In 1811, President Timothy Dwight of Yale, while visiting New York, compiled a list of the city's leading benevolent societies. Without exception they were pragmatic in approach and circumscribed in aim: the Humane Society, for the relief of debtors and the destitute generally; the German Society, to aid German immigrants; the Dispensary, to provide free medical care for the poor; the Marine Society, to relieve the "distressed masters of ships, their wives and orphans." Two years later, in 1813, *A Gazetteer of the State of New-York* published another list of the city's benevolent institutions; again almost all had pragmatic and secular ends.[1]

In 1833, however, when Edwin Williams published his guide book, *New-York as It Is in 1833*, the list of religious charities in New York City was far longer than its secular counterpart.[2] The philanthropic imagination of the 1820's and 1830's was engrossed by Sunday schools, by Bible, missionary, and religious tract societies. The most urgent charity now seemed to be that of converting to evangelical Protestantism the unbelieving, wherever they lived, whatever their

[1] The *Gazetteer*'s list included the Albion Benevolent Society, the Association for the Relief of Disabled Firemen, a House Carpenters' Society, the Kine-Pock Institution, a lying-in hospital. Dwight, *Travels*, pp. 440–441; Spafford, *Gazetteer*, p. 250.

[2] Williams, *New York as It Is*, pp. 59–82.

status in society—from the merchants and sailors of the American cities to Burmese, Ceylonese, and Indians. Older charities, often with ostensibly secular goals, displayed, as well, a decidedly evangelical character. Religion had become millennial, and thus uncompromisingly reformist.

This change in American religious beliefs is fundamental to an understanding of the rise of the city mission. We can trace its source, at least in part, to two developments at the turn of the century. The first was the great revival enthusiam which began in the 1790's and continued into the 1830's (the germinal period of the early city missions). In these decades Americans elaborated and increasingly accepted a theology which served to justify the activism this new piety demanded. The second influence in shaping the city mission impulse was the parallel rise of missionary zeal in England during these same years; it was inevitable that Americans should admire and copy the institutional experiments undertaken by English evangelicals.

[1]

Beginning with the late 1780's and 1790's, a wave of revivals swept across frontier America. By the early 1800's, this new religious enthusiasm had appeared also on the east coast, finding converts in every major eastern town and city, reshaping the religious life of entire areas in New England and New York State. No longer a rural phenomenon, appealing primarily to uneducated farmers, these revivals converted ministers, prominent merchants, and lawyers, college presidents, faculty, and students. New York City and Philadelphia experienced significant revivals. President Timothy Dwight of Yale saved his college, and even his state, from skepticism and the Republicans. Lyman Beecher "sparked" the north shore of Long Island and much of Connecticut, his zeal finding converts even in aristocratic and Unitarian Boston. Few denominations or areas remained unaffected; conservative Scotch Presbyterians from the highlands of Virginia and North Carolina, sophisticated liberals such as Dwight and Nathaniel Taylor of Yale, Arminian Methodists, Baptists of all persuasions, even the evangelical wing of the Protestant Episcopal Church felt the impact of these revivals and the urgency of their emphasis upon the conversion experience and the necessity of Christian action.[3]

Church membership grew rapidly; in 1800, church historians have estimated, one person in every fifteen had belonged to a Protestant church; by 1835, one out of every eight did. Church membership, given the tremendous rise in population during these years, had far more than doubled. For denominations where statistics exist, the picture is clear-cut. In 1802, 87,000 adults held full membership in Methodist churches. By 1812, the number reached 196,000, and by 1836, 362,000.

[3] William Speer, *The Great Revival of 1800* (Philadelphia, 1872); Ashbel Green, *Report on the Revival of Religion, 1815* (Philadelphia, 1815); Lyman Beecher, *The Autobiography of Lyman Beecher*, ed. by Barbara M. Cross (2 vols.; Cambridge, Massachusetts, 1961), Vol. I; Sidney Mead, *Nathaniel W. Taylor, 1786–1858* (Chicago, 1942); Charles Keller, *The Second Great Awakening in Connecticut* (New Haven, 1942); Whitney R. Cross, *The Burned-Over District* (Ithaca, New York, 1950); Winthrop S. Hudson, *American Protestantism* (Chicago, 1961). Concerning these revivals, one of their more prominent converts, New York Presbyterian Gardiner Spring, wrote: "From the time I entered College, in 1800, down to the year 1825, there was an uninterrupted series of these celestial visitations, spreading over different parts of the land. During the whole of these twenty-five years, there was not a month in which we could not point to some village, some city, some seminary of learning, and say: 'Behold what hath God wrought.'" Gardiner Spring, *Personal Reminiscences* (2 vols.; New York, 1866), I, 160. I have purposely avoided discussion of the temporal connection between the western and eastern aspects of this religious awakening. Both clearly had indigenous and characteristic roots.

That same year, Presbyterian membership reached 127,000. By 1834, 641,000 Americans were Methodists, 248,000 Presbyterians.[4]

In the wake of these revivals came the organization of countless missionary societies founded specifically to spread God's word to the unbelieving. The duty of those already converted seemed clear enough. "Blest with the light of his truth ourselves," Nathaniel Bowen told the New York Bible and Common Prayer Book Society in 1812, "we are bound to cause it to shine to the utmost possible extent on all who sit in darkness around us. The obligation is too evident to be proved."[5] These hopefully saved Christians sought to reach all those destitute of religion, whether because of poverty, indifference, or physical isolation. Their newly founded missionary organizations sent preachers, Bibles, and tracts to newly settled areas where churches and ministers were few, to residents of poorer rural communities along the eastern coast —and to the poor of their own cities.[6]

[4] United States, Department of Commerce, Bureau of the Census, *Historical Statistics of the United States, Colonial Times to 1957* (Washington, D.C., 1960), pp. 226–229; Edwin Scott Gaustad, *Historical Atlas of Religion in America* (New York, 1962), pp. 43, 52, 57, 78, 91. Figures for church membership in pre-1860 America are at best approximations.

[5] Nathaniel Bowen, *A Sermon Preached before the Bible and Common Prayer Book Society of New-York, in Trinity Church, March 1, 1812* (New York, 1812), p. 23.

[6] The Western Missionary Society was founded by the Pittsburgh Synod in 1802, the Connecticut Missionary Society in 1797 by a combination of liberal Hopkinsians—led by Timothy Dwight—and old-line New England Congregationalists. A similar alliance founded the Massachusetts Missionary Society in 1799. Speer, *Great Revival*, pp. 79–87; Spring, *Reminiscences*, I, 241–244, 264–265; Oliver Wendell Elsbree, *The Rise of the Missionary Spirit in America, 1790–1815* (Williamsport, Pennsylvania, 1928), Chaps. III and IV; Hudson, *American Protestantism*, pp. 78–90; Clifford S. Griffin, *Their Brothers'*

The missionaries supported by these societies, however, could not convert an irreligious nation unaided. A network of Bible, tract, and Sunday school societies augmented their evangelical efforts. In 1809 philanthropic Philadelphians had organized America's first Bible society. By 1815, the country had over one hundred Bible societies, and the following year evangelical Christians united to form the American Bible Society. Religious tract societies worked hand in hand with the Bible societies. Through the distribution of cheap, popularly written literature, they hoped to awaken interest in religion among the irreligious and thus prepare the way for their sister missionary and Bible societies. The Sunday school movement developed at this time—and for similar purposes. The first Sunday schools in the country were established in the 1790's. By 1824, some 50,000 American children gathered weekly for religious instruction. By 1826, the fourteen leading mission, Bible, tract, and Sunday school societies had a combined annual income of $361,804.54.[7]

Americans were not the only ones who worked and prayed in Christ's cause. The millennial and missionary surge of early-nineteenth-century America, while rooted in indigenous needs, took much of its particular institutional direction from an allied evangelical movement which dominated England's religious life during the very years that the Second Great Awakening swept across the United States.

Keepers, Moral Stewardship in the United States, 1800–1865 (New Brunswick, New Jersey, 1960), pp. 24–25; Pomerantz, *New York*, p. 392.

[7] For recent historical studies of these organizations see: Griffin, *Brothers' Keepers, passim*; Charles I. Foster, *An Errand of Mercy, the Evangelical United Front, 1790–1837* (Chapel Hill, 1960), pp. 105–110, 121–150; John R. Bodo, *The Protestant Clergy and Public Issues, 1812–1848* (Princeton, 1954), especially Chaps. IV and VI; and Charles C. Cole, *The Social Ideas of the Northern Evangelists, 1826–1860* (New York, 1954).

Great Britain, beginning in the 1790's and early 1800's experienced a revival of religious pietism which, though quite different in many ways from the American revivals, converted many Englishmen to a new emotional religion and led them consequently to organize and support countless missionary and reform societies. The goal of these movements in both countries was the same—the conversion of the world to evangelical Protestantism and the remaking of the home society into a nation pure and Christian. Evangelicals in both countries utilized the same types of institutions to spearhead their religious crusade. In England the leading societies were religious tract and Bible societies, most prominently the London Religious Tract Society and the British and Foreign Bible Society. They were supported by a host of subsidiary groups, by Sunday school unions, and by foreign mission societies, in addition to their own auxiliaries and associations.[8] And quite early the English evangelicals turned to the conversion and transformation of the urban and industrial poor into devout, productive, and conservative members of society.[9]

This institutional parallel is not surprising. The British evangelical societies served as models in the formation of their sister American organizations. Every prominent American evangelical society—with the exception of the temperance societies—found its progenitor in England: Bible, mission,

[8] For three recent studies of the evangelical movement, see: Ford K. Brown, *Fathers of the Victorians, the Age of Wilberforce* (Cambridge, England, 1961); Standish Meacham, *Henry Thornton of Clapham, 1760–1815* (Cambridge, Massachusetts, 1964); Mary G. Jones, *Hannah More* (Cambridge, England, 1952).

[9] Brown, *Fathers*, pp. 234–284. Some historians have tended to interpret the interest of the English evangelicals in the poor as essentially a device to ensure social control. For a somewhat extreme statement of this position, one which sees English class attitudes and desire for social control transmitted to the United States and figuring largely in the benevolent movement in this country, see Foster, *Errand of Mercy*, pp. 82–100.

and Sunday school societies, tract distribution societies, city missions, and societies especially to train young men as evangelical missionaries. Anxious to assert their indebtedness, the American Bible, religious tract, and Sunday school societies corresponded actively with English evangelical groups, reprinted lengthy excerpts of the English reports in their own annual reports and felt that they shared with their English brethren in the glorious work which presaged the coming of Christ. Many referred specifically to the reception of British annual or monthly reports as the immediate inspiration of their organization.[10]

Communications between England and American pietists were not limited, however, to official reports and to the exchange of religious tracts. In New York and indeed throughout the country, reformers had established warm personal contacts with like-thinking Christians in England. Four New Yorkers in particular—Isabella Graham, Divie Bethune, Thomas Eddy, and John Griscom—all long active in both New York's urban and religious charities, had visited English reformers and corresponded frequently with them. Their

[10] The New York Religious Tract Society (hereinafter referred to as N.Y.R.T.S.), one of the most active early evangelical and missionary societies in the United States, not only claimed the London Religious Tract Society as its inspiration but regularly reprinted lengthy excerpts from the annual reports of the Society and from the reports of other British and European evangelical societies. Many other American reform societies did likewise. See, for example, the Long Island Bible and Common Prayer Book Society, *First Annual Report, 1816* (New York, 1816); The New York Sunday School Union Society, *First Report, 1817* (New York, 1817), p. 7; Bowen, *Sermon . . . Bible and Common Prayer Book Society*, p. 4; Marine Bible Society of New York, *Eighth Annual Report* (New York, 1824); New York Female Auxiliary Bible Society, *Seventh Annual Report* (New York, 1823), p. 3. For a list of evangelical societies active between the 1790's and the 1840's, see Brown, *Fathers*, pp. 329–340.

correspondence began in the 1790's and continued into the 1830's. Other pious New Yorkers visited England to exchange ideas, to inspect English religious philanthropies, and to raise money for American counterparts. John Mitchell Mason and Gardiner Spring, both founders of important American mission societies and leaders in New York's evangelical world, are two other prominent examples of Americans with close ties to the world of English piety and philanthropy.[11]

The written word, nevertheless, proved the most effective means by which English evangelical ideas and institutions found their way across the ocean. Hannah More, Leigh Richmond, and William Wilberforce, the prophets and spokesmen of British Evangelism, were read eagerly by pious New Yorkers. Their tracts were spread broadside across the American frontier and among America's urban poor by tract societies and missionary groups; the authors of the *Dairyman's Daughter* and the *Shepherd of Salisbury Plain* played as great a role as any American religious leader in inculcating the doctrines of a zealous Protestantism throughout America.

[2]

This then was an age of religious enthusiasm and activism, an age of Bibles, tracts, and missions. This was a generation

[11] Graham, *Power of Faith*, pp. 331, 345–352, 381–385, 390–394; Knapp, *Eddy*, pp. 178–214, 216–230, 248–249, 252–257, 265–267, 270–274, 278–281; Griscom, *Memoir*, pp. 101–157, 165–166; John Griscom, *A Year in Europe Comprising a Journal of Observations in England, Scotland, Ireland, France, Switzerland, the North of Italy, and Holland. In 1818 and 1819* (2 vols.; New York, 1823); W. D. Snodgrass, "John Mitchell Mason, D.D.," *The Annals of the Pulpit*, ed. by William Sprague (9 vols.; New York, 1857–1869), IV, 1; Spring, *Reminiscences*, II, 96–140. For a more detailed description of these transatlantic ties see Carroll S. Rosenberg, "Evangelism and the New City" (unpublished Ph.D. Dissertation, Columbia University, 1968), pp. 61–65.

during which missionary and millennial zeal colored virtually every aspect of American life—including urban philanthropy. New Yorkers' initial efforts to provide for the religious needs of their city's poor began gradually during the second decade of the nineteenth century. At first, religious missionaries viewed their activities as a decidedly subordinate trend within the traditional world of New York philanthropy. They thought of their religious work as adding a spiritual factor to, but not replacing, older predominantly secular efforts. Yet there was always strong pressure to broaden their religious approach, to adopt the methods and scope of the evangelical movement. Eventually these pressures created the city mission movement.

The early history of the Society for Supporting the Gospel Among the Poor of the City of New York, a transitional organization linking the older secular charity with the newer pattern of mission work, illustrates clearly these pressures and the gradual changes in outlook and method they were to bring. The Society for Supporting the Gospel was founded in December, 1812, to maintain a chaplain in the city's eleemosynary institutions—in the prisons, almshouse, and city hospital. Until this time, neither the city nor the state had appointed a chaplain to care for the souls incarcerated in these institutions.

But in 1813 even pious philanthropists still thought of religious charity in limited terms; they did not expect their chaplain to be a missionary to all the poor of the city, nor that he should seek to promote a general religious revival as did frontier missionaries and later city missionaries. He was to function solely as a religious appendage to established secular institutions, conducting regular religious services for the inmates of New York's public institutions, distributing Bibles among them, and praying with the penitent and dying. The missionary was not, despite the organization's name, to visit the poor generally, nor even to oversee the religious development of those whom he had known in a public institution, once they were released from it.[12]

This was an age, however, when ministers increasingly courted revivals among their congregations, when they were judged both by fellow clergymen and earnest laymen in terms of the number of conversions they had gained and the number of revivals they had led. The missionaries and the younger members of the Society for Supporting the Gospel could not help judging themselves and their Society in these terms. The Reverend Ezra Stiles Ely—the Society's first missionary—and his successor, John Stanford, both viewed themselves as true missionaries and sought actively to convert the irreligious and indifferent. Although forced to limit their ministry to the inmates of public institutions, they adopted within this restricted field evangelical methods surprisingly similar to those of the frontier missionary, and not unlike those later adopted by the highly evangelical followers of Lyman Beecher and Charles Grandison Finney. They visited the penitent or the dying inmate frequently, and refused to rest until they had convinced him of his sinfulness and impending damnation.[13]

[12] Society for Supporting the Gospel Among the Poor of the City of New York (hereinafter referred to as S.S.G.P.), *First Report of the Trustees*, reprinted, Ezra Stiles Ely, *Visits of Mercy*, II, 178–180; S.S.G.P., *Annual Reports, II-IV, 1815–1817* (New York, 1815–1817).

[13] Ezra Stiles Ely's diary for the nearly three years of his chaplaincy was reprinted as *Visits of Mercy*. Such conversion accounts are liberally sprinkled throughout, as they are in the diary John Stanford kept during a much more lengthy service as chaplain. The Stanford diary is reprinted in large part in Charles G. Sommers, *Memoir of the Reverend John Stanford, D.D., Late Chaplain to the Humane and Criminal Institutions in the City of New York* (New York, 1835). The manuscript diary, which is only a little more

Like the annual reports of later evangelical city missions, their reports were filled with accounts of deathbed conversions and of the prayerful agonies and resultant conversions of former atheists and indifferent Christians. This, not simply the holding of perfunctory Sunday services, was the true aim of their ministry as they and the Society came to see it. Aided in their evangelical labors by such members of the Society as Leonard Bleecker, Divie Bethune, and Anson G. Phelps (all deeply evangelical Christians and all later active supporters of the city mission movement), they strove with ever greater intensity to save the souls of all found in the city's institutions.[14] It was but a short step for evangelical Christians to seek the conversion of the poor throughout the city.

In 1816, New Yorkers took that step, founding three separate organizations to bring religion to the city's poor. These were the Young Men's Missionary Society of New York, the New York Evangelical Missionary Society of Young Men, and the Female Missionary Society for the Poor of New York.[15] This date is not surprising. For that very year many of the same pious New Yorkers who founded these benevolent associations had also worked actively to establish the American Bible Society, the American Education Society and, a year later, the American Sunday School Union.

These societies were an integral part of the Second Great Awakening's missionary and millennial enthusiasm. Each had originated as a fund-raising auxiliary of one of New York's mission or Bible societies. But as the evangelical zeal of the

---

complete than the printed one, is deposited in the Manuscript Division, New York Historical Society.

[14] S.S.G.P., *Annual Reports, II-IV; passim;* and *First Report of Trustees.*

[15] For a more detailed description of these societies see Rosenberg, "Evangelism and the New City," pp. 72–89.

Awakening intensified, the members and directors of these societies began to feel dissatisfied with simply raising funds for other pious organizations. They wished themselves to send ministers, Bibles, and tracts to America's frontiers and isolated rural areas. In 1816, for instance, the Young Men's Missionary Society of New York broke away from its parent society, the New York Missionary Society, and commenced an independent program. Within two years, the Society had undertaken the support of twelve missionaries along a vast frontier area, stretching from western New York State to Illinois, through western Pennsylvania and Virginia to Alabama. The New York Evangelical Missionary Society of Young Men, a society founded by a somewhat more "liberal" group of Presbyterians, supported missionaries in northeastern Pennsylvania, in Genesee County, New York, and in "still more undefined and extended desolations in the State of Georgia." These missionaries held Sunday services, baptized and married, established churches, organized Sunday schools, and distributed Bibles and tracts, seeking everywhere to counteract the infidelity and irreligion that seemed inevitably to accompany frontier life. The societies' supporters hoped that their ministers would in addition be able to extend the revival fervor and claim new conquests in the millennial war against atheism and irreligion.[16]

[16] The Young Men's Missionary Society of New York (hereinafter referred to as Y.M.M.S.N.Y.), *Third Annual Report, December, 1818* (New York, 1819), pp. 1–15; New York Evangelical Missionary Society of Young Men (hereinafter referred to as N.Y.E.M.S.Y.M.), *Proceedings of the First Anniversary of the New-York Evangelical Missionary Society* (New York, 1817), p. 3; Philip Whelpley, "Address to the New-York Evangelical Society of Young Men," *Proceedings of the First Anniversary of the New-York Evangelical Society of Young Men, 1817* (New York, 1817), pp. 12, 15; Shepherd Knapp, *A History of the Brick Presbyterian Church in the City of New York* (New York, 1924), pp. 243–244.

Not all the societies' missionaries, however, labored in small towns or among isolated farms; a few dedicated ministers sought their converts in the dank and crowded tenements and shanties of New York's developing slums. In 1815, the Female Missionary Society for the Poor of New York sent their first missionary to Corlear's Hook. Two years later a missionary supported by the Young Men's Missionary Society of New York joined him in working among the city's destitute. In 1818, the New York Evangelical Missionary Society of Young Men hired two more city missionaries—one to labor among the black population of Bancker Street, the second at Corlear's Hook.[17]

At first these missionaries visited from tenement to tenement, distributed tracts and Bibles, and held Sunday services wherever they could find a room or a "congregation"—however transitory. During his first two months at Corlear's Hook, for instance, Reverend John Miller, missionary of the Young Men's Missionary Society of New York, visited ninety-seven families "in the abodes of ignorance, poverty and distress." During his first year as missionary for the Female Missionary Society, Ward Stafford gathered between four and six hundred children into his Sunday school and preached regularly to the unchurched in a rented room near the Corlear's Hook shipyards. Gradually, however, the missionaries and their societies began to seek more permanent relations with the poor. In 1817, the Young Men's Missionary Society of New York founded their first permanent chapel and free church on Broome Street in the heart of Corlear's Hook. In October, 1818, the Female Missionary Society dedi-

[17] N.Y.E.M.S.Y.M., *Proceedings of the First Anniversary*, pp. 3–5, 17; Female Missionary Society for the Poor of the City of New-York and its Vicinity (hereinafter referred to as F.M.S.), *Second Annual Report* (New York, 1818), p. 5; Y.M.M.S.N.Y., *Third Annual Report*, pp. 16–18.

cated their first mission chapel on Bancker Street. The following year they helped establish a second mission church near Corlear's Hook, the Allen Street Presbyterian Church.[18]

The early full-time missionaries received more than financial assistance from their sponsoring organizations, for the three societies soon concluded that active proselytizing efforts by the members themselves were necessary if religion were to reach the urban poor: Christians must systematically visit the poor in their homes; only through such individual commitment could their efforts meet with success. The active members of the Female Missionary Society had already discovered this when their efforts to found several Sunday schools at Corlear's Hook had led them to visit extensively in the area's tenements seeking to recruit pupils. Their missionary, Ward Stafford, actively encouraged the women to expand their initial visiting efforts. In his first report to the Society's managers Stafford requested that the members organize volunteer ward-visiting committees and systematically visit the city's poorer neighborhoods, distributing tracts and Bibles, ascertaining the religious state of the families they encountered—and their temporal needs as well.[19]

Indeed Stafford was responsible for leading the Female Missionary Society on the path which all the later and longer-lived city missions were to follow—a path toward a characteristic blend of temporal and religious philanthropy. Stafford was convinced that both sorts of charity must work hand in hand if the poor of New York were to be converted and brought into Christian churches. The ladies of the ward committees, Stafford explained, should offer temporal aid,

[18] Y.M.M.S.N.Y., *Third Annual Report*, pp. 16–18; Ward Stafford, *New Missionary Field, A Report to the Female Missionary Society for the Poor of the City of New-York and its Vicinity, at their Quarterly Prayer Meeting, March, 1817* (2d ed.; New York, 1817), pp. 23–24.
[19] Stafford, *New Missionary Field*, pp. 29–31.

clothing, and food for the sick and hungry, when they visited to pray and distribute Bibles. "Particular pains," Stafford advised, "should be taken to approach the destitute, especially the vicious, in times of affliction. Places inaccessible to Christians at other times are then approached with perfect ease." Even in the case of less desperate need, Stafford urged, wise housekeepers could advise the poor on efficient methods of buying and preparing food, making clothes, and preparing for the hard times of winter. "To manage their temporal concerns to advantage many need information, advice and direction, which without the least difficulty, might be given by a kind and judicious neighbor." In this way the Female Missionary Society might win the confidence of the poor, bridge the gulf which existed between the prosperous churchgoer and the destitute slum dweller, and gradually bring these unfortunates within the fold of their Sunday schools and mission chapel.[20]

Willingness to labor for the souls of the poor, even to feed and clothe their bodies, did not mean, however, that the well-to-do Christian, in 1817, necessarily felt either sympathy or closeness for the objects of his charity. Despite Stafford's reference to neighborly advice, the poor described in the reports and sermons of the three societies remained alien objects of a traditionally condescending philanthropy—a degraded class, distasteful to the respectable and discriminating Christian. These early city mission societies regularly spoke of the "vicious poor," of their "desperate depravity," of their urban mission area as "this wilderness of sin." "Almost all the sufferings of the poor in this and other cities," Ward Stafford confidently asserted in 1817, "are the immediate effect of ignorance or vice." [21]

[20] *Ibid.*, pp. 30–32.
[21] *Ibid.*, pp. 11, 17, 22, 42; F.M.S., *Second Annual Report*, p. 5; and *Fifth Annual Report*, pp. 8–9.

Such a censorious attitude helped shape the societies' policies. The Young Men's Missionary Society, for instance, drew a sharp distinction between the frontier and rural objects of their missionary zeal and their urban "clients." They sent their missionaries to the frontier in the hope that they would foster revivals among those rural settlers, converting hundreds, changing the tone and character of frontier society. They believed and expected that if God's grace favored their efforts, crude, perhaps irreligious farmers would be transformed into zealous Christians—thus into sober and responsible pillars of a stable rural society.[22] But not so the subjects of their urban mission. Far from hoping to remake Corlear's Hook, the managers expected only that their missionaries would offer religious solace to sick and dying Christians and establish Sunday schools so that youthful slum dwellers might be exposed to religious influences. They did not expect to convert the "vicious" poor nor bring a general sense of religious zeal and immediacy to so "degraded and unlikely a locale."[23] There is no feeling in these reports—as there were to be in the reports of city missions during the Age of Jackson—that the religious conversion of the poor was not only possible, but was also a necessary prerequisite to the elimination of poverty from urban America. In sharp contrast with the pietists a generation later, these early missionaries accepted slums and poverty without feeling that the existence of a class of permanently destitute cast doubt upon the equity of their social and political institutions.

The seeming ambivalence of the New Yorkers' attitudes toward the unchurched of their city's slums was only to have been expected. For the mission societies stood at a transition point in both theological and social attitudes, reflecting the eighteenth century's distaste for and yet resigned acceptance of the poor, and the nineteenth century's evangelical concern

[22] Y.M.M.S.N.Y., *Third Annual Report*, p. 3.   [23] *Ibid.*, p. 16.

for their spiritual improvement. The societies reflected as
well the concern conservative New Yorkers felt toward the
steady increase in the numbers of the city's poor. Religion
seemed to offer the only real solution to these varied problems. By converting and thus socializing the children of the
uneducated and irreligious poor, they would at once save individual souls and preserve social stability. That conversion
would bring with it prosperity—or at least self-sufficiency—
seemed too apparent to be questioned.

However, the evangelical movement was still young in
1816 and 1817. Only the most devout and active were moved
to seek the conversion of the poor in their own city. The
Evangelical Missionary Society, the Female Missionary Society, and the Young Men's Missionary Society seem by the
mid-1820's to have dissolved or discontinued their city mission
efforts. But in origin and aims they foreshadowed the influences which led a decade later to the formation of more
permanent and influential city missions.

[3]

The New Yorkers who had founded these first city missions were orthodox Calvinists, some of them rigid Scotch
Presbyterians. Formally they accepted the Calvinist doctrines
of predestination and of total human depravity. Every man,
orthodox Calvinists believed, deserved the punishments of
hell, and nothing any man did could effect his own salvation.
Yet God, they believed, in His benevolence determined to
save some sinners. These souls He infused with grace, reawakening their fallen nature. Overwhelmed by this flood
of grace, seeing themselves and God for the first time with
new reason and understanding, this blessed minority threw
themselves upon God's mercy and were saved. Calvin likened
this experience to God raping the soul. God, not man, Cal-

vinists of all shades argued, was the prime and sole mover in conversion, acting from motives awful and unknowable.

God had determined from the beginning of time the saved and the damned. Why, then, establish missions to convert sinners? Did orthodox Calvinist founders of New York's mission societies, men such as John Mitchell Mason and John Romeyn, or even Gardiner Spring or Ezra Stiles Ely, believe that God needed them to help effect His salvation of certain sinners? Yet if logic denied them a role in the salvation of men, why the compulsion, not only to distribute Bibles and support missionaries, but also to gain immediate converts during revival meetings? Why the feeling that upon the sum of their individual efforts rested the coming of the millennium?

Most religious organizations in the early years of the Second Great Awakening entertained, as we have seen, quite modest views of the success they might achieve. The Massachusetts Bible Society characteristically reported in 1814:

The operation of the Bible, is necessarily gradual and noiseless. Its province is the heart, and its best fruits are those mild and humble virtues, which ask no notice but from the eye of God. Striking effects cannot therefore be related, and ought not to be expected. It is enough to know, that we have sown the good seed of divine truth, and we may leave it with confidence to HIM, whose grace descends as the dew. . . .[24]

Quite a different tone began to appear, however, in the years after the close of the War of 1812. In 1818, for example, the Young Men's Missionary Society of New York, organized by New York's most orthodox Scotch Presbyterians,

[24] Bible Society of Massachusetts, *Report of the Executive Committee of the Bible Society of Massachusetts, prepared for the Anniversary of the Society, June 2, 1814* (Boston, 1814), p. 4.

wrote in a new spirit of the activities of their missionaries along the frontier:

Others are now on their way to aid the Lord against the mighty. Many precious souls, it is hoped, have, through their instrumentality, been rescued from the power of the prince of darkness, and have received an inheritance among those who are sanctified through faith in Jesus Christ.[25]

That same year the Female Missionary Society for the Poor of the City of New York wrote in its annual report:

God has promised to give his Son the Heathen for his inheritance, and the uttermost parts of the earth for his possession; and are there not some among the destitute of our own city for whom Christ died? Some elect who must yet be gathered in? The very circumstance that God hath put it into the hearts of his people to erect a house for public worship in so vicious a part of our city, argues a strong probability that he hath some souls there that must be sought out.[26]

Both God and the conversion experience had seemingly changed. The God of these zealous Christians was not the God of Calvin acting with arbitrary and inscrutable power upon powerless man, but rather a God that must await the voluntary actions of a group of respectable Christians to gather in those He had willed to save. And Christians too had changed. Over the decades they had seemingly gained a power sufficient to help save their fellow sinners.

William G. McLoughlin, an eminent historian of religion in America, recently suggested that,

in the evangelistic fervor engendered by the [first Great] Awakening pietists of all kinds gradually abandoned the emphasis on a limited atonement and worked their way toward the doctrines

[25] Y.M.M.S.N.Y., *Third Annual Report*, p. 3.
[26] F.M.S., *Second Annual Report*, p. 5.

of free will, free grace and immediate salvation open to all men. By the end of the eighteenth century the unique American systems of itinerant evangelism and mass revivalism had evolved to provide the techniques for regenerating a whole society (and through missions, the whole world).[27]

This "evangelization" of Calvinism has been traced by Church historians in the thought and writings of a few prominent liberal theologians.[28] Scholars have less frequently suggested, however, that the Second Great Awakening and its revivalistic zeal affected in a similar manner the religious beliefs of orthodox Calvinists generally—and that it did so as early as the second decade of the nineteenth century.

Certainly this was the case among pious New Yorkers. Even among those who considered themselves most orthodox, man's ability seemed increasingly important; God seemed increasingly willing to help those who would help themselves (and others) in finding a way to salvation. New Yorkers began to place greater and greater emphasis upon the technique and significance of sanctification. The experience of grace was only a first step, indispensable though it may have been, to a life of pious activism. One might indeed, with no more than the minimum amount of distortion necessarily created by such schematic interpretations, regard all of American theology between Samuel Hopkins and Charles Grandison Finney as a constant search for forms in which to express and justify the

[27] William G. McLoughlin, "Pietism," p. 168.
[28] To list only a few who have been subjects of modern historical scholarship: Sidney Mead, *Nathaniel W. Taylor;* Barbara Cross, *Horace Bushnell, Minister to a Changing America* (Chicago, 1958); Barbara Cross, "Introduction," Beecher, *Autobiography;* McLoughlin, *Modern Revivalism: Charles Grandison Finney to Billy Graham* (New York, 1959); Charles E. Cuningham, *Timothy Dwight, 1752–1817, A Biography* (New York, 1942).

generation's increasingly unavoidable commitment to evangelical action.[29]

Both in terms of personal influence and ideas, Finney was a genuine culmination of this impulse; not surprisingly, he was a major influence both personally and intellectually in the shaping of New York's first permanent city missions.

In the winter of 1834–1835, while pastor of the Chatham Street Chapel, Finney gave a series of sermons on revivals. His object was, in part, to inspire an immediate revival in New York City, and in part to state clearly his religious and methodological beliefs. He succeeded in both.[30]

In one sense Finney seemed merely to be appropriating some of the tenets of Hopkinsian liberalism (such as man's natural ability to know and serve God) and forcing them to their logical conclusions. Salvation, Finney insisted in the very

[29] For a detailed account of this gradual emotional and theological development in the lives of five influential supporters of New York's early religious charities (Isabella Graham, Divie Bethune, John Stanford, Gardiner Spring, Anson Phelps) see Rosenberg, "Evangelism and the New City."

[30] These lectures or sermons give the historian an excellent opportunity to analyze the religious doctrines which Finney personally preached in New York and which apparently had a deep effect upon New Yorkers' religious beliefs and practices. The sermons were copied, more or less verbatim, by Joshua Leavitt and published weekly in Leavitt's revivalistic *New York Evangelist;* New Yorkers could refer to Leavitt's copies only a few days after they had heard Finney himself give the sermon. Finney then edited Leavitt's transcriptions and published them as a book, *Lectures on Revivals of Religion*, which appeared in May, 1835; *Lectures on Revivals* quickly became an evangelistic best-seller, selling 12,000 copies in its first three months of publication. *Lectures on Revivals* has recently been reissued, edited by William McLoughlin and including a lengthy introduction by McLoughlin: Charles Grandison Finney, *Lectures on the Revival of Religion*, ed. by William G. McLoughlin (Cambridge, Massachusetts, 1960). The following references to *Lectures on Revivals* will be to the McLoughlin edition.

first lecture of his winter revival series, was not a miracle in which the Holy Ghost descended and radically altered the debased nature of man. There is nothing, he argued, in the act of conversion or justification that is "beyond the ordinary power of nature. It consists entirely in the right exercise of the powers of nature." In terms Gardiner Spring would have had difficulty in refuting, Finney insisted that "when mankind become religious they are not enabled to put forth exertions which they were unable before to put forth. They only exert the powers they had before in a different way, and use them for the glory of God." [31] It was man's moral inability, Finney asserted, again using Hopkinsian terms, man's sinful preference for the world, not a debased nature, that stood in the way of his salvation, and ultimately condemned him to hell. Man's salvation waited only upon the revival or awakening of his moral faculties. On this point Finney could have claimed the support of liberal Hopkinsians in New York and throughout the east. [32]

But here agreement ended. Only the Holy Ghost, Hopkinsians insisted, could miraculously awaken man's moral faculties. Man could pray and study. He could not save himself; God alone knew whom He had willed to save. As he had in countless earlier western revivals, Finney thundered in the winter of 1834, "*Religion* [by which he meant salvation or conversion] *is the work of man*. It is something for man to

[31] Finney, "What a Revival of Religion Is," *Lectures on Revivals*, pp. 13, 9–13.

[32] As Finney stated in terms very similar to those used, for instance, by Gardiner Spring at the beginning of Spring's New York ministry, "God induces him [man] to do it [obey God]. He influences him by his Spirit, because of his great wickedness and reluctance to obey. . . . Men are wholly indisposed to obey; and unless God interpose the influence of his Spirit, not a man on earth will ever obey the commands of God." *Ibid.*, p. 9.

do. . . . It is man's duty. It is not a miracle, or dependent on a miracle in any sense. It is a purely philosophical [scientific or natural] result of the right use of constituted means—as much so as any other effect produced by the application of means." [33] Man's moral faculties would respond to natural, humanly contrived stimuli. These, then, were Finney's two revolutionary doctrines: salvation is a natural and understandable process, and man is capable of being the active agent.

Finney substituted for the miraculous descent of the Holy Ghost the new revival methods which he and other religious liberals had developed and, in particular, the simple and oft-repeated statement that man could act, that he could save himself. All the components of salvation, Finney insisted, existed within man and within his world. God held out the means of salvation to all men. It was the responsibility of sinful man to grasp it for himself. Pietists of a slightly older generation like Isabella Graham and John Stanford had insisted that man was an active agent to the extent that he could pray for a new heart; once saved, they believed man had then to work actively to become holy. Finney claimed that salvation itself was the product of human effort and determination. As he told his New York audiences:

The agency is the sinner himself. The conversion of a sinner consists in his obeying the truth. It is therefore impossible it should take place without his agency, for it consists in *his* acting right. He is influenced to this by the agency of God, and by the agency of men.[34]

[33] *Ibid.*, pp. 9, 13. McLoughlin in an editorial footnote points out that to Finney's generation, the term "philosophical" carried the implication "scientific or natural."

[34] *Ibid.*, p. 18.

Finney's new man was thus a voluntary agent. He could will to accept God's proffered salvation or to reject it. The ultimate responsibility for his salvation or damnation rested not with God or with God's will, but with the sinner.[35]

Man could will, similarly, to save others or refuse to save others. Man, as well as God, played a role in the conversion of sinners. Finney argued that, in creating a natural process of saving mankind, God had willed to work through human agents to save sinners. These agents could be the revival minister or missionary, who sought through exhortation and warnings to awaken the sleeping Christian.[36] But, Finney urged, the human agent could be the pious layman as well. The believer could bring about revivals of religion in others simply by his prayers, or better, by prayer accompanied by missionary activities. Indeed, Finney told his New York audience, if revivals did not come, if sinners were not saved it was because Christians had not prayed and had not worked, not because God had predestined their damnation.

Finney, throughout his sermons, emphasized again and again that the individual lay Christian, even a lay Christian

---

[35] "Men are not mere *instruments* in the hand of God," Finney stated, going on to assert that man could in fact refuse to be saved even when God desired to save him. *Ibid.*, pp. 18–20.

[36] Again, Finney emphasized not only the power of the minister to provoke revivals—a feat which Finney asserted a true minister could perform at any time—but that the minister's actions were not remotely ordained by God, but wholly volitional. "Truth is the instrument [of God in conversion]. The preacher is a moral agent in the work; he acts; he is not a mere passive instrument; he is voluntary in promoting the conversion of sinners." *Ibid.*, p. 18.

Essentially related to this position was Finney's belief that the individual was responsible not only for saving his own soul, but those of all around him. If sin existed, it was because Christians had not worked and prayed. Finney, "The Prayer of Faith," *ibid.*, p. 84.

without formal education, and of low social and economic status, could bring on a revival. If this lay Christian had deep faith and his minister lacked faith or was bound to a literal Calvinism, then that layman could be far more effective than the minister in saving souls. (Throughout the sermons one also finds frequent pejorative references to the wealthy and to higher education, as well as indications that Finney felt that his congregation was frequently tempted by the vices of social climbing and emulation of the rich.) In the fourth of his lectures on revivals, for example, Finney pointedly placed responsibility for the sins and the spiritual deadness of New York upon the shoulders of his audience, the practicing Christians of New York.

Brethren . . . Elders of the church, men, women, any of you, and all of you—what do you say? . . . You see why you have not had a revival. It is only because you don't want one. Because you are not praying for it, nor anxious for it . . . I appeal to your consciences. Are you making these efforts now, to promote a revival? [37]

At last evangelical Christians had a minister who boldly asserted that they and their missionaries had the power to save sinners. What Philip Whelpley, and what the conservative Calvinist officers of the Young Men's Missionary Society of New York, had written in 1816 concerning the missionary duties of the Christian need no longer be inconsistent with formal religious doctrine. Finney had provided them with a theological rationale. Christians had a religious duty to go about the city saving sinners; their missionary endeavors might be the difference between the salvation and damnation of countless souls. Finney seldom let a sermon pass without pointing out to his audience their duties as city missionaries.

[37] Finney, "When a Revival Is to Be Expected," *ibid.*, p. 36.

Will you spend the winter in learning *about* revivals, and do nothing *for* them? I want you as fast as you learn anything on the subject of revivals, to put it in practice, and go to work and see if you cannot promote a revival among sinners here. . . . We call on you to unite now in a solemn pledge to God, that you will do your duty as fast as you learn what it is, and to pray that He will pour out his Spirit upon this church and upon all the city this winter.[38]

The city mission movement was more than a pragmatic response to the new problems of urban poverty. Its specific motives and methods were shaped in large measure by the religious enthusiasm of the opening decades of the nineteenth century and the social expectations characteristic of Jacksonian America.

[38] Finney, "What a Revival of Religion Is," *ibid.*, pp. 22–23. See also "When a Revival Is to Be Expected" and "How to Promote a Revival," *ibid., passim.* Indeed all of Finney's lectures were meant to instruct his audience on methods of stimulating a revival in New York or any other area. They were meant for immediate application, not for theological analysis. See, for example, two other sermons, "Means to Be Used with Sinners" and "How Churches Can Help Ministers," *ibid.*, pp. 140–155, 223–249.

CHAPTER 3

New York City
Tract Society

On the evening of February 19, 1827, a group of prominent philanthropists organized New York's first permanent city mission, the New York City Tract Society. Within a few years, hundreds of the Society's volunteer workers were systematically visiting every section of the city, leaving tracts and Bibles, and praying with the receptive. Though initially concerned with the spiritual condition of all classes and groups in New York, the City Tract Society soon began to devote an increasing portion of its time and resources to the religious and temporal needs of the city's poor.

This shift in purpose resulted from the impact of the city and growing numbers of the urban poor upon an institution at first exclusively religious in inspiration and universal in approach. The Society's contact with New York slum dwellers occurred in a generation when articulate Americans were becoming committed to the values of equalitarianism and at a time when urban poverty was assuming an increasingly threatening character. This configuration of circumstances helped elicit an inevitably activist response from concerned New Yorkers—but an activism directly rooted in religious conviction. The history of the New York City Tract Society illustrates a developing urban consciousness in a period which was as much the Age of Finney as that of Jackson.

[1]

The origins of the New York City Tract Society lay far back in the evangelical movement. They can be traced to 1812 and the founding of the New York Religious Tract Society, one of many such evangelical societies established during these years. The original aims of the Religious Tract Society, as the Society announced them in its first annual report in 1812, were to select religious pamphlets "consistent with the Reformation," print them cheaply in bulk, and then distribute them throughout the country. The objects of the distribution campaign were to be the "poor and the negligent." [1] The poor, to religious New Yorkers in 1812, in contradistinction to later city mission supporters, were not immigrants in the city slums, but rather those of the middle and lower-middle classes who had moved away from established religious centers, either to the trans-Appalachian frontier or to new communities developing in the east. They were poor because they were not as yet able to support a minister or establish a church. The negligent were those, either in the city or the country, poor or well-to-do, who chose not to perform these pious acts. The Religious Tract Society hoped that by saturating "destitute" areas with religious literature and by pressing tracts upon the irreligious, they could soon convert the nation to evangelical

[1] The Constitution of the New York Religious Tract Society, reprinted in N.Y.R.T.S., *Fourth Annual Report, 1815* (New York, 1816), p. 22; N.Y.R.T.S., "First Annual Report, 1812, presented 1813." The first ten annual reports of the N.Y.R.T.S. (the first two of which exist only in manuscript) are in the archives of the New York City Mission Society, 105 East 22nd Street, New York City. For English origins of the tract movement, see Brown, *Fathers*, pp. 244–245; Foster, *Errand*, Part I; and Chap. 2, above.

Christianity. The aims of the Religious Tract Society were thus identical with those of the equally pious Bible, mission, and Sunday school societies which Christians were establishing throughout the east during the first two decades of the nineteenth century.[2]

The Religious Tract Society's membership was remarkably similar as well. The men who founded and managed the Religious Tract Society in 1812 were, with few exceptions, already active members of New York's varied mission, Bible, and Sunday school societies. And they would soon take the lead in establishing these organizations on a national basis. These activists included the city's leading revival ministers, Philip Milledoler, John Mitchell Mason, Gardiner Spring, Samuel H. Cox, John Romeyn, and Philip Whelpley, and her most zealous and philanthropic laymen, Divie Bethune, Philip D. Keese, Arthur Tappan, Thomas Stokes, Richard Varick, John Caldwell, and Leonard Bleecker.[3]

The initial goal of the Religious Tract Society was to supply the religious needs of its own state. And these were great. New York in the opening decades of the nineteenth century was still a frontier state. Large areas had just been opened to settlement, and its population multiplied as immigrants from New England and Europe moved up the Hudson Valley and then, as the Erie Canal was completed in the 1820's, into the heartland of the state.[4] The Religious Tract Society hoped

[2] N.Y.R.T.S., "Second Annual Report"; N.Y.R.T.S., *Fourth Annual Report*, pp. 18-19. See, as well, the activist appeals for support of mission work by the Society's corresponding secretary, Zachariah Lewis, in the two newspapers he edited, the New York *Commercial Advertiser* and the *American Missionary Register*.

[3] For a brief discussion of these men, their varied evangelical interests and their theological position, see Rosenberg, "Evangelism and the New City."

[4] Ellis, *Short History*, Chaps. XIV and XVI; Cross, *Burned-Over District*, Book II.

through tract distribution to keep this population true to Christianity and, hopefully, to the Calvinism of the eastern seaboard.[5]

Despite this frontier emphasis, the New York Religious Tract Society did not ignore its own city. At first, however, the officers of the Society did not feel that city tract distribution differed in any way from that of their frontier work. The Society sought through the efforts of individual members to reach all classes and sections of the city. Members circulated tracts among their friends, left them on steamships and stage coaches, gave them to strangers in the street, to their servants, to the clerks in their offices, to the inmates of the city's charitable institutions. Their object was not to meet any specific temporal needs, but to convert all to Christ.[6]

Gradually, however, the Society's contact with the city's poor became more intimate and direct. Individual members began to seek out the needy in hopes of educating and ultimately converting them. James Eastburn, for example, a Society manager, had as early as 1814 and 1815 begun to visit working-class streets, leaving tracts and talking with the residents. (Eastburn had first become aware of the city's poor and their religious needs when he had helped to establish charity Sunday schools in slum neighborhoods.) By 1816, Eastburn's visiting and observations led him to propose at the Society's annual meeting that Society members begin to distribute tracts directly to the city's poor—and to all—he urged: to the intemperate, the vicious, and the irreligious, as well as to "the neglected poor, the sick and the dying." [7] Certainly such ministers and pious laymen as Samuel H. Cox, his close friend,

[5] N.Y.R.T.S., "First Annual Report," no page; and *Third Annual Report, 1814* (New York, 1815), pp. 5, 13–14.

[6] N.Y.R.T.S., *Fifth Annual Report, 1816* (New York, 1817), p. 13.

[7] *Ibid.*, p. 40.

Gardiner Spring, John D. Keese, and Divie Bethune were all well aware of the existence of city slums and the misery of their inhabitants.

The reports of the Society's own auxiliaries also drew attention to the existence of widespread misery and irreligion in American cities. One of the Religious Tract Society's oldest and largest auxiliaries, the Female Tract Society of Providence, Rhode Island, for example, chose the factory workers of Rhode Island's newly established mill towns as its mission field.[8] The Female Juvenile Society of the Cedar Street Presbyterian Church in New York and the Samaritan Society of New Orleans also chose the urban laboring classes as their mission field.[9] But the auxiliary most active in working with the urban poor was the Religious Tract Society's own Female Branch. Members visited the poor in their homes, leaving tracts and praying with the more receptive. Others, connected with the African Free School, distributed tracts among the city's black population. Finally in 1826, these experiences led them to announce "a plan for district visiting" in all sections of the city.[10] At this time, the ladies were not in a financial position to undertake so ambitious a program. Only a few years later, however, such a visiting plan was adopted by the ladies' new parent organization, the New York City Tract Society.

[8] *Ibid.*, pp. 31–32; N.Y.R.T.S., *Sixth Annual Report, 1817* (New York, 1818), pp. 37–39.

[9] N.Y.R.T.S., *Fifth Annual Report*, pp. 11–12; and *Eighth Annual Report, 1819* (New York, 1820), p. 16.

[10] Female Branch of the N.Y.R.T.S., "Constitution and Minutes, 1822–1826," entry for September 29, 1826. Significantly, the ladies traced their interest in visiting to the influence of the "excellent Local System of the Revd. Dr. Chalmers." Female Branch, *Second Annual Report, 1824* (New York, 1824), pp. 31–32; *Third Annual Report, 1825* (New York, 1825); and "Minutes, 1825–1827," entry of March 25, 1827.

While distribution and visitation work revealed the existence of poverty and slums to New Yorkers—to many for the first time—it did not immediately transform the Society's original goals. Even when working with the city's poor, the Society's interest remained almost exclusively religious. The poor were still poor because they were without religious comforts; charity was still defined as tract distribution and prayer.

At the same time, however, the Society's mode of operation was undergoing a major change. Begun as a single organization to print and distribute tracts throughout America, the Religious Tract Society soon found that its New York City membership could not, unaided, supply the religious needs of the entire frontier. After only three years of operation, the Society had found itself four hundred dollars in debt, while its tracts had yet to reach many communities, even in its own state. To improve both its financial and distributing arrangements, the Religious Tract Society began systematically to encourage the formation of auxiliary tract societies. These auxiliaries were to raise money with which to purchase tracts from the parent organization and then to distribute the tracts themselves, thus assuring an income to the parent society, which undertook the printing, and relieving it of the task of distribution.[11] So successful was the Religious Tract Society in this program that by 1816 it was able to expand greatly the number of tracts it printed. Two-thirds of the tracts printed were sold to its own auxiliaries, a ratio it maintained for the next decade. That same year it showed its first profit.

Yet financial embarrassment continued to plague the Soci-

[11] N.Y.R.T.S., *Fourth Annual Report*, pp. 6, 17–18. In doing this, the N.Y.R.T.S. was clearly following the example of the London Tract Society, which relied heavily upon its auxiliaries for financial support and for the distribution of its tracts. Foster, *Errand*, pp. 77, 87–88; Griffin, *Brothers'*, Chap. V.

ety. Beginning in 1820, tract sales reached a plateau. Many of
the auxiliaries, to save the expense and delay of transportation
from New York City to the west, printed their own tracts;
others shifted affiliation from New York to the newly established and vigorous New England Tract Society of Boston.[12]
Indeed these two organizations, each committed to saturating
the west with religious literature, soon found themselves in
competition for auxiliaries and financial support. Since both
were "Presbygational" organizations and both suffered from
financial embarrassment, it was not long before they united
in 1825 to form the American Tract Society. This new organization limited itself to printing low-cost religious tracts,
to be bought and distributed by its network of far-flung
auxiliaries. Thus the principal responsibility for distributing
tracts to the "needy" and the "negligent" now passed to these
auxiliaries.

The founding of a national organization did not result in
the members of the old New York Religious Tract Society
losing interest in their own city. Indeed, at the urging of a
number of New York members of the American Tract Society and with the help of the Female Branch, leaders of the
former Religious Tract Society intensified their distribution
of religious literature in New York City. At first they attempted to work through the American Tract Society. Supplied with tracts printed by the national society, individual
members visited the city's markets and the waterfront and
gave out tracts to artisans, sailors, and to passersby. But they
soon realized that such sporadic distribution was not adequate
to the growing religious needs of their own city.[13] New

[12] N.Y.R.T.S., *Tenth Annual Report, 1821* (New York, 1822),
pp. 5, 14, 21, 32.
[13] N.Y.C.T.S., *First Annual Report, Presented February 6, 1828*
(New York, 1828), p. 11.

York's population increased each year, swelled by European immigration and by young men and women from rural America. Suddenly cut off from accustomed religious ties and moral influences, these new city dwellers formed a spiritual flotsam in an ever-growing and potentially corrupting city. With an unstable population increasing each year, Christians could not delay; New York City desperately needed its own tract society.[14]

[2]

Thus on the evening of February 19, 1827, acting through the Young Men's Auxiliary Tract Society, the leaders of the old Religious Tract Society reassembled to form a new organization, the New York City Tract Society. Former presidents, treasurers, and managers of the Religious Tract Society, the leading philanthropists and evangelical Christians of the city attended: Richard Varick, Thomas Stokes, Arthur Tappan, Marcus Wilbur, Moses Allen and the Reverends John Stanford, Charles Sommes, James Milnor, and Gardiner Spring. Zachariah Lewis, the last president of the Religious Tract Society, became the first president of the new organization. They maintained their ties with the American Tract Society and organized the New York society as an auxiliary of the national group, its function being simply to distribute tracts throughout New York City.[15]

Indeed, the aims and methods of the City Tract Society at first closely resembled those of the Religious Tract Society and the American Tract Society. The managers of the City Tract Society, like those of the other two groups (they were, to a large extent, identical in these early years), saw themselves and their organization as part of a world-wide evangelical crusade. Their objectives were the gaining of converts to

[14] See, for example, *ibid.*, p. 21.   [15] *Ibid.*, List of Officers, no page.

evangelical Christianity, the strengthening of the faith of
fellow Christians, and the exerting of a moral influence upon
society generally. At first the managers made no concerted
effort to contact the city's poor. They were not secular reformers, seeking to solve the problems of crime or pauperism.
They sought rather the conversion and moral improvement of
all groups and classes in New York, the affluent as much as,
if not more than, the poor. They chose to work in the city
simply because it was one area, familiar to them, that the
American Tract Society had not included in its distribution
program. They did not, in 1827, as would many later religious
philanthropists, choose New York because it was an area
peculiarly corrupt and sinful but because it was a city.[16]

The program of the early City Tract Society reflected these
evangelical aims. Most of the managers and active members
agreed in considering the great social and religious problems
of New York to be Sabbath-breaking, intemperance, and
swearing. Such problems were to be found among New
Yorkers of all social classes. And City Tract Society supporters were confident that tract distribution could reform
the manners and morals of the ungodly. The officers of the
new society established six permanent committees to distribute
tracts to varied groups and areas in the city—to those whose
conversion might play a significant role in promoting the millennium. These were the sailors and ship captains of the waterfront, artisans and shopkeepers in the city markets, the city's
charity Sunday school scholars, the inhabitants of its public

[16] N.Y.C.T.S., Constitution of the New York City Tract Society,
Article 8, bound in the Society's *First Annual Report*; and also *First
Annual Report*, p. 12; *Third Annual Report, Presented February, 1830*
(New York, 1830), pp. 9, 19–20; and *Fourth Annual Report, Pre-
sented April 18, 1831* (New York, 1831), pp. 9–10, 12, 14.

institutions, its suburban population (often without a minister or church), and the passengers on the steamboats which plied the Hudson River and the coast of southern New England. These were for the most part not the very poor, the city's slum dwellers. The tract distributors sought to convert those most like themselves: businessmen and families from the countryside around New York, shopkeepers and mechanics who kept their shops open on Sunday. They sought as well the conversion of those traditional objects of religious charity, the sick, the criminal, the paupers of the almshouse.[17]

These committees were staffed not by salaried city missionaries but by the City Tract Society's own members. Every member of the Society was an active participant on one of the distributing committees. Arthur Tappan, for example, one of New York's wealthiest wholesalers, was a member of the Society's waterfront distributing committee, regularly visiting the piers and warehouses along the lower East River. William Dodge, another prominent merchant, was an active member of the steamboat committee. Merchant Zephaniah Platt and physician James C. Bliss, along with city chaplain John Stanford, composed the committee on humane and criminal institutions. On Sundays, between morning and evening church services, these tract distributors fanned out through the city. Along the waterfront they admonished sailors for drinking or swearing. In the public markets they urged shopkeepers to observe the Sabbath. Finding a group of boys headed for the play areas of the city for a game of ball, members of the committee on the outskirts of the city scolded them and sent them off to the nearest Sunday school. This pattern of tract distribution was informal, conceived as it was by men who still

[17] N.Y.C.T.S., *First Annual Report*, pp. 19–20; and *Second Annual Report, Presented February 4, 1829* (New York, 1829), pp. 8, 20, 21.

thought in terms of the small and relatively simple city they remembered from the opening years of the century.[18]

In 1829, however, the managers of the City Tract Society decided upon a radically new program, one which drastically changed their organization's activities, aims, and structure. At the Society's second annual meeting, Arthur Tappan rose to suggest that the Society form committees whose duty it would be to distribute a tract each month to every New York City family; the Society's *ad hoc* methods seemed grossly inadequate to the city's growing religious needs. The membership approved Tappan's plan and ordered the creation of committees to distribute tracts systematically in each of the city's wards.[19] The committees were to consist of the tract

[18] N.Y.C.T.S., *First Annual Report*, pp. 12–21; *Second Annual Report*, pp. 11–16; *Third Annual Report*, p. 18; *Fourth Annual Report*, pp. 16–17; and *Seventh Annual Report, Presented April 16, 1834* (New York, 1834), pp. 36–37.

[19] N.Y.C.T.S., *Third Annual Report*, pp. 9–10. The Society and Tappan were influenced in this choice by the decision, that same year, of the several national evangelical societies to saturate the Mississippi Valley with religious tracts, Bibles, and ministers. The N.Y.C.T.S.'s *Third Annual Report* contains the comment, "Are there not multitudes of families . . . even in our own city, who neglect all the means of grace, . . . and whom it is as truly our duty to supply with Tracts as any in the Valley of the West?" (p. 10). Undoubtedly of great influence, as well, was the system of district visiting adopted by the British evangelicals. They had supported a system of district visiting for a number of years, but in 1828 a representative group of evangelicals united to form the General Society for Promoting District Visiting. The purpose of the new national society was to establish "a regular system of domiciliary visitation . . . by which every poor family might be visited at their habitations, from house to house, and from room to room." Brown, *Fathers*, pp. 239–241. The proximity of the dates when English and New York evangelical groups both chose to distribute tracts systematically, monthly, in specific, well-defined districts, and the history of the close relationship between the two groups, suggests that Tappan and the New York Society were almost certainly influenced by the British precedent.

distributors for that particular ward; each tract distributor would have approximately sixty familes in his district. He was to visit every family at least once a month. Besides leaving tracts, the visitor was to discuss the family's religious life, urge church membership and regular attendance upon all, and offer to enroll the family's children in a convenient Sunday school. All sections of the city should be visited, Society managers consistently urged—even the poorest.

Over the next few years, the tract distributor's new role gradually changed and expanded. At first, in 1829 or 1830, these pious visitors had simply given out tracts and urged their allotted families to embark upon a religious life.[20] Slowly, however, individual visitors became deeply involved with the religious life of particular households. They were no longer satisfied if a family simply accepted religious tracts, or even read them. The distributors sought now the conversion of at least one member of each family. Beginning in that year visitors first reported selecting individuals each month for special prayer and missionary efforts.

In 1833, the Society officially recognized this new dimension in the distributor's role. That year the City Tract Society's officers formally instructed the visitors not simply to leave tracts, but to pray earnestly for and with each family. Indeed the officers implied that the tract distributor had failed in his duty unless he held prayer and Bible-reading sessions with his families and worked zealously for their conversion.[21]

[20] During the early years of the tract distribution effort, the N.Y.C.T.S. attributed conversions simply to the impact of the tract and not to the visitor's efforts to convert the individual (of which activity there is little evidence in the early 1830's). See N.Y.C.T.S., *Third Annual Report*, pp. 11–16; and *Fifth Annual Report, Presented March 14, 1832* (New York, 1832), pp. 1–22.

[21] N.Y.C.T.S., *Sixth Annual Report, Presented 1833* (New York, 1833), pp. 13, 10–14.

The official publications of the City Tract Society reflected these changes. Increasingly the Society's annual reports contained lengthy descriptions of conversions and of tract distributors' efforts to awaken sinners to the need for salvation. The tract distributor would press a tract upon the unregenerate soul, talk to him of his sins and of man's dependence upon Christ's mercy. At first the man or woman might refuse the tract, rebuff or insult the distributor, but finally would be overcome by consciousness of sin and the justness of eternal punishment. During the sinner's ordeal of anguish and fear, the tract distributor prayed with him, forcing him to recount his sins, picturing the torments of hell, but affirming, at the same time, the balm of Christ's love held out to all who would seek it. Joyously, the tract distributor reported each conversion to the City Tract Society. Proudly the Society printed the account in its next annual report.[22] Indeed, beginning in 1833, the annual reports regularly included a list of the number converted each month, a policy the Society continued until the 1860's.[23]

These institutional changes reflected radical alterations in the City Tract Society's formal aims and theological emphases. By 1831 and 1832, the Society's officers and members had begun to see their tract distribution as part of a great religious revival, sweeping across America and bringing with it the millennium. Indeed, as early as 1829 (the year, significantly, that the Society adopted its plan to distribute systematically to all in the city) the City Tract Society managers announced, "Christian Friends! This is no time for halting. It is an age of

[22] For examples of descriptions of conversions, see N.Y.C.T.S., *Seventh Annual Report*, pp. 13, 17, 27–28; *Ninth Annual Report, Presented 1836* (New York, 1836), pp. 21, 24; and *Twelfth Annual Report, Presented December 19, 1838* (New York, 1839), p. 44. Such descriptions dot the Society's reports throughout the 1830's.

[23] N.Y.C.T.S., *Sixth Annual Report*, pp. 25–27.

great events, the millennial day is approaching." After four years of tract distribution in each ward in the city, they concluded: "Never have your Board been so thoroughly convinced that, in this system, when it shall be seized with the united energy of the Church, they have the lever which shall move the foundation of Satan's empire in this city." By 1835, the City Tract Society's officers boasted of the changes which had transformed their organization. No longer was it simply a society that coldly distributed tracts. Its volunteers had become missionaries of Christ, struggling for the salvation of each individual they encountered. In 1834, the Society's Board of Managers had written of the duties and aims of the visitors:

The object before them has been the conversion of the entire city to the faith of Jesus Christ. It is a great work, and to the eye of sense, insurmountable obstacles oppose its accomplishment. But in reliance upon the arm of God, the work *can* be done: it *must* be done. They have endeavored, therefore, to impress upon the minds of those engaged in it, that the mere distribution of Tracts is only a subordinate part of the work, and that the high hopes of the friends of this cause will only be realized, when, in imitation of the great apostles of the Gentiles, every distributor shall, with the spirit of his Master, go from house to house "warning every man, and teaching every man, night and day with tears." [24]

The City Tract Society now considered itself "a society to carry the Gospel by the living voice, as well as the written word 'to every creature' . . . and . . . in the hand of God . . . to save all."

These views of their organization and its religious objectives marked a drastic change from those expressed in 1812 by the

[24] N.Y.C.T.S., *Second Annual Report*, p. 21; *Sixth Annual Report*, p. 9; *Eighth Annual Report, Presented March 11, 1835* (New York, 1835), p. 12; and *Seventh Annual Report*, p. 11.

founders of the New York Religious Tract Society. They had urged the distribution of tracts because the written word would obviate the need for personal preaching. Religious literature, as distinct from the sermons of itinerant, frontier ministers, would not excite the emotions or appeal to man's corrupt senses. Rarely did the Religious Tract Society refer to the individual conversions which resulted from its distribution work, never to the revivals which flared up throughout New York State during the very years the Religious Tract Society was most active in that area. Such attitudes bore little resemblance to the missionary zeal and the millennial hopes expressed a decade later by the leaders and workers of the newly founded City Tract Society.

What factors explain these changes? Basically they were the three we have already discussed. First was the Second Great Awakening and the evangelical movement within American Protestantism. Second and more specifically were the great urban revivals of Charles Grandison Finney. And, finally, there were the changes which had taken place in New York City itself during the generation between 1812 and 1832.

The managers and members of the City Tract Society, with a handful of exceptions, belonged either to the Presbyterian or to the Reformed Church of New York. Naturally, they considered themselves orthodox Calvinists and adhered to the doctrines of the Westminster Confession. For many of them, however, this adherence had become increasingly formal. While their religious zeal in no way decreased, their theological orientation lay less and less in the direction of orthodox Calvinism, more and more in the direction of the new evangelism.

In particular the Society espoused a belief in unlimited atonement, in the ability of Christians to act as agents in the conversion of sinners, and in the importance of revivals in bringing the millennium. No longer did the officers of the City Tract Society insist (as their orthodox predecessors had in 1812) upon God's infinite justice in condemning to hell the vast majority of mankind. More and more this traditional Calvinism was tempered by confidence in Christ's desire to save all men. "But Christ is full of compassion," the Society's managers wrote in 1834, "and unwilling that any should perish." [25] Salvation, made possible by Christ's amnesty, now depended upon man seeking out Christ, confessing his sins, and claiming His mercy. The countless conversion accounts in the Society's annual reports make clear the unfaltering belief that Christ wished to save all mankind.

Equally clear was the conviction that pious tract distributors were agents in the conversion process. Hence the logic in their attempting to seek the conversion of every family in the city. God, the City Tract Society's officers believed, blessed their members' prayers, their tracts, their very conversations, making the Society's volunteers agents of His saving grace. The Society's visitors came, indeed, by the mid-thirties to see their agency in the conversion of individual sinners as a necessity in bringing the millennium. The changes in religious beliefs which were foreshadowed early in the century in the official statements of such mission societies as the Young Men's Missionary Society of New York or the Female Missionary Society for the Poor of the City of New York clearly reached maturity in the assumptions and attitudes of the New York City Tract Society.

This new enthusiastic theology was in the air in the late 1820's and 1830's. Its optimism, its vigor, its faith in individual action were appropriate to the mood of the highly ambitious, materialistic, and rising port of New York. But specific events in the years between 1827 and 1835 crystallized these new be-

[25] N.Y.C.T.S., *Seventh Annual Report*, p. 9.

liefs for New Yorkers. During these years Finney conducted his great eastern revivals.

Throughout these years Finney maintained close personal ties with a number of the managers and officers of the New York City Tract Society. Perhaps his earliest eastern supporter was Arthur Tappan; by 1826 and 1827 such other advocates of tract distribution as Lewis Tappan, Anson G. Phelps, and William and David Dodge had all become ardent Finney disciples. Zephaniah Platt, one of the Society's officers and most active tract distributors, while living in western New York, had been a personal convert of Charles Finney.[26] Both through such personal contacts and in his theology, Finney embodied and promoted this growing and pervasive enthusiasm, this increasing emphasis on human ability.

No sooner had Finney arrived in the east to preach in Wilmington, Delaware, in 1827 than Anson G. Phelps and the Tappans arranged a secret meeting between the youthful revivalist and New York's orthodox Presbyterian clergy. They hoped, in this way, to win Finney an entree to the city's pulpits, whose pastors were united in their suspicion of Finney's "new measures." When this failed and the regular ministry refused to invite Finney to preach in the city, the Tappans, against the wishes of their own pastor, asked Finney to preach as summer replacement at their Laight Street Presbyterian Church. In the years that followed, in order to provide Finney with a regular church, Anson G. Phelps, with financial support from the Tappans, purchased several churches for Finney and his congregations. It was from these churches that Finney led his two great New York revivals, one from the fall of

[26] Charles G. Finney, *Memoirs of Rev. Charles G. Finney, Written by Himself* (New York, 1876), pp. 275–277, 280–283; McLoughlin, *Modern Revivalism*, pp. 50–51.

1829 to midsummer of 1830, the second beginning in 1832 and extending until his departure for Oberlin in 1835.[27]

These revivals had the effect of presenting the new theological beliefs dramatically to New Yorkers. Thousands came to hear Finney's lectures and to attend his evening prayer and Bible meetings. The number of converts grew, impressing even the indifferent and hostile, and soon the revival spread to other churches. Merchants gave their clerks time off to attend Finney's meetings, while special early morning services were held for the businessmen themselves. By 1832, Finney's New York City converts had established seven new churches.[28]

Finney taught new methods, as well as new ideas. Indeed many of the missionary techniques adopted by the City Tract Society's distributors of prayer, conversation, and Bible-reading were first developed by Finney during these revivals. It was he who urged Christians to overcome their natural reticence and to seek conversions among the unregenerate. It was his custom, for instance, during his revival meetings to

[27] McLoughlin, *Modern Revivalism*, pp. 51–53. For a description of these new evangelical churches, see Susan Hayes Ward, *The History of the Broadway Tabernacle Church, from Its Organization in 1840 to the Close of 1900, Including Factors Influencing Its Formation* (New York, 1901), pp. 21–32, and L. Nelson Nichols, *History of the Broadway Tabernacle of New York City* (New Haven, 1940), pp. 52–55, 61–63.

[28] For an important firsthand description of Finney's New York revivals, see his *Memoirs*, pp. 272–283, 320–325. These new Presbyterian (later Congregational) churches organized as free churches, that is, without the customary pew rental fee. They hoped to appeal to the middle and lower-middle classes, perhaps even to the artisans and the poor of New York, a group established churches had made little effort to incorporate into church membership. Cf. Finney's remarks on the work of the Dey Street First Free Presbyterian Church. Finney, *Memoirs*, p. 283.

station converts throughout the church. They were to observe if any person near them was particularly moved and, if so, urge him to stay after the meeting for special prayers. (And their enthusiasm was unquestionable; Arthur Tappan, for example, one evening seized the lapel of a prospective convert and refused to let go until his prisoner had promised to attend special prayer meetings that same evening.[29] City Tract Society visitors reported countless zealous acts of this kind when seeking the conversion of a resident of their assigned district.) Finney also urged his converts to visit homes throughout the city, especially in the poorer sections surrounding the Chatham Street Chapel.[30]

It was in 1829, the year that Finney began his revival in New York (following similar revivals in Philadelphia and Rochester), that Arthur Tappan, already a Finney disciple, proposed the universal distribution of tracts in New York. In 1830 and 1831, during and immediately following Finney's forceful sermons urging New Yorkers to go through the streets seeking the conversion of all, the City Tract Society visitors began to do just that, to pray and struggle for the justification of every family in their district. That same year, 1830, the Society predicted that its visitors would "with the blessing of God, destroy every vice and nourish every virtue." [31] In the premillennial enthusiasm of 1830 the Society intended this prediction quite literally.

A close relationship would also appear to have existed between Finney's preaching and the willingness of New Yorkers

[29] *Ibid.*, pp. 322–323.

[30] Finney sent his disciples out to some of New York's worst slums. They went from house to house urging people to attend Finney's meetings and afterwards visited those who had gone, seeking to secure their conversion. This work closely resembled the visiting conducted by the New York City Tract Society.

[31] N.Y.C.T.S., *Seventh Annual Report*, p. 24.

to volunteer as tract distributors and city missionaries. In 1830, following Finney's first New York revival, the number of the Society's tract distributors suddenly increased from roughly fifty to nearly five hundred. This number continued to grow slowly over the next few years. During the winter of 1834–1835, the winter of Finney's second New York revival, over one thousand men and women actively engaged in tract distribution and missionary activities.[32] Samuel Halliday, for example, during the next three decades one of New York's best-known and most active city missionaries, reported that it was Finney's revivals that had led him into missionary work. Moreover, he recalled years later, almost every member of his church had felt Finney's influence and become an active Christian worker as a result.[33]

Finney's influence is apparent not only in the increased number of the City Tract Society's volunteer distributors but also in their changed activities and self-image. New York's regular ministers, in many cases conservative in both theology and social views, would not and could not visit all over the city, praying with the unchurched. Lay tract distributors thus assumed the role of revivalists to their city.[34] The division

[32] N.Y.C.T.S., *Second Annual Report*, "List of Officers," no page; *Fourth Annual Report*, p. 18; *Sixth Annual Report*, pp. 9–10; *Seventh Annual Report*, p. 9; *Ninth Annual Report*, p. 13; and *Eleventh Annual Report, Presented December 20, 1837* (New York, 1838), p. 210. At all times, at least half of the tract distributors were women. Clearly this type of religious activity offered activist women a socially acceptable area in which to expend their energies.

[33] Halliday, *Winning Souls*, pp. 7–12, 20–29.

[34] There was apparently some hostility between some members of the regular ministry and the officers and workers of the Tract Society. This ill-will was undoubtedly influenced by the regular clergies' hostility to Finney and his revivals and the growing split within the Presbyterian Church between revival and conservative groups. In 1836, indeed, Finney withdrew from the Presbyterian

of New York into tract districts gave each distributor his own "parish," his own flock to exhort and convert. Finney had repeatedly insisted in his winter sermons that the lay Christian must act to promote conversions and revivals, if his minister would not. Thus encouraged, the tract visitors—as they were now called—began to proselytize actively and to bring their converts to regular churches fully prepared for membership.[35]

The Society's officers did all they could to encourage volunteer workers to view themselves as city missionaries. In each annual report, they carefully recorded the numbers converted in each ward. The ministers whose lengthy sermons marked each annual meeting of the Society also stressed the importance of the layman's new role. Only if each individual Christian worked as a missionary, the Reverend Smith told the tract distributors in 1835, only if he were "willing to labor and 'travail in birth' for his dying fellow men," could the millennium come.[36] Conscientiously the lay tract distributor strove to be worthy of this new responsibility. Often he would spend his mornings in prayer and supplication—and in the af-

----

Church to accept the pastorate of the Broadway Tabernacle, organized with the financial support of the Tappans, Dodges, and A. G. Phelps as a Congregational Church. Beginning in 1834 the N.Y.C.T.S. began to criticize the regular churches for their failure to support the Society's efforts to secure a city-wide revival, and also for failing to bring religion to the city's poor. N.Y.C.T.S., *Seventh Annual Report*, p. 50; and *Eighth Annual Report*, p. 35. With revival-minded ministers, however, the Society and its workers maintained the closest relations.

[35] N.Y.C.T.S., *Seventh Annual Report*, p. 31; *Eighth Annual Report* pp. 12, 49; *Sixth Annual Report*, pp. 11–21; and *Eleventh Annual Report*, p. 80.

[36] The Reverend Smith (no first name given), quoted in N.Y.C.T.S., *Eighth Annual Report*, pp. 12, 5–12. See similar remarks made later that year by the Reverend E. F. Hatfield, *Ninth Annual Report*, pp. 6–8.

ternoon distribute tracts with "an assurance that I was not alone, neither going in my own strength." When he visited the poor—ignorant and often without a Bible, let alone money to purchase a regular church pew—he must have seemed indeed a minister of God.[37]

Finney's radical doctrines thus drastically altered the New York City Tract Society's distribution methods, its collective self-image as well as the self-image of the individual tract visitor. But this was only a beginning. An inevitable result of the membership's decision to distribute tracts systematically throughout the city was their discovery of urban poverty. By 1835, tract distributors were regularly visiting slum families.[38] Their first reaction, as in the case of a distributor in the city's seventh ward, was one of horror at such poverty and ignorance. "In visiting the abodes of the sick and afflicted this past month, I have witnessed an increased amount of wretchedness. Almost every-day brings me in contact with cases so appalling and distressing that it requires a nerve of steel to prevent the mind and body from sinking under perpetual excitement." They found ramshackle buildings housing as many as seventy persons, streets crowded with children who neither worked nor attended school, their parents poverty-stricken, drunken, and illiterate. "To see their degradation," as one distributor wrote, "perfectly astonished me." Concerned, visitors wrote touchingly of women seeking to survive in unheated and unfurnished garrets, of children barefoot and hungry. By

[37] Report of a tract visitor, N.Y.C.T.S., *Ninth Annual Report*, p. 31; and *Seventh Annual Report*, p. 19.
[38] That year the Society's newly hired, salaried city missionaries, for the first time, included visiting the poor and distributing charity as one of their regular duties. J. B. Horton, "Report for the Seventh Ward," N.Y.C.T.S., *Eighth Annual Report*, p. 23; T. T. Pond, "Report for the Eleventh Ward," *ibid.*, p. 37; John H. Bulin, "Report for the Thirteenth Ward," *ibid.*, p. 40.

the mid-1830's, many tract distributors were working exclusively in slum neighborhoods.[39]

As the tract visitors became increasingly familiar with the city's slums, they realized that their inhabitants would never become members of the city's regular churches—in part because of the slum-dwellers' own ignorance, destitution, or irreligion, in part because of the indifference, indeed hostility, of New York's clergy and laity. They began, accordingly, to offer special services for the poor; they organized Sunday schools, weekly and bimonthly Bible classes, and prayer meetings for inhabitants of the city's worst tenements. At times they were amazed at their own success. A visitor in the fifth ward, who had established a prayer meeting for the seventy tenants of the infamous Arcade apartment house, reported that his work had been so popular that the tenants had requested him to begin a Bible class as well. "A moral change has evidently taken place in this colony," he reported. "This month we report two hopeful conversions as the result of this labor." [40]

By the mid-1830's, then, they had begun to see the conversion of the urban poor as an important task and their Society as a real link between the city's churches and the poor. The Society's annual reports frequently referred to Christ's admonition that "the poor have the Gospel preached to them." The Society, as an Albany clergyman testified at their annual

[39] N.Y.C.T.S., *Ninth Annual Report,* pp. 15, 23–25, 30; and *Eighth Annual Report,* pp. 18, 23, 34–35.

[40] N.Y.C.T.S., *Tenth Annual Report, Presented December, 1836* (New York, 1837), p. 35. In March of 1835, William Bradford, one of the Society's city missionaries, wrote of his systematic visitations and distribution of charity, "the distributors felt this to be the only system by which they could effectively preach the Gospel to the poor and destitute of this populous city." N.Y.C.T.S., *Eighth Annual Report,* pp. 15, 34–35.

meeting in 1835, "goes to the people. It really flies across the great gulf which they would never pass. It goes to the sick, the infirm, the bedridden, the aged, the stupid, the ignorant and careless, the infidel, the scoffer, the hardened and the tender-hearted." [41]

Inevitably, the visitors began to go among the poor armed with food, money, and clothing as well as with tracts and prayers. At first such charity was distributed informally by individual visitors; the annual report for 1833 contains mention of one of the first such incidents. A tract distributor, visiting a crowded city tenement, came upon a bedridden invalid. His wife, busy caring for her husband and three children, could not work to support the family. The rent was due. They had pawned all their possessions and could not buy food for the day. "I have now no prospect but starvation and death," the man declared. The distributor paid the rent and brought food and clothing for the family. That year, the City Tract Society secretary concluded his annual report with the casual statement: "The Poor and the Sick have in very many instances been sought out and their wants supplied." [42]

With each year the City Tract Society became increasingly involved in distributing such temporal goods along with its religious literature, prayers, and exhortations. The Society authorized tract visitors to pay rent, to bring food and clothing to the destitute, and to find jobs for the unemployed. In 1834 tract distributors reported supplying clothing to Sunday school children and bringing fuel and food to poor families.

[41] N.Y.C.T.S., *Seventh Annual Report*, p. 50.

[42] Throughout 1832 and 1833, most of the Society's charitable work was carried out in an extremely random fashion. The Society apparently made no attempt to organize either sources of charitable aid, or their search for those who needed aid. N.Y.C.T.S., *Sixth Annual Report*, pp. 13, 5, 20, 27.

Some dedicated their efforts toward aiding the destitute black population of the city. A few visitors established night schools to teach the freedmen to read and write. Increasingly the visitors' tasks began to resemble those of early twentieth-century social workers. The Society's managers gave institutional recognition to this new charitable role when they began to appeal in their annual reports to pious New Yorkers to create a special fund—separate from that earmarked to support tract distribution—which the visitors could call upon in their new philanthropic role.[43]

Significantly, all these early objects of charity were examples of what contemporaries would call the worthy poor: the sick, the aged, the widowed, and the orphaned who suffered through no fault of their own. Within the religious context of the time, these poor were placed on earth by God to strengthen their own character through suffering and perhaps more importantly to provide wealthy Christians with an opportunity for charitable acts. (Significantly as well, these early objects of concern were drawn from groups basically in sympathy with the Protestant values of contemporary society, and thus relatively receptive to the visitors' conversion efforts.)

But gradually both the objects of charity and the tone of the Society's reports changed. During 1835 and 1836, the tract distributors came increasingly to blame poverty on the deliberate acts of the poor themselves, and especially on the sin of intemperance. In 1835, tract distributors began a census of the number of saloons in their districts. Amzi Camp, superintendent of the poverty-stricken sixth ward, reported count-

[43] N.Y.C.T.S., *Seventh Annual Report*, pp. 1–14, 30–34, 41; *Eighth Annual Report*, pp. 15, 23–24, 34–35; *Ninth Annual Report*, pp. 15, 23–25, 30; *Tenth Annual Report*, pp. 22–25, 36, 46–47, 54–59, 64–65, 71; and *Eleventh Annual Report*, pp. 80–87.

ing over three hundred saloons in his district, forty on a single street. Increasingly the tract distributors came to correlate poverty with intemperance. "Both parents were intemperate, of course very poor." "The husband of this worthy woman was a *drunkard—he died a drunkard,* and the *drunkard's poverty* and the *drunkard's curse* came upon his family." "There are in my district *ten groceries,* producing poverty, wickedness, and death in the families around." [44]

Gradually the City Tract Society's early optimism faded. The objects of their efforts were no longer a troop of young boys seeking relaxation in a Sunday ball game or an artisan found working on the Sabbath. Now the Society worked among drunkards, among slum dwellers in wretched garrets and hovels.[45] The City Tract Society's attitude toward the approaching millennium, toward its own city, and toward the poor began ever so slightly to change. The tract distributors still concerned themselves primarily with the conversion of the individual soul. Their goals, despite these *ad hoc* charitable efforts, remained centered in the spreading of the Gospel. They still compared their work with that of rural tract distributors. But increasingly a note of concern, almost of despair, would creep into their reports. How could the Society convert this throng of destitute, often alien, persons? How could they relieve their needs, temporal and spiritual, and bring them into the community of respectable, Protestant Americans? The financial panic and depression which struck the city in 1837 and the years following sharpened this sense

[44] N.Y.C.T.S., *Eight Annual Report,* pp. 14–15; *Ninth Annual Report,* pp. 17, 20, 24; and *Tenth Annual Report,* p. 41.

[45] N.Y.C.T.S., *Ninth Annual Report,* p. 17. In 1837, for instance, a woman visitor, whose district was a black slum, wrote: "When I first approached the district . . . my spirit sunk within me, regarding the field altogether inaccessible to a tract visitor. . . . I commenced with trembling." N.Y.C.T.S., *Eleventh Annual Report,* p. 27.

of helplessness and despair. The Society's visitors between 1837 and 1843 devoted their efforts almost exclusively to meeting the most pressing physical needs of the destitute and homeless. As they did so, their sense of the endlessness of the city's needs increased, sharply altering the sense of confidence and optimism which had characterized the first visiting committees.[46]

Yet religion continued to hold out hope. In the mid- and late thirties the City Tract Society and its membership still believed that God's grace could remake their city. The Society's principal concern remained the religious conversion of the individual. This was the path through which the millennium would come. Their efforts to convert all of New York's inhabitants dominate the annual reports and statements of individual distributors through the 1830's.

[46] See below, Chap. 7.

CHAPTER 4

New York Female
Moral Reform Society

In the spring of 1834, a group of earnest New York women established the New York Female Moral Reform Society. Its aim was the reform and ultimate conversion of New York's prostitutes and, more generally, the advocacy of moral perfection throughout American society. In this Victorian generation, such a society represented necessarily an extreme wing of evangelical Protestantism. Its leaders, converts and personal acquaintances of Charles Grandison Finney, were motivated by the revivalist's insistence that all sin, even the oldest, must be driven from the land; every Christian, they believed, must work zealously to purify American society. Only then could the millennium come. Clearly, an absorbing interest in the physical well-being, or even in the religious conversion, of New York's poor had no place in the goals of the Society's founders.

Yet within but a few years of its organization, the Female Moral Reform Society had become one of the city's more active eleemosynary institutions. Its members and their paid agents visited tenement apartments, distributed food and clothing, and sought jobs for the unemployed. This transformation, like the similar metamorphosis of the New York City Tract Society, grew out of a desire to convert all men, and the motivation such a conviction provided created situations in which at least some respectable New Yorkers came into contact with the poor of their own city. This work with the city's poor grew increasingly prominent in the Society's program as the unattainability of their original goal—the conversion of New York's prostitutes and the purification of American sexual morality—became gradually apparent.

The history of the Moral Reform Society demonstrates with peculiar clarity another and comparatively neglected aspect of ante-bellum American reform movements—the new role of women. Women played an important part in all of the religious reform groups of this evangelical generation; they were the workers, the fund raisers, the emotionally committed supporters of tract and Bible societies, of Sunday schools, and of charity sewing societies. In these activities, the women of America's new middle class found ways to expand the roles traditionally allotted them—and to express as well a normally unspoken hostility toward the male and his dominant role.

[1]

Charles Grandison Finney began his first New York revival in the fall and winter of 1829; it continued into the spring of 1830. That same spring a youthful Princeton divinity student, John R. McDowall, arrived in New York City to spend the summer as a volunteer city missionary for the American Tract Society.[1] In these two events lay the origins of the

---

[1] John R. McDowall, the son of a minister in Fredericksburg, Lenox County, Midland District, Upper Canada, was born February 20, 1801. He attended Schenectady College and then Princeton. While at Princeton, 1828–1829, McDowall was active in a number of evangelical and missionary societies. Joshua Leavitt, *Memoir and Select Remains of the Late Reverend John R. M'Dowall* (New York, 1838), pp. 1–89, 99.

American Female Guardian Society, its nationwide moral reform crusade, and its long-lived city mission work.

Undoubtedly influenced by its New York City auxiliary, the American Tract Society sent McDowall to the Five Points, already notorious for its crowded tenements, its crime rate, and its numerous and sordid brothels. McDowall, assisted by his brother, a fellow divinity student, visited tenements, distributed Bibles and tracts, established a Sunday school, and gave temperance lectures. Eventually the brothers even began to visit the Five Points houses of prostitution, leading prayer meetings when they could and remonstrating with both the women and their customers.

Deeply moved by his summer experiences, McDowall decided not to return to Princeton that fall, but to remain in New York as a city missionary. Although he lacked any formal sponsorship or financial support, McDowall began to organize Sunday schools and Bible classes in the city's prisons and almshouse. The dynamic young man quickly found supporters. A number of respectable New York women, many converted during Finney's winter revival, came to McDowall's aid; they taught in his Sunday schools and Bible classes, visited the prisons and hospitals, led prayer meetings, and distributed religious literature. These volunteer workers gradually became interested in the "affecting" problems of the female convicts.[2] Most of these women, McDowall's visitors soon discovered, were prostitutes. Upon their release from prison or hospital, no honest occupation offered an alternative to their old ways; their lives revolved around the brothel, the prison, and the hospital. In 1831, hoping to disrupt this vicious cycle, and hoping also to provide an opportunity for exerting

[2] *Ibid.*; cf. New York Magdalen Society, *First Annual Report of the Executive Committee of the New York Magdalen Society, Instituted January 1, 1830* (New York, 1831), p. 5.

some Christian influence upon these lost souls, a number of McDowall's female supporters—aided by such active and generous evangelicals as Arthur and Lewis Tappan—established the New York Magdalen Society and opened a "House of Refuge." The house would serve, they hoped, as a stopping place for the penitent harlot. Here she might be subjected to the benevolent influence of religion and at the same time be taught new skills; at last, she might assume a responsible place in society.[3]

McDowall and his supporters had established their home with little or no publicity and, consequently, without criticism from even the most fastidious. This pleasant state ended abruptly when McDowall published his first annual report as missionary of the Magdalen Society. The young man proclaimed indignantly that there were some ten thousand prostitutes in New York; many of the brothels' regular clients, he asserted, belonged to prominent and seemingly respectable families. Lewdness and impurity tainted all sectors of American society. True Christians, McDowall asserted, must wage a thoroughgoing crusade against violators of the Seventh Commandment.[4]

[3] *McDowall's Journal*, II (December, 1834), 89. The relation of this early Magdalen Society to the evangelical movement generally, and to the N.Y.C.T.S. specifically, can be seen in its first list of officers and directors. The Society's first president was Arthur Tappan; its directors included A. G. Phelps, William Colgate, Thomas Stokes, George P. Shipman, and Moses Allen. New York Magdalen Society, *First Annual Report . . . 1830*, inside title page and p. 7.

[4] John R. McDowall, *Magdalen Report*, reprinted *McDowall's Journal*, II (May, 1834), 33–38. The radical and atheistic *Free Enquirer*, highly critical of New York's missionary and charitable societies, took special note of McDowall's report. While somewhat skeptical of his statistics, the editors were pleased to point to the seeming inability of Christian doctrine to reform New York men. *Free Enquirer*, July 23, 1831, pp. 313–314.

The report shocked and irritated respectable New Yorkers, not only by its facts, but also by its tone of righteous indignation, and by its implied criticism of New York's leading families. McDowall immediately became the target of an indignation equally righteous. The young ex-Princetonian was, it seemed clear to many New Yorkers, an irresponsible scandalmonger, an obscene seeker after notoriety.[5] Hostility quickly spread from McDowall to the Society he had founded; its female members were subjected to abuse and threatened with ostracism. The Society quickly retreated, denying responsibility for the report; the ladies closed their home and disbanded their organization.[6]

But McDowall would not retreat. Seeking to rally support, he published a second report, *Magdalen Facts*, reaffirming and enlarging upon his original statements. In this report, McDowall called not simply for increased zeal in converting prostitutes, but also for a general and uncompromising moral crusade, one which would ruthlessly excise sin from all of American society.[7] McDowall began as well to publish a monthly, *McDowall's Journal*, its purpose to urge what was from the first a largely rural audience to turn to God, to purify their own hearts, and to work toward the moral perfection of American society.[8]

To secure financial support, McDowall urged the creation

[5] Flora L. Northrup, *The Record of a Century* (New York, 1934), pp. 13–14; cf. *McDowall's Defence*, I, No. 1 (July, 1836), 3; *The Trial of the Reverend John Robert McDowall by the Third Presbytery of New York in Feb., March, and April, 1836* (New York, 1836).

[6] [Thomas Hastings, Sr.], *Missionary Labors through a Series of Years among Fallen Women by the New York Magdalen Society* (New York, 1870), p. 15.

[7] John R. McDowall, *Magdalen Facts* (New York, 1832).

[8] Only two volumes of *McDowall's Journal* were published, covering the period January, 1833, to December, 1834.

of local, church-centered, reform societies. Within the year, a number of such groups had been founded in New York, connected for the most part with the city's more evangelical churches. (A number of these had been themselves newly founded in response to the enthusiasm of Finney's revivals.) These groups hoped, of course, to reform prostitutes, but also to warn other God-fearing Christians of the pervasiveness of such sin and the need to oppose it. Prostitution was after all only one of many offenses against the Seventh Commandment; adultery, lewd thoughts and language, and bawdy literature were equally sinful in the eyes of God. *McDowall's Journal* served as a vehicle for such warnings and admonitions. After nearly a year of silent support for *McDowall's Journal*, the female members of the several moral reform societies felt sufficiently numerous and confident to organize a second city-wide moral reform society, and to open a new house of refuge.[9]

Thus on a spring evening in May, 1834, a small group of women met at the revivalistic Third Free Presbyterian Church to found the New York Female Moral Reform Society.[10] Its founders and many of its active members—or their

---

[9] Between the demise of the New York Magdalen Society and the organization of the New York Female Moral Reform Society (hereinafter referred to as N.Y.F.M.R.S.), McDowall was connected—as agent—with a third society, the New York Female Benevolent Society, which he had helped found in February of 1833. For a more detailed account, see Carroll Rosenberg, "Evangelism and the New City," Chap. V.

[10] "Minutes of the Meeting of the Ladies' Society for the Observance of the Seventh Commandment held in Chatham Street Chapel, May 12, 1834," in ledger book entitled "Constitution and Minutes of the New York Female Moral Reform Society, May 1834 to July 1839," deposited in the archives of the American Female Guardian Society (hereinafter referred to as A.F.G.S.), Woodycrest Avenue, Bronx, New York. (The Society has the executive com-

fathers or husbands—were closely associated with Finney, whose wife, Lydia Andrews Finney, was the Society's first directress. After she moved with her husband to Oberlin in 1835, leadership was assumed by Mrs. William Green, the wife of one of Finney's closest supporters. The two clergymen instrumental in the founding of the organization, Dirck C. Lansing and John Ingersoll, were disciples of Finney and well known for their revival enthusiasm. The Tappan brothers, so active in their advocacy of Finney's evangelical goals, acted for many years as sponsors and financial advisors to the ladies.[11]

With such close ties to Finney and his new theology—and the commitment it implied to Christian action—the ladies of the Moral Reform Society occupied an extreme wing in the evangelical movement. They were not content to remain at home, satisfied with educating their children in the ways of piety and with praying for the millennium. Finney's preach-

---

mittee minutes from May, 1835–June, 1847, and from January 7, 1852– February 18, 1852.) See also *McDowall's Journal*, II (January, 1834), 6–7. The Society continues to exist, caring for children from broken or disturbed homes. Its current name is the Woodycrest Youth Service.

[11] For early officers and managers, see *McDowall's Journal*, II (January, 1834), 6–7, and II (September, 1834), 65. For a list of early "male advisors" to the N.Y.F.M.R.S., see Leavitt, *Memoir*, p. 248. For the connection between the Society, its supporters, and Finney, see L. Nelson Nichols and Allen Knight Chalmers, *History of the Broadway Tabernacle of New York City*, pp. 49–67, and McLoughlin, *Modern Revivalism*, pp. 50–53. McDowall's own connection with Finney and his New York City supporters was apparently quite close. Tappan paid McDowall's expenses when he first came to work with the American Tract Society. Anson G. Phelps, as a member of the N.Y.S.P.P., first interested McDowall in visiting the penitentiary and establishing a Sunday school there. When McDowall was finally ordained, it was at the Finneyite Spring Street Church. Leavitt, *Memoir*, pp. 99, 151, 192.

ing had convinced them that silence in the face of sin amounted to complicity. Like the New York abolitionists— many, of course, Finneyites and some such as Leavitt and the Tappans also supporters of the moral reform cause—they felt themselves unable any longer to compromise with the devil; sin must be assailed wherever and in whatever form it existed. Condemnation by the polite and dead-of-soul could not be permitted to affect such resolves. As they stated in the first edition of their moral reform journal:

As Christians we must view it in the light of God's word—we must enter into his feelings on the subject—engage in its over-throw just in the manner he would have us; and we shall feel we ought to have done in the great day of judgment. We must look away from all worldly opinions or influences, for they are per-verted and wrong; and individually act only as in the presence of God.[12]

Seen in these transcendent terms, their duty was inescapable.

[2]

The program adopted by the Female Moral Reform Soci-ety in the spring of 1834 embraced two quite different, though to the Society's founders quite consistent, modes of attack. One was absolutist and millennial, an attempt through publications to convert the entire nation to perfect moral purity. At the same time, however, the Society sponsored a parallel and somewhat more pragmatic program, one aimed at converting and reforming the lewd and presumably lost women of the city. Though strikingly dissimilar in method and geographic scope, both efforts were unified by an un-compromising zeal for driving sin from America and promot-ing the millennium.

The vehicle for the Society's crusade to purify all America

[12] *Advocate of Moral Reform*, I (January–February, 1835), 6.

was their monthly journal, the *Advocate of Moral Reform*. In December of 1834, shortly after the establishment of their organization, the ladies acquired *McDowall's Journal*. Renaming it the *Advocate for Moral Reform*, they made it their official journal.[13] Within three years, the *Advocate* had become one of the nation's most widely read evangelical papers, and by 1837 boasted 16,500 regular subscribers. By that time the Society's managers had come to see its publication as their most important activity.[14]

The female editors of the *Advocate* remained true to the program enunciated by John McDowall in 1832. The *Advocate*, like *McDowall's Journal*, openly addressed itself to the problems of illicit sexuality and the circulation of lewd and suggestive literature, art, and songs. Country readers were warned again and again that both prostitution and seduction were far more common than they imagined, that country girls, seduced and abandoned, provided the principal source of New York's harlots. Mothers were entreated to educate their children in a knowledge of the Seventh Commandment and to permit neither sons nor daughters to leave home without being warned of the dangers awaiting them.[15] Column after closely printed column was filled with stories illustrating the perils besetting the virtue of innocent country girls.

The forthright details (explicit seduction scenes, for example) in some of these incidents were shocking enough to

[13] The Society, in taking over the *Journal*, hired McDowall as general agent and missionary. N.Y.F.M.R.S., "Executive Committee Minutes, December 31, 1834." See also *Advocate of Moral Reform*, I (January–February, 1835), 1.

[14] N.Y.F.M.R.S., "Executive Committee Minutes, June 6 and June 25, 1835, June (n.d.) 1836"; N.Y.F.M.R.S., *The Guardian or Fourth Annual Report of the New York Female Moral Reform Society, Presented May 9, 1838* (New York, 1838), pp. 4–6.

[15] See, for example, *Advocate of Moral Reform*, I (October and November, 1835), *passim;* II (January, 1836), 3; III (February 15, 1837), 211; IV (January 15, 1838), 14; and IV (April 15, 1838), 59.

contemporaries; far more controversial, however, was the Society's decision to continue the factual exposés which McDowall had begun in his journal. McDowall, to the consternation of many respectable New Yorkers, had urged readers to inform him of men they knew to be guilty of visiting brothels or of seducing innocent girls—especially men prominent in their community's religious or public life. McDowall, in printing these letters, left little doubt in his readers' minds as to the transgressor's identity; he used the initials of such "hypocrites" and provided the names of the towns or counties in which they lived.[16] The lady managers of the Society decided, when adopting *McDowall's Journal*, to continue such articles and letters. They stated defiantly in the first issue of the *Advocate:*

We think it proper even to expose names, for the same reason that the names of thieves and robbers are published, that the public may know them and govern themselves accordingly. We mean to let the licentious know, that if they are not ashamed of their debasing vice, we will not be ashamed to expose them. Whenever we can possess ourselves of well-authenticated facts in connection with names, we shall soon let it be known what stand we shall take in relation to this vice.[17]

[16] See, for example, *McDowall's Journal*, I (March, 1833), 20; I (October, 1833), 75–76; II (January, 1834), 7–8; and II (April, 1834), 25–28. Public reaction, especially, one assumes, among certain groups in society, was violent and personal. McDowall reported receiving countless obscene and threatening letters. *Ibid.*, I (December, 1833), 103. A New York State Grand Jury finally condemned the magazine as "an obscene and demoralizing publication," a decision applauded by respectable New York religious journals. *McDowall's Defence*, I, No. 1 (July, 1836), 3.

[17] See, for example, *Advocate of Moral Reform*, I (March, 1835), 13–14; I (April, 1835), 18, 20; II (January, 1836), 3–4; II (February, 1836), 17–19; III (January 15, 1837), *passim;* and III (February 15, 1837), *passim.*

As converts of Finney, the ladies were convinced that sin existed only because the saved had not struggled and prayed against it. They felt an individual and immediate responsibility to fight sin in all its manifestations, even those of adultery and fornication. It was this pietistic commitment which sanctioned the Society's defiance of customary social taboos; absolute moral imperatives made it possible, indeed necessary, for the ladies to speak the unspeakable.[18]

Not surprisingly, the great majority of the *Advocate*'s rural subscribers lived in that belt of New York counties termed by contemporaries the "burned-over district." From its inception the New York Female Moral Reform Society had wooed the pious women of New York State and New England. In June of 1835, the Society's executive committee hired a minister to travel through western New York "in behalf of *Moral Reform Causes*." [19] The following year the committee sent two emissaries—the editor of the *Advocate* and a paid female agent —on a thousand-mile tour of the New England states. Visiting women's groups and churches in Brattleboro, Deerfield, Northampton, Pittsfield, the Stockbridges, and many other towns, the ladies rallied their sisters to the moral reform cause and helped organize some forty-one auxiliaries. Each succeeding summer saw similar trips by paid agents and managers of the Society.[20] By 1839, the New York Female Moral Reform

[18] It would be inappropriate in this context to attempt to explicate possible subconscious motivations which compelled the exhilarating concern with sexual morality exhibited by these particular women. Such concerns were, however, formally consistent with an activist and millennial world view.

[19] N.Y.F.M.R.S., "Executive Committee Minutes, June 25, 1835," p. 38.

[20] N.Y.F.M.R.S., "Executive Committee Minutes, October 4, 1836, and May 22, 1837, and September 11, 1839," pp. 4–7, 59, 85. Indeed, as early as 1833 a substantial portion of John McDowall's support

Society boasted some 445 female auxiliaries, principally in greater New England.[21]

The numbers and financial strength of the auxiliaries soon began to reshape the structure of the Moral Reform Society. Its dependence upon auxiliaries outside the city was intensified, moreover, by the financial difficulties the New York Society faced following the Panic of 1837.[22] With many of their staunchest city supporters bankrupt or in straitened circumstances, the ladies were forced to turn to their auxiliaries for financial aid. The *Advocate* regularly printed appeals for money, and the executive committee began to distribute special circulars asking for contributions.[23] In 1839, the Society's executive committee voted to reorganize as a national society; the New York group would be simply one of its constituent societies.[24]

At the same time that the Society's managers had launched their uncompromising war against the licentiousness which seemed to pervade the New England countryside, they began, as well, their more sharply focussed campaign against New York City's houses of prostitution.

---

seemed to come from rural areas. See, for example, *McDowall's Journal*, I (August, 1833), 59–62.

[21] N.Y.F.M.R.S., "Executive Committee Minutes, October 4, 1838," p. 118; Northrup, *Record*, p. 22.

[22] For the effect of the Panic on New York's evangelical Congregationalists see Nichols and Chalmers, *History of the Broadway Tabernacle*, pp. 67–72.

[23] N.Y.F.M.R.S., "Executive Committee Minutes, October, 1837 to February, 1838," *passim.*

[24] N.Y.F.M.R.S., "Executive Committee Minutes, May 10, 1839," pp. 1–3; and "Quarterly Meeting, July, 1839." Power within the new national organization was so divided that the president and board of managers were members of the N.Y.F.M.R.S. while the vice presidents were chosen from the rural auxiliaries. The annual meeting was held in New York City, the quarterly meetings in one of the towns of Greater New England.

In the fall of 1834, the Society's managers appointed John McDowall as their official agent and missionary and hired two young missionaries to assist him.[25] Paralleling McDowall's original mode of operation, these missionaries visited the female wards of the almshouse, the city hospital, and jails, leading prayer meetings and distributing Bibles and tracts. Far more of their time, however, was spent in systematically visiting—or, to be more accurate, descending upon—brothels, praying with and exhorting both the inmates and their patrons. The Society's missionaries went everywhere, from the exclusive brothels on the west side, boasting elegant interiors and a distinguished carriage trade, to the filthy houses at Five Points and Corlear's Hook. The missionaries were especially fond of arriving early Sunday morning—catching women and customers as they awoke on the traditionally sacred day. The missionaries would announce their arrival by a vigorous reading of Bible passages, followed by prayer and song.[26] Their reception at the more genteel establishments was relatively polite and even encouraging. The women often expressed deep regret at their life of sin and blamed an early and unwise love for their undoing. The women and customers of the lower-class slum brothels, however, met them almost uniformly with curses and threats.

The ladies did not depend completely on paid missionaries for the completion of such tasks; accompanied by pious male volunteers from the city's revival churches, the members of the Female Moral Reform Society themselves invaded the city's hapless brothels. (The executive committee minutes for Janu-

[25] *Advocate of Moral Reform*, I (January–February, 1835), 4; Northrup, *Record*, p. 19.

[26] *Advocate of Moral Reform*, I (March, 1835), 11–12; I (August, 1835), 59; and I (November, 1835), 86; N.Y.F.M.R.S., "Executive Committee Minutes, April 30, 1836," p. 54.

ary of 1835, for example, contain a lengthy discussion of the properly discreet make-up of groups for such active visiting.) [27] The members went primarily to pray and to exert moral influence. They were not unaware, however, of the disruptive effect that frequent visits of large groups of praying Christians would have. In a *Circular to the Ladies of the United States*, the managers urged that "Companies of pious males or females should visit [such] houses from day to day. . . . This will leave them no peace in their sins—will have the effect of breaking up their houses—will prevent visitors from going there through fear of detection." [28]

In conjunction with such visiting, the Moral Reform Society opened a "House of Reception," a refuge for prostitutes seeking to reform. It was not meant, the managers firmly announced, to be a home for the morally incapable, a permanent refuge for those seeking to hide from the world. Rather, they envisioned their home as a "house of industry" where the errant would be taught new trades and prepared for useful jobs. When the managers felt their repentant charges prepared—both morally and with new skills—to return to society, they attempted to find them jobs with Christian families —and so far as possible—away from temptation.[29]

Despite this melioristic approach, the ultimate objects of the Reform Society were spiritual, not temporal. Certainly the causes of prostitution—as the ladies understood them—were varied, ranging from betrayed innocence and inexperience to economic need and moral depravity. But religious conversion was, in every case, a necessary part of a permanent cure. The prostitute lived as an enemy of God; each day without re-

[27] N.Y.F.M.R.S., "Executive Committee Minutes, January 24, 1835," p. 31.
[28] *Advocate of Moral Reform*, I (January–February, 1835), 7.
[29] *Ibid.*, I (September 1, 1835), 72; Northrup, *Record*, p. 19.

pentance corrupted her further. Only God's redeeming grace could secure her reformation and eternal forgiveness. A partial or temporary reform could often be effected, the ladies admitted, by finding a girl a job or by returning her to her family, but only God's grace and a consciously experienced salvation brought true reform.[30] The Society's managers strove at all times to convert their charges. Besides the daily prayers common to Christian homes of the day, the managers held weekly prayer meetings at the House and not infrequently would stop their bimonthly executive committee meetings when the Holy Spirit seemed near to call their "family" to pray with them.[31]

Despite such pious efforts, however, few prostitutes reformed; fewer still appeared, to their benefactresses, to have experienced the saving grace of conversion. Indeed, the number of inmates at the Society's House of Refuge, as it came to be called, was always small. In March of 1835, for instance, the Executive Committee reported only fourteen women at the House. A year later, total admissions had reached but thirty, only four of whom were considered saved. As late as April, 1836, after almost two years of rescue efforts, the officers could characterize only four inmates as "serious and industrious." [32]

Almost a year earlier, indeed, the managers had considered remodeling their House of Refuge into a "Stranger's Hotel." By offering temporary lodgings to "honest but destitute" women, as the managers put it, they hoped to protect the

[30] *Advocate of Moral Reform,* I (April, 1835), 17; I (May, 1835), 35; and IV (January 1, 1838), 13.
[31] N.Y.F.M.R.S., "Executive Committee Minutes, December 24, 1834, January 24, 1835, and January 12, 1836."
[32] *Advocate of Moral Reform,* I (March, 1835), 11; N.Y.F.M.R.S., "Executive Committee Minutes, April 5, 1836, May 30, 1835," pp. 52, 55.

virtuous from the city's temptations. They did not abandon their House at this time, however, but moved it instead to a more respectable uptown neighborhood, hoping that rural surroundings might be more conducive to reform work.[33] Another year of failure, however, convinced the managers and their executive committee that hopes of reforming the fallen were delusive. The final debacle came in the summer of 1836 when the regular manager of the House left the city because of poor health. In his absence, the executive committee reported unhappily, the inmates seized control, and discipline and morality deteriorated precipitously. The managers reassembled in the fall to find their refuge in chaos. Bitterly discouraged, they dismissed the few remaining unruly inmates and closed the building.[34]

While discouraged in its attempts to reform the city's prostitutes, the Society had during these same years become increasingly conscious of New York's peculiar spiritual and material needs.

At the same meeting in which the executive committee decided to close the House of Refuge, it voted to open an employment agency for destitute but honest women, hoping to prevent prostitution by offering the still virtuous an honorable alternative. A few months later, the committee voted to hire two female missionaries to distribute religious tracts to families throughout the city, and a male missionary to visit the poor in the almshouse and penitentiary. Most importantly for the future of the organization, in December of 1836, the executive committee constituted itself a visiting committee, each of its members agreeing to visit families in the city, preaching piety and strict observance of the Seventh Commandment.[35] (It

[33] Northrup, *Record*, p. 19.
[34] N.Y.F.M.R.S., "Executive Committee Minutes, October 4, 1836."
[35] N.Y.F.M.R.S., "Executive Committee Minutes, December 6, 1836," p. 69.

was hardly coincidental that these same months saw an intensification of the City Tract Society's melioristic efforts.)

These decisions widened the Society's contact with the destitute and unemployed of the city, though this had been by no means the Society's original intent. Each institutionalized commitment tended to develop a tenacious life of its own, inadvertently projecting the Society ever deeper into the problems of urban poverty. This is demonstrated clearly in the evolution of the Society's employment agency. The work of this agency grew so rapidly that within six months of its founding, the ladies in charge declared themselves unable to cope with the overwhelming number of job applications.[36] So important did the task of finding jobs for unemployed women seem to the executive committee that in June, 1837, they voted to change drastically the statement of purpose that appeared in their by-laws to include a statement of their new charitable efforts among the urban poor. The amendment explained,

One special object of this Society shall be to extend the hand of Christian kindness to respectable unprotected females, especially the fatherless and the orphan, and when such shall apply with the proper testimonials an effort shall be made to obtain employment for them in such families as may be safely recommended.

Within a few years hundreds of women turned each month to the Society's employment bureau not only for jobs but also for aid. "The poor," the executive committee commented, "seemed to regard the Society and rooms a public depot for charity." [37]

The activities of the visiting committee increased each year

[36] N.Y.F.M.R.S., "Executive Committee Minutes, April 21, 1837," p. 82.

[37] N.Y.F.M.R.S., "Executive Committee Minutes, June 19, 1837, February 1, 1843." The Society did not record how many of these women received jobs through the Society.

as well. Indeed by the spring of 1837 members of the executive committee spent so much of their time in house-to-house visiting that the managers voted to pay each member a monthly salary. (Twenty-four dollars was the figure agreed upon, no nominal sum at this time.) [38] At first the visiting committee's efforts paralleled those undertaken by the City Tract Society's workers during that organization's early years. Both organizations began programs of house-to-house visiting with the sole object of spreading evangelical religion. The sick, the dying, housewives and their small children, and the aged all received particular attention—as did families with adolescent daughters and adults professing belief in unorthodox theologies. [39]

From the first, the families visited seem to have been principally middle and lower-middle class. Some visitors showed a definite hesitancy in approaching the homes of the well-to-do. This demonstrates, I think, the class assumptions and make-up of the Society's membership—and of a number of contemporary evangelical societies as well. These societies represented the newly established—in many cases families whose roots were not in the city but in New England or western New York. (Though conclusive evidence is of course lacking, it seems likely that their participation in the Society's activities was an assertion of the legitimacy of their own roles through a defensive attack on the implied godlessness of established families who did not live as Christians should. One gathers this impression with particular clarity in reading the Society's attacks on the city's more fashionable bordellos, and their well-to-do clients.) By the late 1830's especially,

[38] N.Y.F.M.R.S., "Executive Committee Minutes, May 22, 1837," p. 85.
[39] *Advocate of Moral Reform*, IV (January 15, 1838), 14–15; IV (February 15, 1838), 29–30; and IV (March 1, 1838), 37.

when the enthusiasm of the revivals had begun to wane, many of the Reform Society's lady tract distributors began to report an increasing hesitancy when preparing to visit New York's more elegant homes. As one visitor wrote:

Felt some reluctance at entering a large and elegant house. I knew that my errand, though a noble one, would receive only the contempt of the rich and the great. . . . The ladies were out, and had the opportunity for conversation with the servant. . . . Her mind was extremely tender. She took the paper with eagerness, and asked immediately for tracts. . . .[40]

A few casual humiliations tended to confirm the ladies' natural tendency to visit the middling classes of society. Gradually, however, as their knowledge and experience broadened, they began to visit even the poor and soon to think of themselves as missionaries specifically to the city's poor.[41]

During the late 1830's their work among the poor grew steadily. Visitors began to report canvassing tenement houses or helping families "respectable but poor." [42] On November 9, 1840, the executive committee could specifically define missionary work among the poor as the chief function of the visiting committees. "The duties," they explained, "of those employed as visiting committees shall be to devote their time to faithful missionary labor in the destitute portions of our city." [43]

Important as the visiting committee's own efforts were in

[40] See the comments of two Society visitors in *ibid.*, IV (March 1, 1838), 37.

[41] The visitors had hesitated at first at this step. One member of the visiting committee remarked early in 1838 that she did not usually visit the very poor. "We knew not what treatment we were to expect in these wretched houses." Finally, however, she visited some twenty slum families. *Ibid.*, IV (February 15, 1838), 30.

[42] *Ibid.*   [43] *Ibid.*, VI (November 9, 1840), 44.

reaching the poor and thus reshaping the Society's policies, external events conspired to force upon them a measure of responsibility for feeding and clothing the needy. In July of 1837 (but a few months after the disintegration of the ladies' House of Refuge) a number of eastern banks failed, precipitating the Panic of 1837 and the subsequent depression which lasted until the mid-1840's. The Society, already in contact with the poor through its employment agency and visiting committee, acted to meet the emergency. The New York Female Moral Reform Society first began to distribute charity to the poor the February following the crash. From that date, the minutes of the executive committee indicate a rapid expansion of this work.[44] By the year's end, indeed, the Society's members were fast becoming expert observers of New York's slum conditions. The visiting committee repeatedly reported finding great destitution, in some cases approaching starvation, among the laboring classes. The funds of New York's ward-relief committees, the visitors found, had become completely inadequate. Hundreds were turned away each day as provisions dwindled at local soup kitchens. The visiting committee saw little choice but to attempt insofar as it could to supplement the efforts of the established ward-relief committees.[45]

Though its scale increased, this work remained inherently random and—in a sense—inadvertent. Its object was still the conversion of the individual soul. The visiting committee sought out tenement families to pray with them, to urge church attendance, if possible to convert them. If such families

[44] From 1838 on, the executive committee received regular reports from the visiting committee on living conditions among the poor. A.F.G.S., "Minute Book No. 2, 1839–1840," *passim*.

[45] See, for example, *Advocate of Moral Reform*, IV (January 1, 1838), 7; IV (February 15, 1838), 29–30; IV (March 1, 1838), 37; and IV (March 15, 1838), 46.

happened to be destitute, without food or clothing, if there were sick children or a dying grandparent, then the visitors were quick to give what help they could: quilts, sheets, food, medicines.[46] And, of course, the ladies of the visiting committee were exposed to the problems of only a minority among the poor, those who seemed "virtuous" and receptive to the word of God. The moralism which informed their view of the world also helped determine the objects of their charity. A Society visitor, for example, walking down Ann Street, in the heart of one of the city's worst slums, was shocked by the extreme poverty of the inhabitants. "But alas!" she reported, "few were found deserving of relief, nearly all were reduced to their present suffering by a course of vice." [47] As was the case with many contemporary religious charities, the Society had true access only to families whose attitudes agreed in most cases with their own. With Catholics, many immigrants, the criminal, and the atheistic, the Society had little if any contact. These poor were simply outside the ladies' experience, and the contacts which did occur brought only misunderstanding and hostility.

Though the ladies remained dedicated supporters of the moral reform crusade, the American Female Guardian Society had changed perceptibly in the years since 1834. Gone was the joyous optimism which anticipated the momentary coming of Christ's Second Kingdom. The ladies no longer asserted—or, presumably, felt—that their organization could drive prostitution from the land and purify American sexual morality. They had begun to assume the more limited goal of helping, insofar as they could, to care for the city's deserving poor.

[46] N.Y.F.M.R.S., "Executive Committee Minutes, February 7, 1838, February 15, 1838, March 1, 1838, October 24, 1838, February 11, 1841."

[47] *Advocate of Moral Reform*, IV (March 1, 1838), 37.

[3]

This pattern of development closely resembled in its institutional evolution the pattern followed by New York's other city missions. But in one aspect the Society was unique. That was its founders' conscious—indeed at times aggressive—assertion of the rights and superior virtues of the female sex.

The urge to go about as self-proclaimed and zealous missionaries of the Lord affected many pious church-going women during the 1830's. But most devoted their energies to such socially acceptable causes as Sunday schools, Bible and tract distribution, foreign missions, or the temperance crusade. The moral reform movement, widely criticized as indelicate if not improper, required from its members a different, perhaps deeper, commitment. Undoubtedly the individuals joining the Society did so for personal reasons, and one assumes their "extreme" personalities were atypical; yet it seems clear that they expressed more general, if less consciously felt, sentiments. In a real sense, the moral reform crusade can be seen as part of a growing self-awareness among middle-class American women, as part of an ordinarily unexpressed desire for an expansion of their role.

The moral reform movement provided a number of outlets for the middle-class woman, released from the labors of the farm by residence in town or city and freed of much household drudgery by servants. The Society broke down the barriers which restricted her to the home. It provided her with a journal written and managed by women and devoted to discussions of immediate interest to the pious American woman. It offered her, through her moral influence in the home and community, a significant part in bringing the millennium. And, by attributing prostitution to men's lechery, it gave a significant number of women a socially acceptable avenue for expressing hostility to men. But far more than this, the Society, in its war against the double standard, offered the American woman—while still remaining within the security of the family unit—a means through which to control the behavior of men.

The American Female Moral Reform Society demonstrated this unspoken feminism in its own institutional history. Its women founders had established their Society in the face of the determined opposition of the city's religious leaders, the religious press, and most of New York's respectable men. Quite early, moreover, they adopted the policy of staffing their organization exclusively with women. From the first only women had been officers and managers of the Society. And after a few years, these officers began to hire women in preference to men as agents and employees. (They did this although the only salaried charitable positions held by women in this period tended to be those of teachers in girls' schools, or supervisors of women's wings in hospitals and homes for juvenile delinquents.) In February, 1835, for instance, the executive committee hired a woman agent to solicit subscriptions to the *Advocate*. That summer they hired another woman to travel through New England and New York State organizing auxiliaries and giving speeches to women on moral reform. In October, 1836, the executive officers appointed two women as editors of their journal—undoubtedly among the first of their sex in this country to hold such positions.[48] In 1841 the committee decided to replace their male financial agent with a woman bookkeeper. By 1843 women even set

[48] N.Y.F.M.R.S., "Executive Committee Minutes, February 20, 1835, October 4, and October 5, 1836," pp. 32, 59, 63; and *Fifth Annual Report*, p. 5.

type and did the folding for the Society's journal. All these jobs, the ladies proudly—indeed aggressively—stressed, were appropriate tasks for women.[49]

Perhaps most importantly, the American Female Moral Reform Society gave its members a sense of female solidarity, a sense of worthiness and autonomy outside woman's traditionally confining role. Its members, their officers frequently told them, formed a united phalanx of 20,000 women. All were daily engaged in a battle to protect their own sex and purify the world by enforcing female moral standards upon the male community.[50]

The key to this *esprit de corps*—it would seem from the tone and rhetoric which characterized almost every issue of the *Advocate*—was a deep-seated hostility toward men, toward their violation of the Seventh Commandment, and, as well, toward their superior position in the home and in soci-

[49] A.F.G.S., *Eleventh Annual Report for the Year 1845* (New York, 1845), pp. 5–6. For details of replacing male employees with women and the bitterness of the male reaction, see A.F.G.S., "Executive Committee Minutes," *passim*, for early 1843. Nevertheless, even these aggressively feminist women did not feel that women could with propriety chair public meetings, even those of their own Society. In 1838, for instance, when the ladies discovered that men expected to attend their annual meeting, they felt that they had to ask men to chair the meeting and read the women's reports. Northrup, *Record*, pp. 21–25.

[50] The executive committee minutes and the *Advocate* are dotted with statements of an aggressively militant type, such as when, in 1837, the American Seventh Commandment Society, a male group, suggested at the time of its organization that the ladies could now properly retire from the field. This they testily refused to do. "We regard ourselves," they replied, "as acting on the behalf and in the name of a large portion of our sex to whom we have virtually pledged ourselves and as occupying ground which none but women could so appropriately or efficiently fill." N.Y.F.M.R.S., "Executive Committee Minutes, October 24, 1836, June 28, 1837," pp. 64–65, 88; and *The Guardian*, p. 3.

ety generally. Titles such as "Licentious Males More to be Despised than Licentious Females" were typical.[51] Equally common were the letters from rural subscribers castigating particular men for callously seducing an innocent girl, causing her ruin, yet retaining favor in the most polite society. Most letters protested particular incidents, but a significant number voiced a bitterness and hostility toward men disproportionate to the particular circumstances involved. The Society's journal provided an avenue for women to express such normally suppressed feelings. Remarking on the double standard and men's attitude toward the seduced woman, one not atypical rural subscriber complained to the Society in 1834,

Honorable men; they would not plunder; a mean action they despise; an imputation on *their honour* might cost a man his life's blood. And yet they are so passingly mean, so utterly contemptible, as basely and treacherously to contrive . . . the destruction of happiness, peace, morality, and all that is endearing in social life; they plunge into degradation, misery, and ruin, those whom they profess to love. O let them not be trusted. Their "tender mercies are cruel." [52]

A similar tone, though more cautiously expressed, characterized many of the Society's official pronouncements. "It makes us indignant," the editors of the *Advocate* wrote in 1835, "that our sex should any longer be imposed upon by men, who pass as gentlemen and yet are guilty of loathsome and disgusting conduct. It is a justice which we owe to each other, to expose their names." An even sharper note of hostility was sounded in a resolution unanimously adopted at one of the Society's quarterly meetings. "Let the condemnation

[51] *Advocate of Moral Reform,* I (November, 1835), 84.
[52] Letter, *McDowall's Journal,* II (April, 1834), 26–27. For similar letters, see *Advocate of Moral Reform,* I (January–February, 1835), 7; I (April, 1835), 22; and I (December, 1835), 91.

of the guilty of our sex remain entire; but let not *the most guilty* of the two—the deliberate destroyer of female innocence—be afforded even an 'apron of fig leaves,' to conceal the blackness of his crimes." Editorials constantly urged women to refuse men of questionable reputation admittance to their homes, to reject proposals of marriage from such men, to drive them out of respectable society.[53]

This hostility toward men, so marked in the Moral Reform Society's rhetoric, yet limited by the accepted form of explicit moral outrage, occasionally manifested itself in even more basic and ultimately revealing criticism. An editorial in the *Advocate* in 1838, for instance, expressed a deeply felt resentment against the power asserted by many husbands over their wives and children. The Society admonished:

A portion of the inhabitants of this favored land are groaning under a despotism, which seems to be modeled precisely after that of the Autocrat of Russia. . . . We allude to the tyranny exercised in the HOME department, where lordly man, "clothed with a little brief authority," rules his trembling subjects with a rod of iron, conscious of entire impunity, and exalting in his fancied superiority.

The Society's editorialist continued, perhaps even more bitterly, "Instead of regarding his wife as a help-mate for him, an equal sharer in his joys and sorrows, he looks upon her as a useful article of furniture, which is valuable only for the benefit derived from it, but which may be thrown aside at pleasure."[54] Such behavior, the editorial carefully emphasized, not only was common, experienced by many of the Society's own members—even by the wives of "Christians" and of

[53] *Advocate of Moral Reform*, I (April, 1835), 20; I (January-February, 1835), *passim*; I (September, 1835), 70; II (February 8, 1836), 20; and IV (January 1 and January 15, 1838), 6, 14.

[54] *Ibid.*, IV (February 15, 1838), 28.

ministers—but also was accepted by society and even justified by men; was it not sanctioned by the Bible?

At about the same time, the editors of the *Advocate* went so far as to print a lengthy attack upon "masculine" translations and interpretations of the Bible, and especially of Paul's epistles. These appeared in a letter written by Sarah Grimké, noted feminist and abolitionist. Calling upon American women to read and interpret the Bible for themselves, she asserted that God had created woman the absolute equal of man. But throughout history, man, being stronger, had usurped the natural rights of women. He had subjected wives and daughters to his physical control and had evolved religious and scientific rationalizations to justify this domination. "Men have endeavored to entice, or to drive women from almost every sphere of moral action." Miss Grimké charged,

"Go home and spin" is the . . . advice of the domestic tyrant. . . . The first duty, I believe, which devolves on our sex now is to think for themselves. . . . Until we take our stand side by side with our brother; until we read all the precepts of the Bible as addressed to woman as well as to man, and lose . . . the consciousness of sex, we shall never fulfil the end of our existence.[55]

Yet such overt criticism of woman's traditional role, such explicit hostility toward men was atypical (containing as it did an attack upon the Protestant ministry and orthodox interpretations of the Bible). This went far beyond the consensus of the *Advocate*'s rural subscribers. The following issue contained several letters sharply critical of Miss Grimké and of the managers, for printing her editorial.[56] And indeed the

[55] *Ibid.*, IV (January 1, 1838), 3–5. For a recent study of the Grimké sisters, see Gerda Lerner, *The Grimké Sisters From South Carolina; Rebels against Slavery* (Boston, 1967).

[56] *Advocate of Moral Reform*, IV (April 1, 1838), 55, and IV (July 16, 1838), 108.

Advocate never again published the work of an overt feminist. Spokesmen for the Society had always been careful to disown explicit attacks on traditional family structure and orthodox Christianity. Indeed their tone in defending tradition was not infrequently bitter and aggressive as, for example, when one of the Society's missionaries reported meeting "a 'Fanny Wright,' in a woman from Philadelphia. . . . Miserable wretch! She talked like a fool about abrogating the marriage covenant. Her talk was so abominable that she was sent from our presence." [57]

The American Female Guardian Society's primary motive and object was the advancement of evangelical Protestantism. Only within this context did they express their feminist sympathies. Overt woman's rights advocates, on the other hand, not infrequently espoused questionable theological doctrines, or else were outrightly atheistic. Anticlericalism had its part in the woman's rights movement as did radical criticism of such social institutions as the family, divorce, and male suffrage. The feminist sentiments expressed by the New York managers and their rural auxiliaries were far more covert— and thus presumably characteristic of a far broader grouping in American society. Rather than being rallying cries for revolutionary programs in woman's rights, these statements were the expression, often barely conscious, of a newly sharpened resentment of women's traditional social and family roles—a resentment we can perhaps associate with the social and economic changes taking place in America during "The Age of Jackson."

[57] *Ibid.*, I (March, 1835), 12. It should be noted that this particular missionary was male.

CHAPTER 5

New York Protestant Episcopal City Mission Society

Both the New York City Tract Society and the American Female Guardian Society were essentially evangelical in motivation and world view. Their involvement with New York's slum dwellers originated, as we have seen, not in the hope of elevating the temporal condition of the poor, but as an incidental skirmish in a more general and uncompromising onslaught against sin.

Not all of New York's religious philanthropists felt this millennial urgency. During the same years that the missionaries of the City Tract and Female Guardian Societies first undertook their struggle against sin, New York Episcopalians also began to work in Manhattan's slums. But their preconceptions and motivations were hardly identical; these benevolent Churchmen sought answers to the same problems as their evangelical contemporaries but found many of the elements of their solution within a distinctly catholic and institutional tradition.

But not every aspect of their response to poverty was uniquely Episcopal. By the 1820's and 1830's, many American Episcopalians had begun to adopt some of the "new methods" of their evangelical contemporaries; like them, they hoped both to save the unchurched and to increase church membership. Indeed, these pious Churchmen hoped that such adopted mission endeavors might bring new vitality to an Episcopal Church weakened by both the American Revolution and the Second Great Awakening. Certainly they could not ignore the pietistic enthusiasm which so moved their fellow Americans. The parallelism of response in denominations so different in traditions only emphasizes the pervasiveness and strength of Jacksonian America's new spirit of religious and social activism.[1]

[1] Relations between High- and Low-Church Episcopalians and between High Churchmen and the evangelical denominations suggest a relation between evangelical and Church missionary organizations more involved than simple emulation and exchange of ideas. Many of the Episcopal missionary and philanthropic societies (for example, the New York Protestant Episcopal Sunday School Union, The Bible and Common Prayer Book Society, the Protestant Episcopal Tract Society, even the New York Protestant Episcopal City Mission Society) seem to have been founded by High Churchmen in competition with the evangelical organizations. Indeed, all ante-bellum Episcopal philanthropic and missionary societies were founded and supported by "High Church" Bishops Hobart and Onderdonk. Leading Low Churchmen such as Stephen Tyng and James Milnor associated themselves not with Church organizations but with their evangelical counterparts—the American Sunday School Union, the American Bible Society, the American Tract Society. They did so in the face of diocesan pressure to support Church organizations, and indeed they evinced certain hostility toward such exclusively Episcopal societies. Cf. James Grant Wilson, ed., *The Centennial History of the Protestant Episcopal Church in the Diocese of New York 1785–1885* (New York, 1886), pp. 373–374, 389–395; Arthur Lowndes, *A Century of Achievement, The History of the New York Bible and Common Prayer Book Society for One Hundred Years* (New York, [1909]); John S. Stone, *A Memoir of the Life of James Milnor, D.D., Late Rector of St. George's Church, New York* (New York, 1849); John Pintard, *Letters*, I, 39, 44–45, 90, 192; II, 134–135; III, 5, 27–28, 80, 175, 177, 261; and IV, 55; Henry Anstice, *A History of St. George's Church in the City of New York, 1752–1811–1911* (New York, 1911), pp. 89–90.

On a June evening in 1831, at a joint anniversary meeting of Christ Church's Male and Female Missionary Associations, Benjamin Onderdonk, newly elected Bishop of the New York diocese, rose and urged the formation of a new benevolent society—an Episcopal city mission.

Episcopalians, he argued, must expand their traditional missionary aims. For years, Christians had been concerned with the need for sending missionaries to Asia and Africa and aiding struggling new parishes in their own western lands. Yet the poor on Manhattan Island had received at best desultory attention; New York was a great and neglected mission field. Onderdonk proposed that the churches of the diocese join in supporting a new society "to preach the Gospel to those without it in New York City itself." [2] Well-to-do New Yorkers traditionally left the city during the hot and unhealthy summer months; nothing was done until September. Then, however, support for the proposed society was enthusiastic, and organizational meetings were quickly held. New York's first Protestant Episcopal City Mission Society began operations early in November, 1831. [3]

The tradition of American Episcopalians caring for the destitute and outcast was almost as old as English colonization in the Western Hemisphere and began with the work of the Society for the Propagation of the Gospel in Foreign Parts. The Society assumed responsibility for the religious instruction, general education, even the physical needs of the black

[2] New York Protestant Episcopal City Mission Society (hereinafter referred to as P.E.C.M.S.), "Minutes leading to the formation of the New York Protestant Episcopal City Mission Society," manuscript ledger, New York Protestant Episcopal City Mission Society, 35 Bleecker Street, New York City (all manuscripts cited, unless otherwise noted, are deposited with the Society).

[3] P.E.C.M.S., "Minutes, Public Meeting, Christ Church, September 15, 1831"; *Churchman*, I (September 24, 1831), 107. For reports of other meetings, see *Churchman*, I (October 1, 1831), 111; I (October 8, 1831), 115.

slave, of the American Indian, and, along the eastern seaboard, of the urban poor. Individual parishes aided this London-based organization in its work. In the Episcopal south, the church vestry supervised the distribution of county charity. In New York City, Trinity—in colonial times the city's only Episcopal Church—organized a charity day school for the children of New York's day laborers and artisans. The pupils were provided not only with instruction, but with food, clothing, even money when their families appeared sufficiently needy and deserving.[4]

Such philanthropic work continued, indeed increased, during the early decades of the nineteenth century. By 1821, for example, New York Episcopalians had helped found a black Episcopal congregation and two free Episcopal churches for poor farmers and squatters in northern Manhattan. Episcopal ministers visited poor neighborhoods, holding Sunday services in areas unable to support a church. Church women organized charity sewing societies, making clothing and bedding for the poor of their parishes and distributing the funds raised by annual fairs and bazaars.[5]

By far the most important and intense contact that New York's Episcopalian church members had with their poorer neighbors came through the parish Sunday school. As originally conceived, both in England and the United States, the Sunday school was a charity school, an attempt to bring reli-

[4] Frank J. Klingberg, *Anglican Humanitarianism in Colonial New York* (Philadelphia, 1940); Carl Bridenbaugh, *Mitre and Sceptre, Transatlantic Faiths, Ideas, Personalities, and Politics, 1689–1775* (New York, 1962); Wilson, *Centennial History*, pp. 370–371; John P. Peters, *The Annals of St. Michaels Protestant Episcopal Church, New York, Compiled on Order of the Vestry* (New York, 1907).

[5] Pintard, *Letters*, IV, 82–83; Peters, *St. Michaels*, pp. 41, 44, 48–49, 69, 238–240; William Wilson Manross, "The Episcopal Church and Reform," *Historical Magazine of the Protestant Episcopal Church*, XII (1943), 339–366.

gion, morals, and a modicum of secular education to the children of the poor. The children of church members—and this applied to evangelical as well as Episcopal churches—did not attend Sunday school; they received their religious education at home and from the sermons they attended each Sabbath. Sunday school classes were, accordingly, held in most cases away from the church building itself, in lofts or rooms rented in poorer neighborhoods.[6]

By 1833, New York Episcopalians supported twenty-four Sunday schools, with an enrollment of 6,161 pupils. The Sunday school teachers, volunteers from among the regular church members, saw their activities as charitable, indeed missionary, labors. In addition to teaching the elements of reading and writing, they visited the homes of their "sabbath scholars," preaching to and praying with adults and children alike, and in this way familiarizing themselves with the temporal needs of their slum-dwelling students. The judicious distribution of temporal charity soon became an important and consciously acknowledged part of the Sunday school movement.[7]

A number of individual Episcopal churches, moreover, established charity day schools for the general education of

[6] Manross, *The Episcopal Church in the United States, 1800–1840* (New York, 1938), pp. 200–201; Anstice, *St. George's*, pp. 87–91; C. H. Brewer, *Early Episcopal Sunday Schools* (Milwaukee, 1933), p. 20.

[7] Brewer, *Sunday Schools*, p. 24; General Protestant Episcopal Sunday School Union, *Fifth Annual Report* (New York, 1831), p. 46; John Henry Hobart, *The Beneficial Effects of Sunday Schools Considered* (New York, 1818); James Milnor, *Address Delivered Before the Superintendents, Teachers and Pupils of the Sunday Schools Attached to St. George's Church, November 9, 1817* (New York, 1817). Indeed, one of the first publications of the Protestant Episcopal Sunday School Union was a series of 800 cards to aid teachers in instructing the illiterate to read. New York Protestant Episcopal Sunday School Society, *First Annual Report of the Board of Managers, December 31, 1817* (New York, 1818).

the poor within parish boundaries and in adjacent neighborhoods.[8] The most active of these was not established by a particular church, however, but by the diocese itself; this was the Protestant Episcopal Public School, an outgrowth of the charity school established by Trinity during the colonial period.[9] By 1832, it enrolled 336 children. That same year the school's trustees tabulated—and fortunately for historians, published—a list of the occupations of their pupils' parents. Thirty of the three hundred were domestics, seventeen were seamstresses, twenty-four cartmen, and twelve laborers. Twenty-four were carpenters, six printers or hatters. Few of the parents could be classed as members, even marginally, of the petty bourgeoisie.[10] (Presumably the more affluent or pretentious among New York's employed classes sent their children to socially acceptable pay schools.) Yet it is logical to assume that the day school's student body was drawn from a higher income group than that of the usually illiterate children who attended only the Sunday schools—and who were attracted in many cases by the small charities of their volunteer teachers. Day school parents could dispense with their children's labor and were sufficiently motivated by middle-class values to think school attendance worthwhile.

By the 1820's and 1830's, then, at least some New York Episcopalians had become aware of the conditions in which

[8] Among the more active of these charity day schools were those supported by Grace Church and by St. Michael's. Peters, *St. Michaels*, pp. 59–66; William Rhinelander Stewart, *Grace Church and Old New York* (New York, 1924), pp. 106–107.

[9] Wilson, *Centennial History*, pp. 370–371; Benjamin T. Onderdonk, *A Plea for Religious Charity Schools* (New York, 1825). For a recent study of Trinity School, see Edward Stewart Moffat, "Trinity School, New York City, 1709–1959" (unpublished Ph.D. dissertation, Columbia University, 1963).

[10] *Churchman*, I (January 7, 1832), 167; and II (November 24, 1832), 350.

New York's working people lived, and had already established institutions to extend both spiritual and material help. The Episcopalian City Mission Society could, at its formation, call upon this background of pragmatic benevolence.

Yet the Protestant Episcopal City Mission Society, indeed all New York's missions, faced the same fundamental problem. Who in the city's vast and growing tenement districts should be the principal objects of their efforts? And if one decided how to choose deserving objects of charity, it was still not clear how they might best be aided.

New York had its very poor—the victims of either vice or misfortune—slum dwellers, often irreligious. New York Episcopalians had already encountered this class, as the parents of Sunday school scholars or as their slum neighbors. But New York had as well a broad spectrum of clerks, artisans, and shopkeepers, who, within the social usage of the time, were also considered to be among "the poor." They were potential church members; yet this potential was ordinarily unrealized, for they could rarely afford the high pew rentals and fine clothing demanded by attendance at the city's fashionable churches. It was to this class—the upright yet not quite established economically—that a free church, with a day school, library, bazaars, and other social activities, would appeal. Successful communication with this class demanded techniques entirely different from those appropriate for work with the city's most depressed classes. Programs capable of cementing the loyalty of one group might well alienate the other. Supporters of New York's Episcopal City Mission Society had first to decide which class among the poor they wished to help. Was their goal the establishment of a well-attended and decorous free church? Or the creation of a permanent mission to New York's outcast?

Knowledgeable Episcopal laymen and ministers were well

aware of the heterogeneous nature of New York's dependent classes. And this very awareness implied a policy choice for the new Society. Indeed, during the summer months between Bishop Onderdonk's call for the founding of a city mission and its actual organization in the fall, New York Episcopalians raised the question; the pages of the *Churchman* for July and August are dotted with letters discussing the appropriate objects for the new Society's benevolence.

One writer, signing himself "Lazarus," represented the city's small tradesmen.[11] His emphasis was sharp and in a sense critical. Though the comfortable might not realize it, he warned, many of the city's Episcopalians were effectively barred from church attendance by excessive pew rentals. This had been Lazarus's own experience. Although born an Episcopalian, the demands of his firm, coupled with the city's high cost of living, had made it impossible for him to afford the exorbitant pew rentals prevailing in New York's Episcopal churches. His problem was an unpleasant but not uncommon one; he had either to join a free church of another denomination or give up church attendance. Countless newcomers to the city, he explained, young clerks and business people from rural America or England, faced precisely this dilemma. Individuals of this type provided easily the most promising object of religious benevolence; there could be little doubt that efforts to bring them into the church would be rewarded with success. They needed only to be offered convenient and attractive free chapels. The projected city mission society, Lazarus hoped, would vigorously undertake this pious work. Others, however, had different visions of the new Society's task. It would, they hoped, reach beyond these church-going, newspaper-reading, small tradesmen and "act upon" the great mass of the city's unchurched and irreligious poor.[12] (Like their

[11] *Ibid.*, I (July 9, 1831), 63.
[12] *Ibid.*, I (July 16, 1831), 66; and I (August 13, 1831), 83.

evangelical counterparts, Episcopalian philanthropists regarded the new Catholic immigrants as unchurched.)

It was clear that the free church and the mission station were real—and in a sense exclusive—alternatives; yet the problems inherent in embracing both modes of action were not so clearly understood. At the time of its founding in the fall of 1831, the Society's managers hoped that their new organization could act as both a free church and as a mission to the outcast poor, attracting day laborers as well as clerks to the Episcopal Church. The problem was to find a neighborhood and a building in which that might be accomplished. The executive committee felt they had done so when they selected an old Presbyterian church on Vandewater Street, deserted when its congregation moved uptown; it seemed admirably suited to the fulfillment of the Society's broad goals.

Vandewater Street lay just six blocks west of the piers and warehouses of Front Street and the East River. It was located, as well, at the northern edge of the east side's crowded commercial district and adjacent to "the Swamp," the center of New York's leather-processing industry. The new church was thus convenient to a cross section of New York's population; all but the wealthy worked in or passed through these streets— laboring men, clerks, and petty shopkeepers, skilled artisans, sailors, and transients. The houses that immediately surrounded the new mission church, on the other hand, sheltered a much narrower social stratum. Lying only a few blocks east of the Five Points, Vandewater and the adjacent streets were filled with immigrant lodging houses and the tenements of cartmen, day laborers, the chronically unemployed, and the criminal.[13] It was an area which few established churches

[13] Scoville, *Old Merchants*, pp. 252–253; Norcross, *New York Swamp*, pp. 65–68; Ernst, *Immigrant Life*, pp. 39–40, map, p. 43. Actual sketches of Vandewater Street as it appeared during the 1830's and 1840's can be found in: William Perris, *Maps of the City of New-York*, Vol. I (New York, 1852). Perris gives "pictographs" of

felt interested in serving. It was, however, precisely the sort of neighborhood which the managers and executive committee of the Society had sought out; commercial and residential, slum and lower-middle class, it encompassed virtually all classes of the unchurched.

On November 19, 1831, Bishop Onderdonk consecrated the now unused Presbyterian church as the Church of the Holy Evangelists, the Protestant Episcopal City Mission Society's first mission station. Three weeks later, Reverend Benjamin Cutler, previously rector of the Episcopal Church in Quincy, Massachusetts, assumed his duties as the new mission's pastor.[14]

The following months were active and encouraging ones for Cutler and the Society. The church regularly held three Sunday and one weekday service. Culter formally and informally conferred with his parishioners; he married and baptized, and provided, indeed, all the normal Episcopal pastoral services for an extensive area without churches or clergymen. After three months, he could report encouraging results. Cutler had attracted an average of four hundred persons to his Sunday services and secured forty communicants as continuing members of the Church of the Holy Evangelists.[15]

The most active components of this rapidly growing mis-

---

all buildings on each city block, telling the size and construction material. See also anonymous photograph of Vandewater Street, Map and Print Collection, New-York Historical Society; David Valentine, *Manual of the Corporation of the City of New York, 1864* (New York, 1864), sketch opposite p. 316.

[14] *Churchman*, I (November 12, 1831); Benjamin T. Onderdonk, *A Sermon . . . Preached at the Consecration of the Mission-Church of the Holy Evangelists . . . on Saturday, Nov. 19, 1831* (New York, 1831).

[15] P.E.C.M.S., *First Quarterly Report of the Executive Committee, March 4, 1832* (New York, 1832), pp. 5–6; *Churchman*, I (December 10, 1831), 150.

sion church were its Sunday and infant schools. The Sunday school and the visiting of its volunteer teachers, the Society's founders firmly believed, had always been the source of the Church's closest and earliest contacts with the poor. The Society's executive committee thus considered the establishment of a well-attended Sunday school as fundamental to their mission chapel's success. Even before purchasing the Vandewater Street church, the executive committee had organized a school committee, had begun to recruit Sunday school teachers, and had bought prayer books and Bibles for Sunday and infant day schools. No sooner had the Bishop consecrated the Church of the Holy Evangelists than it opened its first Sunday school class on November 20, 1831.[16] Within a few weeks, one hundred children were in regular attendance. By the spring of 1832, the school committee could report a total of 275 children enrolled; the Board of Female Visitors conducted a daily infant school with an average attendance of seventy.

The families reached through these schools were among the poorest in the city. And, indeed, the managers took genuine pride in their ability to work with and help these destitute children, the offspring of the "depraved" as well as the "worthy." In May of 1832, for example, Bishop Onderdonk, as chairman of the Society's school committee, reported with due satisfaction that "by far the largest number [of the students] are children of poor intemperate and decayed families." [17]

[16] P.E.C.M.S., "Executive Committee Minutes, November 14, 1831."
[17] P.E.C.M.S., "First Annual Report, 1832," reprinted in *Churchman*, I (February 4, 1832), 182. Also see *Churchman*, I (January 21, 1832), 175; P.E.C.M.S., "First Report of School Committee," printed in *Churchman*, I (May 5, 1832), 234; P.E.C.M.S., *First Quarterly Report of the Executive Committee*, pp. 5–7; Letter to Editor from "B," *Churchman*, II (May 5, 1832), 234–235.

These Sabbath scholars had not migrated naturally or spontaneously to the classroom. Sunday school teachers, visitors, and the Society's missionaries had from the first sought out the district's poorest families and most dilapidated tenements. Often they found that a lack of clothing, rather than interest, kept children from school and church; not uncommonly these little urchins lacked shoes, stockings, and other necessities. As early as December 3, 1831, the School Committee issued an appeal through the *Churchman* for contributions of food, clothing, and money for their Sabbath and day-nursery scholars.[18] The seemingly inevitable pattern of city mission work was again being enacted; temporal relief assumed an ever-larger place in the Society's work. The managers soon established a formal Benevolent Society to raise money for this purpose. Souls, it was apparent, could not be saved while bodies remained cold and hungry.[19]

The Society did not, of course, limit its attention to Sunday school children but consistently sought out adult as well as juvenile slum dwellers. During its first year, the Society continued to hope that the most abandoned among the city's poor would become their missionaries' "special parishioners." In his first three months as city missionary, for example, Benjamin Cutler reported having made 132 visits to sordid tenement apartments in the vicinity of his mission chapel.[20]

The cholera epidemic which struck New York in the spring of 1832—only a half-year after the Society's founding—dramatically intensified these efforts.[21] The Mission Society's executive committee immediately expanded the amount of

[18] *Churchman*, I (November 12, 1831), 139; I (December 3, 1831), 146–147; and II (May 5, 1832), 234.

[19] P.E.C.M.S., "First Annual Report," pp. 5–6; and "Second Quarterly Report of the Executive Committee, June 1832," printed *Churchman*, II (June 16, 1832), 258–259.

[20] *Churchman*, II (May 19, 1832), 242.

[21] See especially Charles E. Rosenberg, *Cholera Years, passim.*

outdoor relief it distributed. Individual members visited the tenements surrounding the mission chapel giving clothes, bedding, and food to the poor, while the Society's managers initiated an ambitious program of work relief.[22] In the years following the epidemic, appeals for contributions by their city missionaries appeared with increasing frequency in the pages of the *Churchman*. Although the Society was careful to emphasize its ultimate spiritual aims, it had come to accept and argue explicitly that temporal relief was often a necessary prerequisite to spiritual uplift. In its Third Annual Report, the Society argued:

Although our chief object is to save the soul, yet it has been found that in many cases the Missionary cannot properly enter on the peculiar duties of his visit before he had fed the hungry, or clothed the naked, or nursed the sick, or provided fuel for the destitute: before he has relieved some of the nameless wants of the sons and daughters of physical suffering.[23]

When the Society held its first annual meeting in June of 1832, its executive committee could take pride in a variety of activities already undertaken, in a program more pragmatic than any of those as yet carried out by contemporary evangelical city missions. The Society had established a free church in a notoriously unpromising neighborhood. It had founded a flourishing Sunday school; its infant school had attracted an enrollment of ninety, and volunteer teachers through their Benevolent Committee, were actively visiting and aiding all the poor who lived near the mission chapel.[24]

[22] *Churchman*, II (July 21, 1832), 279; II (August 4, 1832), 287; and III (January 19, 1833), 383; P.E.C.M.S., "Minutes, First Quarterly Meeting, of the Executive Committee, March 31, 1833," printed *Churchman*, III (April 13, 1833), 430.

[23] P.E.C.M.S., "Minutes of the Second Quarterly Report of the Executive Committee, June 3, 1832."

[24] Benjamin Onderdonk, "Address to the Convention," *Churchman*, II (October 13, 1832), 325.

Thus, in the spring of 1832, the executive committee felt prepared to undertake a new and highly ambitious program, one which would greatly expand the Society's activities and contacts with the city's poor. That March, the executive committee voted to divide the city into ten districts, each to contain approximately twenty thousand persons. The executive committee appointed a committee for each district whose responsibility it was to establish a Sunday school, a religious library, and to ascertain the possibility of launching a mission chapel. Each of these committees, the Society hoped, would create a new mission station to parallel the successful religious and charitable work already undertaken at the Church of the Holy Evangelists. In this way the managers hoped they might bring the Episcopal faith to all the city's poor and unchurched.[25]

During the next few years, the Society's members worked actively to implement this program. No group was more active than the local committee for "District E," a rectangle bounded by Grand and Houston Streets, the Bowery, and East River. District E lay just northeast of the city's center and just south of the shipyards and slums of Corlear's Hook. A relatively new section, its population consisted of laborers, artisans, and a sprinkling of petty shopkeepers. Its homes and tenements were small and crudely built. Devoid of churches, containing but one public school, it was hardly one of the city's better residential areas.[26] For these reasons, however, it

[25] P.E.C.M.S., "Executive Committee Minutes, November 8, 1832, November 23, 1832"; Lot Jones, *A Discourse Delivered on the Twenty-Fifth Anniversary of the Church of the Epiphany, New York, January 10, 1858, by the Rector and First Pastor* (New York, 1858). Lot Jones had been pastor of Epiphany from its inception in 1833.

[26] For a detailed contemporary description of this area, see Perris, *Maps*, Vol. II (New York, 1852); *Leslie's Weekly*, III (February 28, 1857), 204.

was, in the opinion of the City Mission Society, a natural location for the establishment of a charity Sunday school—and possibly a mission chapel as well.

No sooner had the committee organized than they conducted a careful canvass of their district, familiarizing themselves with its population and its religious and educational needs. On December 26, 1832, they were able to open their first Sunday school and planned as well to establish a small chapel in a rented loft nearby.[27]

But the members of District E committee were not the only New York Episcopalians interested in this Houston-Grand Street area as a mission field. Most prominent among a number of free-lance Episcopal missionaries was the Reverend John McVickar, a professor at Columbia College, and better known to historians as an influential writer on political economy. McVickar regularly spent his Sundays conducting religious services in the city's poorest neighborhoods. In this way he had come to know the working-class district southwest of Corlear's Hook. At the same time that the committee for District E was organizing its Sunday school, McVickar was preparing to open a mission chapel of his own.

McVickar held his first mission services on January 6, 1833. His congregation met in a poorly lit loft over a fire-engine room on Allen Street; it consisted of but a handful of adults and a few children. McVickar could provide them with only two ragged prayer books—and his own prayers. During the following weeks, however, the mission expanded. McVickar rented a larger room on the corner of Houston and Allen Streets and, with the help of two of his Columbia College students, began a Sunday school.[28]

[27] *Churchman*, II (December 29, 1832), 371.
[28] *Ibid.*, II (January 12, 1833), 379; John McVickar to Charles King, December 4, 1854, John McVickar File, Columbiana Collection, Columbia University, New York City; Jones, *Discourse*, pp. 6–8; for

The Columbia political economist soon presented an account of his work to the executive committee of the Mission Society; he proposed that his chapel—he called it the Church of the Epiphany—be transferred to the Episcopal City Mission Society and that it serve as one of its mission stations. The executive committee quickly adopted his proposal. The Church of the Epiphany, absorbing the tiny chapel and Sunday school already established for District E, became the Society's second mission church.[29]

The Mission Church of the Epiphany soon rewarded the faith of its founders. During its first year of existence, while still crowded into a tiny loft, its regular congregation increased from forty to four hundred and the number of communicants from ten to seventy. The Sunday schools attracted more than three hundred children—and, by the year's end, could boast of the services of some thirty volunteer teachers. With so encouraging a response, the Society decided to formalize and expand these efforts by providing more appropriate facilities; they erected an imposing building to house the growing Church of the Epiphany. It was consecrated on August 24, 1833.[30]

Both new churches, the Holy Evangelists and Epiphany, flourished in the years following their founding; the annual reports of both mission churches regularly presented a pic-

---

a recent scholarly biography of McVickar, see: John Brett Langstaff, *The Enterprising Life: John McVickar 1787–1868* (New York, 1961). See also W. A. McVickar, *The Life of the Reverend John McVickar, S.T.D.* (New York, 1872); Joseph Dorfman and R. G. Tugwell, "The Reverend John McVickar, Christian Teacher and Economist," *Columbia University Quarterly*, XXIII (December, 1931), 353–401.

[29] P.E.C.M.S., "Minutes, Second Annual Meeting, January 14, 1833," *Churchman*, III (August 24, 1833), 507.

[30] P.E.C.M.S., *Third Annual Report*, p. 12; *Churchman*, III (August 31, 1833), 510.

ture of service and popularity. Indeed the congregations of both these Episcopal missions gradually began to assume the character of established parishes. They evolved steadily toward the status of self-sufficient free churches, and away from mission-station dependence. In this development, the fledgling congregations received the active encouragement of the parent society. As early as April, 1833, the executive committee granted mission churches the right to raise and expend money for special parish purposes and to have charge of ordinary repairs. In 1838, the executive committee agreed to permit the individual churches to retain the proceeds of each week's collection. In return, the congregations would assume total responsibility for their churches' operating expenses. (The Society was still responsible for the minister's salary.) "It is of great importance," the Board of Trustees explained, "that these persons should be induced and encouraged . . . to take a deep interest in . . . and exert themselves for the promotion of this Society." [31]

By 1840, the congregations of these mission churches were behaving very much like the congregations of a number of other respectable, if hardly fashionable, churches in and around Manhattan. In that year, the parishioners of Epiphany were first able to assume the entire cost of their Sunday and infant day schools. Indeed they continually expanded the day school, gradually adding higher grades and thus including older children.[32] In 1843 Epiphany's congregation hired an assistant minister to aid their pastor. Between 1837 and 1840, the church undertook, as well, an ambitious program of remodeling; they redecorated the interior of the church, purchased a "valuable" baptismal font, and contributed nearly $3,000 to-

[31] P.E.C.M.S., "Executive Committee Minutes, April 11, 1833"; and "Executive Committee Minutes, January 30, 1838, April 24, 1838."
[32] P.E.C.M.S., *Ninth Annual Report*, pp. 5–7.

ward other phases of the face-lifting. (The women of the congregation took the lead; their sensitivity toward the church's social role made a valuable contribution to it ultimate responsibility.) Epiphany's congregation began, even during the still difficult years of the early 1840's, to give financial support to a number of general diocesan charities.[33] The congregation of the Holy Evangelists, while not as prosperous, was still able to pay its operating expenses, contribute toward the support of its infant and Sunday schools, and to some general diocesan charities.[34]

What kind of parishioners were these, so quick to remodel their church, so willing to support an assistant minister, so eager to contribute to foreign missions? The majority, quite clearly, were not unskilled workers, domestics, the unemployed, and the unemployable. Such individuals might send their children to the mission church's Sunday school, but the church's regular communicants came from a distinctly more

[33] P.E.C.M.S., *Sixth Annual Report for the Year 1837* (New York, 1837), p. 9; and *Ninth Annual Report*, p. 7. Also Lot Jones, "Report of the Church of the Epiphany," *Journal of the Proceedings of the 57th Convention of the Protestant Episcopal Church in the Diocese of New York, 1841* (New York, 1841), p. 133; Lot Jones, "Report of the Church of the Epiphany," *Journal of the Proceedings of the 59th Convention of the Protestant Episcopal Church in the Diocese of New York, 1843* (New York, 1843), p. 152.

[34] Benjamin Evans, "Report of the Church of the Holy Evangelists," *Journal of the Proceedings of the 58th Convention of the Protestant Episcopal Church in the Diocese of New York, 1842* (New York, 1842), p. 117. It is interesting to note the manner in which the Holy Evangelists was actually remodeled. One parishoner, an architect, drew up plans for the interior. Another contributed a marble font; a third, an upholsterer, gave the furnishings for the pulpit and desk. Benjamin Evans, "Report of the Church of the Holy Evangelists," *Journal of the Proceedings of the 59th Convention of the Protestant Episcopal Church*, p. 148.

"elevated" social and economic stratum. The congregation of the Holy Evangelists, their first minister, Benjamin Cutler, reported in 1833, consisted of three major elements. First were Episcopalians who had, amidst the social and emotional turbulence of the metropolis, drifted away from God. The members of the second group were victims of the city—Episcopalians no longer able to afford pew rents as a result of financial reverses. Finally, there were the young men of good family come from the country to make their fortunes. Several years later, Cutler found no reason to modify this analysis. His congregation, he explained, was made up of the

honest, industrious sober and respectable . . . the utterly vagrant and depraved poor either wholly declining or soon discontinuing attendance upon public worship; or else, by their continued attendance, gradually changing their habits and appearance and becoming assimilated with the purer and better classes, with which they were brought into spiritual association.

Many of his parishioners, the minister added, were English emigrants, Church of England communicants before leaving their native island.[35]

This profile of the mission congregation changed very little during the following years. In 1836, E. B. Kellogg, in his annual report to the Board of Managers, stated that the city's honest and industrious artisans and mechanics made up the great bulk of their communicants. "They are," he explained with enthusiasm, "an industrious, respectable, and most interesting class." And certainly they were in their relative economic stability an atypical element among the poor; collections in the mission churches, the executive committee explained in

[35] P.E.C.M.S., "First Quarterly Meeting . . . 1833"; and *Third Annual Report*, p. 5.

1837, had always accounted for a susbstantial portion of the Society's income.[36] The creation of such viable congregations was clearly consistent with the original hopes of the Society's founders, or with at least some of them.[37]

With such encouraging results, the Mission Society's committees were anxious to establish additional free churches. (As early as 1835, the executive committee had considered the matter, and had approached the vestry of Trinity Church in hopes of purchasing a lot for a third mission chapel.) The managers, however, found it difficult to raise even a portion of the $10,000 needed to build another church. McVickar suggested then that the Society follow the same policy he had; they should, that is, establish Sunday schools and informal services in likely sections of the city. If both residents and philanthropists responded favorably, the possibility of creating another church might then be appropriately discussed.[38]

The Society acceded to McVickar's suggestion and in the years that followed held informal church services and established a number of Sunday schools in the northwest section of the city. Here few churches existed and the Society hoped to form a congregation in a neighborhood similar to Vande-

[36] Letter from E. B. Kellogg to Benjamin Onderdonk, reprinted P.E.C.M.S., *Fifth Annual Report for the Year 1836* (New York, 1836), pp. 9–10; and "Executive Committee Minutes, February 23, 1837."

[37] During the first year of the Society's operations, Bishop Onderdonk confirmed this emphasis by stating that the principal purpose of the Society was to provide attractive free churches for immigrants of the Anglican communion and for those "young persons of both sexes, belonging to respectable and pious, but not wealthy families of our communion . . . resorting to this city for purposes of business." *Churchman*, II (October 13, 1832), 325. Cf. James Eastburn, "Sermon," *ibid.*, II (December 15, 1832), 363; and II (April 28, 1832), 230.

[38] P.E.C.M.S., "Executive Committee Minutes, May 18, 1835, and November 11, 1835"; and *Fourth Annual Report for the Year 1835* (New York, 1835), p. 9.

water or Stanton Streets. In 1842, the Society at last was able to establish a third mission church on Christopher Street on the city's west side. It was consecrated on March 15, 1842, the Mission Church of St. Matthew.[39]

We have pictured an enterprise both meaningful and seemingly vigorous. For a dozen years, the Episcopal City Mission Society had sought with increasing energy to reach the great mass of New York's unchurched and often irreligious poor. The Society had established three free churches; it had instituted a network of Sunday schools and an elaborate program of domestic visitation and outdoor relief. Yet, paradoxically, the Society had, by the early 1840's, lost much of its support among the city's regular Episcopal parishes; its treasury was empty, its debts constantly increasing. Finally, in 1847, its financial embarrassments no longer endurable, the Society was forced to disband.

How could this have happened? What factors could have brought about the demise of so ambitious and, in many ways, so successful an undertaking? Beginning in the late 1830's three separate and largely unrelated developments began to compromise the Society's activities, erode its support, shatter its coherence of purpose—all leading irrevocably to its dissolution.

The Panic of 1837 was the most obvious factor impairing the Society's growth. The depression persisted until the mid-1840's, and New York's Episcopal laity was hard hit. Newly established congregations were particularly embarrassed; confronted with heavy mortgages and greatly reduced pew rentals, they repented the ambitious building programs undertaken during the halcyon days of the early thirties. The vestry of

[39] P.E.C.M.S., "Executive Committee Minutes, June 14, 1836, February 23, 1837, May 16, 1837"; *Fifth Annual Report*, pp. 6–12; and *Sixth Annual Report*, pp. 10–12; Wilson, *Centennial Hsitory*, p. 391.

Trinity Church, with its extraordinary financial resources, stepped in to save a number of these new churches.[40]

In November of 1837, at the height of the panic, the Episcopal City Mission Society also called upon Trinity's aid. Bishop Onderdonk, still the Mission Society's president, served as intermediary; the Trinity corporation, he reported to the Board of Managers on the twenty-seventh of November, agreed to lend them $10,000, taking as security mortgages on the two mission churches. The executive committee immediately used half this sum to meet impending mortgage payments. They were forced to dissipate the other $5,000 in paying the Society's normal operating expenses.[41]

By the beginning of 1838, the Society's financial situation had become critical. It owed some $27,000 for the construction of its mission churches; annual interest payments alone amounted to almost $2,000. The salaries of its full-time missionaries meant another annual obligation of some $3,500; operating expenses for the Sunday schools and mission chapels amounted to nearly $1,500. Yet in 1837, the churches and Episcopal laity of the city had contributed only $2,200 to the Society to meet these fixed expenses of nearly $7,000.[42]

The Society had to devise new stratagems. On January 30, 1838, the executive committee asked the mission church congregations to assume financial responsibility for their churches, with the exception of the minister's salary. That same year, the Society's Board of Managers was able to secure an increase in the subvention granted the Society each year

[40] See, for a case study of one of these churches, E. Clowes Chorley, *The Centennial History of St. Bartholomew's Church in the City of New York, 1835–1935* (New York, 1935).

[41] P.E.C.M.S., "Minutes of Special Meeting held at the Church of the Holy Evangelists, November 27, 1837."

[42] P.E.C.M.S., "Executive Committee Minutes, January 30, 1838."

by Trinity (from $1,100 to $1,800).[43] But individual church contributions still lagged; indeed, they decreased during the late 1830's and early 1840's. In 1835, for example, parishioners of the city's several Episcopal parishes had contributed $4,450, in 1842 but $796.56. By 1845, individual church contributions had dwindled almost to nothing; Christ Church, for example, which had been instrumental in founding the Society fourteen years before, gave only nineteen dollars.[44]

By 1843, the Protestant Episcopal City Mission Society faced bankruptcy. Though it owned three churches valued at $50,000, the buildings were heavily mortgaged; each year interest payments of $2,500 had to be met. The executive committee, in their report for 1843, complained that a handful of wealthy Episcopalians maintained the Society, while the average churchgoer ignored its needs. "The Society has not grown as it should have because the average well-to-do Episcopalian has lost interest in its aims and has failed to support it." [45]

The Society was able to struggle on for a few final years, its future increasingly problematical. In June of 1847, however, its condition seemed terminal; the mortgage on the Church of the Holy Evangelists had already been foreclosed, and the building was scheduled to be sold on the twenty-first. The executive committee called an emergency meeting of members and friends. Only Trinity and Grace, among the

[43] For the effect of this decision on the internal development of these churches and for their readiness to accept this responsibility, see pp. 141–142, above; P.E.C.M.S., *Eighth Annual Report for the Year 1839* (New York, 1839), p. 4.

[44] For a summary of the contributions, see P.E.C.M.S., *Annual Reports, 4th–14th (1835–1845)*.

[45] P.E.C.M.S., *Twelfth Annual Report for the Year 1843* (New York, 1843), p. 12.

city's Episcopal churches, favored continuing support for the Society. The other churches refused when requested to hold a special collection to aid the mission society and its work. As the meeting adjourned, the Society's only hope lay in the possibility that Trinity might again step in to assume their obligations.[46] But this was not to be; the Society disbanded in the fall of 1847.

The Reverend John McVickar, a founder and for many years its vice-president, wrote the Society's final report to the diocesan convention. The churches of the diocese, he began diplomatically, had decided to limit their mission work to the poor within their own parish boundaries. Thus their decision to discontinue support of the Mission Society. Without funds, McVickar explained, the Society had been forced to dispose of its property; the church buildings had been given to their respective congregations with the condition that they remain free churches. The Columbia professor, with obvious feeling, sharply questioned the wisdom of these decisions. The poor of the city, he argued, could not be found within the parish limits of the denomination's wealthier churches. The abjectly destitute rarely lived even in the immediate vicinity of those respectable lower-middle-class neighborhoods in which a stable free church congregation might be expected to develop. (McVickar was somewhat overstating this picture of residential exclusiveness.) The demise of the Mission Society implied as well the end of any hope that lower-class New Yorkers might be gathered into the Episcopal fold.[47]

[46] P.E.C.M.S., "Minutes, Special Meeting of the City Mission Society, June 16, 1847."

[47] John McVickar, "Report of the New York Protestant Episcopal City Mission Society," *Journal of the Proceedings of the 63rd Convention of the Protestant Episcopal Church in the Diocese of New York, 1847* (New York, 1847), pp. 90–92.

The Society did not die completely; McVickar and a few dedicated supporters continued to hold formalistic annual meetings so that the Society's charter might not lapse. And this faith was not misplaced. Fifteen years later, McVickar was elected chairman of a meeting of New York Episcopalians which succeeded in revitalizing the dormant Society.[48]

Though the depression was of undoubted significance in bringing a halt to the Mission Society's activities, it cannot alone explain the Society's demise. Church contributions had fallen to $2,200 in 1837, although the Panic did not strike until the year's end nor assume the dimensions of a major depression for yet another year. By 1846–1847, on the other hand, business had revived, and building expanded. At the same time, however, the willingness of Episcopalians to support their city mission reached a new low.

Another explanation can be found in the schism which rent the Episcopal diocese of New York throughout the 1840's. These years marked the height of the tractarian controversy within American Episcopalianism. The opposition provoked by the Oxford theologians in the New York diocese was particularly bitter, a bitterness which corresponded to the power and influence of avowedly High-Church leaders within the diocese. Finally Low-Church leaders succeeded— after a notorious misconduct trial—in ousting Bishop Onderdonk, principal spokesman for the High-Church position in New York—and, unfortunately for the Episcopal City Mission Society, its president and chief backer. (In 1844, Benjamin Onderdonk was accused of "immorality and impurity" by several Low-Church bishops; the following year he was tried by a special ecclesiastical court, suspended, and re-

[48] The P.E.C.M.S. has the minutes of several of these *pro forma* meetings held between June 16, 1847, and April 28, 1864.

moved as bishop of the diocese.) The New York diocese remained without a permanent bishop until 1861.[49]

The heritage of bitterness left by Onderdonk's removal
made any successful organization on the diocesan level extremely difficult. Without a strong bishop to hold the diocese
together, individual churches deserted existing organizations
and showed little willingness to cooperate in joint charitable
and missionary endeavors. Programs associated closely with
Onderdonk inherited the rancor surrounding his name. Low-
Church Episcopalians now felt completely free to support
the interdenominational and evangelical alternatives to the
exclusively Episcopal societies favored by Bishop Onderdonk.
Not surprisingly the clergymen most closely associated with
such evangelical missionary societies and opposed to exclusive Episcopal organizations had also been leaders of the
movement to impeach Onderdonk.[50]

Both the depression of 1837 and the removal of Bishop
Onderdonk were problems in a sense external to the Mission
Society itself. A third factor in its dissolution originated in a
confusion of aims within the Society.

Its leaders had embarked upon two essentially different
kinds of work. One was the attempt to reach those in society
with no stable economic identity and no religious orientation.
Household visits, work with children, temporal relief—all

[49] *The Proceedings of the Court Convened . . . for the Trial of
the Right Reverend Benjamin T. Onderdonk, D.D., Bishop of New
York* (New York, 1845). The trial's most recent historian, E. Clowes
Chorley, "Benjamin Tredwell Onderdonk, Fourth Bishop of New
York," *Historical Magazine of the Protestant Episcopal Church*, IX
(March, 1940), 1–51, concludes that the trial violated the precepts of
common law and the constitution of the Protestant Episcopal Church.
To High-Church Episcopalians throughout the century, Onderdonk
seemed a martyr, the victim of a cynical frame-up.

[50] See Chap. 5, n. 1, above.

these were avenues through which such potential (if un-likely) Episcopalians might be reached. A second kind of work was less ambitious, yet, as we have seen, more reward-ing in its promise of immediate and tangible success. This was an attempt to bring "respectable" artisans, clerks, and small tradesmen within the Episcopal fold; such individuals might be reached by more traditional means—access to free churches and the influence of dignified and improving ser-vices.

Could one organization attain both goals? It did not seem that they could; the Society's managers soon discovered that the pursuit of such divergent aims created tensions within their organization—tensions reflecting America's social atti-tudes during the 1830's and 1840's.

The strain of this ambitious program told first upon the minister who was expected to serve both as pastor to a free church and as missionary to the destitute. Benjamin Cutler, the Society's first city missionary, resigned early in March, 1833. He was, he explained to the executive committee, no longer physically able to serve both as pastor to a free church and as missionary to the poor. At one point, Cutler elabo-rated, he had considered giving up his work among the destitute and concentrating exclusively upon his pastoral duties. But to do so, he felt, would quickly transform the mission church into a "settled and regular parish." And this was not the intention of the Society's founders. Only by undertaking the role both of pastor and of missionary could he hope to accomplish the Society's dual aims.[51]

Yet such a transformation could not be avoided. Grad-ually, the Society came to feel that there was no alternative to treating their mission stations as "settled and regular par-ishes." The very poor, Cutler had pointed out in 1834, did

[51] P.E.C.M.S., "Executive Committee Minutes, March 14, 1833."

not have the makings of regular and reliable parishioners. As the mission churches prospered and their parochial responsibilities increased, the city missionaries had inevitably less and less time to seek out such unfortunates and to endeavor to bring them within the Episcopal flock.

The mission appellation, on the other hand, alienated many of the economically ambitious lower-middle class who comprised the Society's most reliable parishioners. "America's clerks, tradesmen, and mechanics," the Board of Managers warned in 1836, "have every expectation of advancing themselves socially and financially. With few exceptions they will, in a short time, become respectable and prosperous members of society." [52] Certainly such aspiring New Yorkers did not like to think of themselves as worshipping in a charity mission, possibly kneeling next to a resident of the Five Points or Corlear's Hook.

In 1836, the Society formally separated the two functions. The Executive Committee voted to transform the mission churches into regular free churches and to employ a third minister to devote his efforts exclusively to working with the outcast poor.[53] Without fixed parish duties, this clergyman was to circulate at random, leading prayer meetings and distributing charity. In explaining these changes to the Sixth Annual Meeting, the Board of Managers stated:

His duty will be to explore the abodes of ignorance and wretchedness, and to give himself up, in a devoted Christian spirit to the sole task of instructing and amending their wretched inmates . . . his teaching will be from house to house; his sermons, the promptings of the occasion delivered . . . at the bedside of the sick, in the abodes of wretchedness.

[52] P.E.C.M.S., *Sixth Annual Report,* pp. 13–16.
[53] P.E.C.M.S., "Executive Committee Minutes, February 23, 1836, and March 8, 1836."

At the same meeting E. B. Kellogg, the newly chosen missionary-at-large, discussed his own understanding of this new role:

They [the mission churches] have furnished to the most deserving and respectable class of the poor, the means of assembling, like their more favored brethren, for the purpose of our common salvation. . . . The City Mission Churches have, indeed, advanced one step down toward the great valley of the poor, and it is a most important step; but the great multitude is still below, and has not yet been reached.[54]

At first the Society hoped that their missionary-at-large might make the whole city his mission field. By the late 1830's, however, they had limited his efforts to the city's northwest corner (from Canal to Fourteenth Street and from Broadway to the Hudson). Between the spring of 1837 and that of 1838, the Society's missionary-at-large made 3,358 visits "to the sick, the poor, the careless and the vicious," distributing tracts, prayer books, and $500 in charity. His "parishioners" were the same lost souls who attracted the assiduous attentions of his evangelical contemporaries. In 1839, the Society's missionary began to visit prisons and hospitals as well, praying and distributing Bibles and tracts to the sick and the criminal. Within the next two years, he was able to organize several Sunday schools with an enrollment of 250. And the hard-working Kellogg continued to distribute charity, serving as a kind of semiofficial almoner for the charitable of the diocese. In 1841, for example, he received $876 from private persons to distribute among the deserving.[55]

[54] P.E.C.M.S., *Sixth Annual Report*, pp. 12, 17–19, 24.
[55] P.E.C.M.S., *Seventh Annual Report*, pp. 8, 12; *Eighth Annual Report*, p. 13; and *Tenth Annual Report for the Year 1841* (New York, 1841), pp. 9–11.

But when New York's Episcopalians ceased supporting their city mission society, two of its free churches and the position of missionary-at-large died. Only the Church of the Epiphany survived, drawing as it did upon the solidly lower-middle-class streets in its immediate vicinity. The Holy Evangelists and St. Matthews, both established in essentially slum areas, were unable—as the depression lengthened—to maintain a stable congregation; without the support of the city's established churches, they disbanded, or moved.[56]

The Protestant Episcopal City Mission Society had undertaken too much. It could not support three free churches, a roving missionary, and randomly placed Sunday schools. But the tensions that arose within the Society's own churches between the needs of their lower-middle-class parishioners and the poorer recipients of Episcopal charity, even the financial and administrative problems of maintaining two quite different programs, cannot alone explain the steady decrease in contributions to the Society. And it is this drying up of financial support which was, of course, the immediate cause of the Society's dissolution. Why did New York's Episcopalians lose faith in the work of their city mission?

The evidence indicates that their disaffection was related to an increasingly negative attitude toward the poor. This disenchantment becomes apparent in even a casual reading of the Society's official statements. Their words demonstrate not only a gradual shift in attitude toward the poor, but a striking decrease in the optimism which had encouraged the Society in its founding years; one does not willingly support

[56] The Church of the Holy Evangelists, for example, remained on Vandewater Street until 1851, when, bankrupt, Trinity Church rescued it, giving it the building known as "Old St. George's Chapel." Holy Evangelists now became a chapel of St. George's. Anstice, *St. George's*, pp. 191–193, 211–214.

programs which promise only frustration. The increasingly bleak views of the Society's managers toward the prospective objects of their charity seem to coincide with the Panic of 1837 and the lingering depression which it precipitated.

During the euphoric days of the early 1830's—when prosperity seemed a permanent condition of American life—economically secure New Yorkers could view their less fortunate fellow citizens with sympathy and a certain optimism. Many might be converted, and once converted could be elevated socially and economically through education, self-help, and the judicious distribution of charity. The *Churchman* commented in 1832:

This transformation of character we propose to effect by the simple agency of plain instruction and cheering counsel, conveyed through the abodes of the destitute by the familiar visitation of those more elevated in life . . . the ultimate object—is to elevate and better the condition of the poor by inculcating the principles of an efficient morality, and calling forth . . . a spirit of independence and self-estimation which will produce habits of thoughtfulness and reliance on their own resources.[57]

Even the increasing numbers of European immigrants arriving during these buoyant years did little to shake this optimism; immigrants were simply a new and challenging mission field.

As late as the spring of 1837, the Society's Board of Managers continued to deny the existence of classes or castes in America, or that enmity existed between rich and poor. Society, as they saw it, was highly mobile; through misfortune some Americans were unable to provide for themselves, but these were individual, accidental cases. The American artisan

[57] P.E.C.M.S., "Executive Committee Minutes, First Quarterly Report . . . 1832"; *Churchman*, I (November 12, 1831), 135; and II (November 17, 1832), 346.

and laborer seemed surely and inevitably to be rising into the middle class.

In the older countries of Europe there is a CLASS OF POOR: families born to poverty, living in poverty, dying in poverty. With us there are none such. In our bounteous land individuals alone are poor; but they form no poor class, because with them poverty is but a transient evil . . . save paupers and vagabonds . . . all else form one common class of citizens; some more, others less advanced in the career of honorable independence; but none without having in their hands, under God's providence, the means of attaining it; and all, with individual exceptions, going on, by industry and economy, to acquire it.[58]

An encouraging picture indeed; it was hard to imagine social conflict within so beneficent a system.

But even before 1837, traces of bitterness and hostility crept into the statements of the Society's ministers and managers. In 1834, for example, the Reverend Hugh Smith, missionary of the Church of the Holy Evangelists, complained that "the utterly vagrant and depraved poor either wholly declin[ed], or soon discontinued attendance upon public worship." His congregation, he reported, had not the slightest admixture from among the ranks of the extremely poor; it was made up of *the honest, industrious, sober and respectable.*[59] In the spring of 1837 the Society's executive committee warned ominously of "that fermenting mass of vice and ignorance which . . . [threatens] the safety of our social and political institutions."

This discouraging and hostile statement was made at the height of the city's speculative prosperity; the impending depression was not even suspected. The causes of the managers' disillusion seemed to lie both in the difficulty of recruiting

[58] P.E.C.M.S., *Sixth Annual Report,* pp. 15–16.
[59] P.E.C.M.S., *Third Annual Report,* pp. 4–5.

the poor to mission-church membership and, also, in the city's rapidly increasing population of unskilled immigrants. Immigration, the Society complained in the spring of 1837 (in sharp contrast to the optimism expressed in 1832) was clearly bringing with it the social problems which beset European cities. "Whatever is in these foreigners of vice, infidelity or crime naturally settles here, adding new strength to what is evil among us." [60] After six years of effort, New York's Episcopalians had begun to think of the poor not simply as unfortunate neighbors—with whom one might well share one's church pew—but as an alien and inferior class. Only a few among them seemed capable of salvation and these only as a result of extraordinary efforts.

Within another six months the number of indigents in New York had quadrupled. The Panic of 1837, starting in the fall, threw thousands out of work; banks suspended; commercial houses, including some of the city's largest, declared themselves bankrupt. Much of the optimism of the early Jackson years abruptly evaporated. By the late 1830's and early 1840's, the poor had come to seem a class apart, a moral cancer within the body politic, impervious to the moral therapy of religion; a growing undertone of disquiet had become a dominant theme. The characteristics associated previously only with the criminal and the alcoholic, that is, with the "vicious" poor, were now applied generally to the unemployed and indigent. With 1838, the words "poverty" and "vice" appeared almost invariably linked in the Society's publications.[61] No longer did its workers expect to save the adult poor of New York's slums. They hoped at best to

[60] P.E.C.M.S., *Sixth Annual Report*, pp. 20, 21–24.
[61] For examples of the Society's increasing alienation from the poor, see P.E.C.M.S., *Seventh Annual Report*, p. 9; and *Eleventh Annual Report*, p. 6.

"rescue" the children of the poor, substituting the wholesome influence of the Sunday school teacher and the charitable visitor for that of drunken and dissolute parents. "The mass of vice and poverty," their missionary-at-large reported, "is yearly accumulating with frightful rapidity." One could not easily sympathize with such alien-seeming, threatening masses. In its *Fourteenth Annual Report,* the Society explained:

Untaught and unreclaimed, they poison the moral atmosphere amid which they live, they vitiate the characters of the young who come within their influence, they train their thousands of children to the ways of ungodliness, they endanger the safety of our Institutions, and they unsettle all the securities of property.[62]

By 1847 few Episcopalians were willing to give continued financial support to an organization that sought to aid and reform such dubious objects of charity.

Thus a conjunction of factors, the changing city, the depression, the overly ambitious aims of the managers, partisan rancor within the church, and class hostilities, all combined to thwart the brave hopes of New York's first Protestant Episcopal City Mission Society.

New York's Episcopal City Mission differed greatly from its evangelical counterparts both in theological orientation and institutional structure. Yet its managers and supporters were dedicated to the same moral and social values as their evan-

[62] P.E.C.M.S., *Eighth Annual Report,* p. 13; and *Fourteenth Annual Report,* p. 14. The Society's alarms and ambivalences paralleled those experienced by the New York City Tract Society. The fact that the Female Moral Reform Society did not express as critical an attitude toward the poor (even following the 1837 Panic) can perhaps be explained by that Society's latent feminism. The F.M.R.S. aided unmarried women, widows, deserted wives, and mothers. Surely the problems which these women faced could as easily be placed at the door of deficient, unproviding men as attributed to the women's own moral weaknesses.

gelical contemporaries; both groups addressed themselves to the same social problems—the immigration of unskilled rural workers, the employment of women in a changing labor market, disease, crime, vagrancy. Both groups assumed as well that the solution to these social ills lay in religious and moral terms; and both groups in aiding the poor utilized identical institutions and techniques: the charity Sunday school, house-to-house visiting, and outdoor relief. Even the mission church was ultimately adopted by both groups, as evangelicals established such churches in considerable numbers in the 1860's. And, finally, both evangelicals and Churchmen shared a similar ambivalence toward the poor, an ambivalence shaded in ever more pessimistic terms in the years after the Panic of 1837.

PART TWO

Protestants and Five Pointers: The City Mission Movement, 1837-1870

CHAPTER 6

The Victorian City: New York, 1837-1870

In 1837, "the wild mania of speculation" that had characterized the Jacksonian economy helped bring a sharp recession.[1] Farm prices fell; construction decreased sharply. Foreign and domestic investments fell sharply, as did imports. No American city was to suffer more than New York, the nation's financial and commercial center. "The markets begin to look gaunt, and the theaters deserted," *Niles Register* reported in the fall of 1837. "Winter and starvation are yet months off." It would be a decade before New York's workingmen enjoyed consistent employment.[2]

Hard times began even before the Panic. Food prices and rents reached exorbitant levels in the winter of 1836–1837. In March, 1837, protestors took drastic action. After a bitter meeting at City Hall, a mob descended on the city's grain warehouses, looting and destroying. In the years following,

[1] Albert Gallatin, quoted by Henry Adams, *Life of Albert Gallatin* (Philadelphia, 1879), p. 656.

[2] *Niles Register*, quoted by Samuel Rezneck, "The Social History of an American Depression, 1837–1843," *American Historical Review*, XL (1935), 664. For two detailed analyses of the depression (ones not always in agreement), see Bray Hammond, *Banks and Politics in America* (Princeton, 1957), Chaps. XV and XVI, and Peter Temin, *The Jacksonian Economy* (New York, 1969), Chaps. IV and V.

the numbers of unemployed and destitute reached unprecedented levels.[3] Traditional philanthropic resources could not meet these new needs; and for nearly a decade concerned and sympathetic New Yorkers struggled with unemployment, vagrancy, crime, and disease.

In the late 1840's prosperity returned, and New York entered a period of vigorous expansion. The population, relatively stable during the depression, increased explosively. Between 1845 and 1850 the city grew from 371,223 to 515,394, and by 1860 over 800,000 souls crowded Manhattan. Bouyant New Yorkers predicted that within a generation as many as two million would live or work on their island. Increased wealth accompanied this rapid growth. Impressive marble-fronted hotels, shops, and private mansions stretched up Broadway and Fifth Avenue and bordered Washington Square.[4]

Yet many, even among the middle class, were hard pressed by the rapidly increasing cost of living. As in 1836, real-estate prices and rents seemed particularly inflated. "A good convenient dwelling with modern improvements," one observer commented in 1869, "is worth a small fortune on this Island. . . . Nineteen-twentieths of the people here might therefore as rationally expect to have Stewart's income . . . as to find themselves holders in fee-simple of a private dwelling in any 'respectable' quarter of town." (The reference is, of course, to "merchant prince," A. T. Stewart.) By the 1860's,

[3] Stokes, *Iconography*, III, 525–527.
[4] Valentine, *Manual of the Corporation of the City of New York for the Year 1850* (New York, 1850), p. 399; Valentine, *Manual of the Corporation of the City of New York for the Year 1861* (New York, 1861), p. 446; New York *Commercial Advertiser*, January 10, 1845, May 5, 1845, May 19, 1845, January 12, 1846, April 2, 1846; New York *Evening Post* February 20, 1845, August 21, 1847, October 2, 1851; Hone, *Diary* (ed., Tuckerman), II, 245.

New Yorkers had already established a developing commuter pattern; each year a substantial number of business people who worked in downtown Manhattan built homes in Brooklyn, Williamsburg, and the upper reaches of Manhattan Island. Bemused and sometimes alarmed observers already commented routinely on this trend which threatened to make the city proper a dwelling place for the very rich and the very poor alone.[5]

Yet a comparatively small proportion of New Yorkers could make use of ferries and surface railroads to escape the city's high costs. Newly arrived immigrants, women wage earners, blacks, the unskilled generally—all were trapped by ignorance, by segregation, by the need to be close to employment opportunities in the city's congested lower wards. These were the tenants of New York's rapidly multiplying tenements.

New York's poverty had kept pace with her commercial expansion; the rich had grown richer and the poor correspondingly poorer. In 1851, for example, a relatively prosperous year, the Superintendent of the Out-Door Poor gave cash support to 12,000 residents of the city and free fuel to another 26,000. Of the 3,450 inmates of the penitentiary that year, over 2,500 were vagrants, men and women, that is, without any apparent means of support. Large numbers of other penniless New Yorkers found refuge in the city's alms-

[5] Junius Henri Browne, *The Great Metropolis: A Mirror of New York* (Hartford, 1869), p. 86; A. W. White, *Annual Report of the City Inspector of the Number of Deaths and Interments in the City of New York during the Year 1850* (New York, 1851), p. 442; Thomas Butler Gunn, *The Physiology of New-York Boarding-Houses* (New York, 1857), pp. 32, 267–268, 280–281. City missionary Samuel B. Halliday, remarking on this commuter pattern in 1859, commented sadly: "We may be said (comparatively), to have no longer a middling class in this city." Halliday, *Lost and Found*, p. 202.

house, hospitals, and reformatory. Each year these numbers mounted.[6] By 1855, the governors of the almshouse reported that pressure from the unemployed was so great that they had had to reconsider their entire program of outdoor relief.[7] And for each person resorting to public charity, contemporaries observed, many more received aid from private individuals and organizations. City missions, industrial schools, medical dispensaries, and orphanages all grew in numbers and in their scale of work.

The newly arrived immigrant, the black, and what contemporaries called the vicious poor were the most alarmingly visible of New York's slum dwellers. But they were not alone; many of the regularly employed and nativeborn were forced to live in circumstances not terribly different. Wage and employment structures in many of the city's trades were changing drastically. By the 1850's, such traditional New York industries as clothing, shoemaking, piano- and furniture-manufacturing were undergoing consolidation and mechanization; in many cases this brought deterioration in working conditions. While some skilled artisans rose to become contractors or manufacturers, many sank to the level of "mechanics" or "laborers." Such workers toiled long hours for wages which seemed increasingly inadequate. Factory hands worked ten to eleven hours a day, and often brought work home to be finished. As the 1850's progressed, an increasing proportion of

[6] New York City, Almshouse (hereinafter referred to as N.Y.C., Almshouse), *Third Annual Report of the Board of Governors of the Almshouse, New-York, for the Year 1851* (New York, 1851), pp. 2, 4, 7, 8, 127–129. It is difficult to say whether in terms of absolute proportions the number of the rich and poor had actually changed. It was clear, however, that New Yorkers *felt* that the extremes of wealth and poverty had become more marked.

[7] N.Y.C., Almshouse, *Seventh Annual Report of the Board of Governors of the Almshouse, New-York, for the Year 1855* (New York, 1856), pp. 190, 189–194.

workers found their way into factories. In 1855, Brooks Brothers employed three hundred male operatives in its clothing factory; Light, Newton, and Bradbury employed 164 men at cabinetmaking. One hundred and ten men worked at the A. H. Gale company producing an average of 650 pianos a year during the 1850's. Iron and metal foundries and the shipbuilding firms at Corlear's Hook had always employed large numbers of men.[8] By the 1850's, public health advocates agreed in condemning the unhealthy and dangerous conditions which prevailed in many of these enterprises.[9]

Workers often preferred doing piecework at home to the regimentation of the ill-ventilated and poorly constructed factories. And indeed in a number of New York's industries —cigar-making and clothing especially—most production took place in the operatives' homes. German and Jewish families, Irish and native-born women, for example, sewed virtually all the ready-made clothing produced in the city in their own tenement apartments, working fifteen to eighteen hours a day. "Each family," a tailor wrote of the industry as he remembered it during the 1860's and '70's, "employed from one to two hands, all living and working in the same

[8] For descriptions of working conditions in various of New York's industries, see Jesse Eliphalet Pope, *The Clothing Industry in New York*, University of Missouri Studies, I (Columbia, Mo., 1903), 12–44; Egal Feldman, *Fit for Men: A Study of New York's Clothing Trade* (Washington, D.C., 1960); [James Dawson Burn], *Three Years Among the Working-classes in the United States during the War* (London, 1865), pp. 178–189; John R. Commons, "American Shoemakers 1648–1895. A Sketch of Industrial Evolution," *Quarterly Journal of Economics*, XXIV, No. 1 (November, 1909), 72; Ernst, *Immigrant*, pp. 81–82, 249, 252.

[9] See, for example, testimony of Dr. Alexander H. Stevens in New York State Senate, *Report of the Select Committee Investigating the Health Department of the City of New York*, Senate Document No. 49 (Albany, 1859), p. 86.

rooms. There was no water in the building and toilets were situated in the back yard." [10] Conditions two decades earlier were, if anything, worse. Gas lighting was rare, and apartments consisted usually of one, or at most two, rooms. There was of course no indoor plumbing.

Mortality rates rose alarmingly during these decades, a fact concerned New Yorkers inevitably associated with such working and living conditions. In 1856, one out of every twenty-nine New Yorkers died, a rate nearly double that of London. This was in sharp contrast to the comparatively bucolic years at the beginning of the century when but one New Yorker in forty-seven died each year. "Death is making an alarming inroad upon [our] population," the State Legislature's Select Committee appointed to investigate New York's health department reported in 1859. "The average yearly mortality is far beyond its due proportion. There are annually cut off from it by disease and death, enough human beings to people a city, and enough human labor to sustain it." [11]

Most disturbingly, this unprecedented mortality rate could be traced directly to increases in infant and stillborn deaths. In 1850, there had been 10,567 infant deaths to 6,411 adult deaths. Ten years later, the City Inspector reported that more than one-half of New York's immigrant children under five died each year (seven in every ten among those under two).[12]

[10] Quoted in Ernst, *Immigrant*, p. 77.

[11] N.Y.S. Senate, *Report . . . Health Department*, pp. 6, 60. For additional medical testimony concerning the city's health, see John H. Griscom, *Annual Report of the Interments in the City and County of New-York, for the Year 1842* (New York, 1843); Griscom, *The Sanitary Condition of the Laboring Population of New York with Suggestions for its Improvement* (New York, 1845); Citizens' Association of New York, *Report of the Council of Hygiene and Public Health of the Citizens' Association of New York upon the Sanitary Condition of the City* (New York, 1865), pp. vii-xviii.

[12] A. W. White, *Annual Report . . . 1850*, pp. 443–448; Daniel E. Delavan, *Annual Report of the City Inspector of the City of New*

It is hardly surprising that the New York Legislature should have launched a series of investigations of the city's health conditions in the 1850's.[13]

The obvious reason for this dismaying increase in disease incidence, most thoughtful New Yorkers assumed, was the filth in which so many of their fellow Manhattanites lived. (Contemporary medical thought, it should be recalled, tended to explain the etiology of most infectious diseases in terms of miasmata arising from decaying organic matter.) New York had always been a filthy city. But population growth and congestion harshly exacerbated conditions already bad in 1810 and 1820. Rear as well as front lots were being filled, tenements were growing upward, their cellars and garrets crowded. The problems of garbage collection, street cleaning, and the removal of human wastes grew proportionately. Yet the Common Council had made little change in its long-criticized methods of sanitation. Garbage collection contracts, for example, remained political plums, and few of the recipients felt called upon actually to perform their specified duties. Even the well-to-do complained that their garbage remained uncollected for weeks and, when removed, was simply dumped on the corporation piers to rot. Tenement districts posed a particular problem. Huge quantities of garbage ac-

York for the Year Ending December 31, 1860 (New York, 1861), p. 13; L. Emmett Holt, "Infant Mortality and its Reduction, especially in New York City," Journal of the American Medical Association, LIV (1910), 682–690; W. F. Thoms, "Health in Country and Cities," Transactions of the American Medical Association, XVII (1866), 431–434.

[13] In addition to the Senate Select Committee of 1858–1859, the New York State Assembly in 1855–1856 had appointed a Special Committee to study tenements in New York and Brooklyn. New York State Assembly, "Report of the Special Committee on Tenement Houses in New York and Brooklyn," Documents of the Assembly of the State of New-York . . . 79th Session, 1856 (Albany, 1856), Vol. V, No. 199.

cumulated, far in excess of the capacity of the few bins supplied by landlords. Even more alarming was the problem of human waste disposal. New York possessed only an incomplete and not very efficient sewer system. Each night, accordingly, carts filled with "nightsoil" passed through the city streets, finally dumping their reeking contents on the corporation piers.[14]

But for New York's workingmen and their families, these were conditions of life, not simply causes for informed concern. Landlords ordinarily provided a few privies along the side of the building, or in its basement or backyard. Missionary visitors as well as dispensary physicians and other public health advocates were horrified to find backyards where children played and mothers hung up wash, coated with human excreta and swarming with flies. To these monumental sources of filth, New Yorkers added that created in raising over three thousand pigs commercially (and many more informally), in operating a score of slaughterhouses within the city limits, and in permitting private individuals to collect street manure, cart it to areas adjacent to the wharves and there allow it to "age." [15]

Deteriorating conditions of health and environment constituted only one aspect of the slum problem. Perhaps the city's most pressing dilemma were hordes of rootless tenement-bred children. Underfed, uneducated, not infrequently illegitimate, they were deeply alarming to prosperous New Yorkers; these

[14] Thomas K. Downing, *Annual Report of the City Inspector of the City of New York for the Year 1856* (New York, 1857), p. 197; New York *Independent*, II (January 10, 1850), 6; Griscom, *Annual Report . . . 1842*, pp. 188–197.

[15] Delavan, *Annual Report . . . 1860*, p. 53; Downing, *Annual Report . . . 1856*, p. 197; N.Y.S. Senate, *Report . . . Health Department*, p. 74; N.Y.S. Assembly, "Report, Tenement Houses," *passim*.

waifs would be citizens and voters in the not-too-distant future. In 1850, New York's police commissioner shocked the city by reporting that there were almost three thousand vagrant children in New York. The majority were girls, and these, he claimed, survived largely through prostitution. Fifteen years later the American Female Guardian Society's *Advocate and Family Guardian* alleged that 125,000 children lived in the city, "unreached and uncared for, as far as moral and religious training is concerned. Fifty thousand of these are vagrants, roaming the streets and docks by day and by night." [16] A number of charitable organizations were established in the 1850's, with the specific goal of providing homes for these children: the Children's Aid Society, the Juvenile Asylum, the Juvenile Guardian Society, and numerous industrial schools. Not surprisingly New York's city missions began to concern themselves more and more with these wayward youths.

Filth, crime, disease, and vagrancy; these were among the more prominent of the problems facing a growing metropolis. And the city had yet to develop a sophisticated bureaucracy or a communications network capable of dealing with problems of such magnitude. Indeed to its earlier inefficiency, New York now added a burgeoning system of political corruption. Franchises for street railroads were openly bought and sold, and policemen's jobs were an accepted medium of political exchange. The city's only health officer was a political appointee, responsible for selecting the city's garbage collectors and street cleaners. Until the mid-1850's, New York possessed

[16] New York *Independent*, II (January 24, 1850), 13, and (February 7, 1850), 22; *Advocate and Family Guardian*, XXXII (January 16, 1866), 20–21. See, as well, James Dabney McCabe, *The Secrets of the Great City* (Philadelphia, 1868), pp. 189–192, for a more sensationalistic contemporary description.

no regular fire or police department, no independent auditor or comptroller.[17] Most public services—relief, medical aid, even education—had necessarily to be supplemented by private charities.

Older New Yorkers, and many newer ones recently come from the country, bewildered by the dimensions of these problems, tended to explain the new city's disorganization in essentially traditional terms, in terms which allowed them to simplify and understand.

Two images served to perform this function for many articulate New Yorkers: the images of the immigrant and the tenement. The tenement was an unnatural environment, inevitably a breeding place for sickness and immorality; the immigrant brought disease, let his children run ragged and larcenous through the city's streets, voted corrupt aldermen into office, and inhabited the city's filthy and deteriorating slum buildings.

In a real sense, it might be argued, these images, at once picture and rationalization, of slum conditions had not really changed since the 1820's and 1830's. Despite the tremendous increase in the scale of these problems, New Yorkers tended still to emphasize the individualistic and the moralistic in their views of poverty in their city. The immigrant, for example, had played a central role in both periods in middle-class explanations of New York's social disorganization. Temperance too still played a significant role in the social thinking of ar-

[17] Henry E. Davies, *A Compilation of the Laws of the State of New York, Relating particularly to the City of New York. Prepared at the Request of the Common Council and Published under their Direction* (New York, 1855), Chap. 217, pp. 410–415; Limpus, *Fire Department*, pp. 180–238; J[ames] F. Richmond, *New York and its Institutions, 1609–1872* (New York, 1872), pp. 180–190; New York City Board of Aldermen, *Proceedings of the Board of Aldermen, May 1831–1936* (339 vols.; New York, 1835–1937), xxviii, 24–29; Haswell, *Reminiscences*, p. 488.

ticulate New Yorkers. But by the 1850's, the tenement had clearly eclipsed temperance in the minds of many Americans concerned with the quality of urban life. And this change is a highly significant one. For this acceptance of the tenement itself as a social problem implies a growing knowledge of living conditions, a growing commitment to environmental attitudes and explanations. And in the minds of many New Yorkers as well, it indicated a growing commitment to pragmatic and melioristic reform.

New Yorkers' anxieties in regard to the immigrant and the tenement cannot be dismissed as a self-serving oversimplification of a complex and threatening situation; both were very real problems. Over 60,000 passengers arrived at the port of New York in 1840—only 4,000 at Philadelphia and 5,000 at Boston. Many others destined for Manhattan landed in Brooklyn and New Jersey. By the decade's end the number of arrivals had grown appreciably. In May of 1849, 32,700 aliens landed in New York City; in June, another 33,000. The following year 212,796 arrived—117,000 from Ireland, 45,535 from Germany, and 35,000 from England and Scotland.[18] Most continued on to farms and villages inland. Each year, however, an appreciable number remained in the city. By 1849, the number and need of these new arrivals had become New York's single most discordant social reality. It was in this period, for example, that the heretofore uninterested state legislature began to consider the problem specifically, passing laws to protect these new arrivals from exploitation by the city's criminals and marginal businesses and adopting Castle Garden for use as a safer and more orderly point of entry.[19]

[18] Valentine, *Manual of the Corporation of the City of New York for the Year 1849* (New York, 1849), p. 311.
[19] New York State Assembly, *Report of the Select Committee Appointed to Investigate Frauds upon Emigrant Passengers Arriving in this State*, Assembly Document No. 46 (Albany, 1847); New York State, *Laws of the State of New-York Passed by the Seventy-*

Contrary to the impression held by many contemporaries, not all of these immigrants sank into the morass of indigence or of the day laborer's life; by the 1850's even the Irish community had its fledgling social institutions—schools, an orphanage, a ladies' seminary and college, even a militia regiment. Irishmen had already begun to find careers in politics and business.[20] Yet many immigrants did not prosper. Of 2,355 almshouse admissions in 1850, 1,810 were foreign-born and 1,464 of these Irish. Similar ratios held good for the city's other eleemosynary institutions; of 3,728 admissions at Bellevue in 1850, 2,596 reported Ireland as their birthplace; only 647 were native-born.[21] Anti-immigrant feeling maintained itself at a high pitch throughout the decade. Such xenophobic sentiments lay, of course, behind much New York interest in reform and third party alternatives during the 1850's.

Anti-Catholicism was an integral component of this chronic nativism; it is, indeed, difficult to disentangle the two. Increasing numbers of Irish and Germans, their growing political power, the contrasts between their life styles and those prescribed by American Protestantism—all intensified traditional dislike of Catholics and Catholicism.[22] "The Catholic

second Session of the Legislature (Troy, New York, 1848). See also New York City Chamber of Commerce, Report on Emigration by a Special Committee of the Chamber of Commerce, January 5, 1865, cited Stokes, Iconography, V, 1823.

[20] See, passim, Freeman's Journal, the official paper of the New York archdiocese, but especially October 10, 1846, April 24, 1847, May 14, 1859; Ernst, Immigration, pp. 84–98, 135–149; Lossing, New York City, II, 701.

[21] N.Y.C., Almshouse, Second Annual Report of the Governors of the Almshouse, New-York, for the Year 1850 (New York, 1851), pp. 21–30, 117–120, 125, 129.

[22] For two of an innumerable number of examples, see editorials in the Christian Times, February 1, 1866, and The Nation, I (November 20, 1865), 691–692. See also Ray Allen Billington, The Protestant Crusade, 1800–1860 (New York, 1938).

religion was a kind of embodied spirit of evil," a *Catholic World* editorial of 1866 explained bitterly, "and her ministers had to vindicate their title to the rank of men and Christians. Religion, morality, liberty, happiness would be swept from the country if they were not exterminated!" [23] These words were not simply hyperbole; to "evangelical" Protestants it was clear that Catholicism was no real religion. Throughout the 1850's and 1860's, the desire to socialize these masses of Catholic immigrants was a significant and explicit theme in the city mission movement—as in the parallel efforts of New Yorkers supporting the Children's Aid Society and industrial schools.

The immigrant lived in the tenement. And the realities of tenement life mocked the formally expressed ethics and morals of a Christian society and threatened that society as well; disease, crime, and vice all seemed to proliferate in crowded tenement apartments.

In its pioneering housing code of 1867, New York State defined a tenement as any building containing more than three families, living and cooking separately, and having access to common stairs and halls. That year, it was later estimated, New York City contained 15,000 such structures.[24] Nine years earlier, Samuel B. Halliday, city missionary and dedicated public health advocate, asserted that three-quarters of the city's inhabitants lived in tenements. In the first ward, for example, close to the docks where the bulk of the city's immigrants landed, 2,341 of 2,814 families lived in tenements. The ward averaged fifteen families per building, a dismayingly large number given the sanitary and engineering abilities

[23] *Catholic World*, III (1866), 389.
[24] Lawrence Veiller, "Tenement House Reform in New York City, 1834–1900," in *The Tenement House Problem*, ed. by Robert W. DeForest and Lawrence Veiller (2 vols.; New York, 1903), I, 69–119.

of New York's construction firms in the 1850's (and the assumption by most Americans that home-owning was the normal and indeed moral pattern of family life, urban as well as rural). The tenth ward—in what is now known as the Lower East Side—averaged seventeen families per building.[25]

The pattern of tenement dwelling which we saw just beginning to develop in the 1830's had, by the 1850's and 1860's, reached a stable and characteristic form. Two quite different kinds of tenements characterized New York's slums: those which concerned contemporaries termed the "reconstructed tenant house" and those called "especially constructed tenements." The reconstructed tenant house was a natural and unplanned consequence of changing residence patterns and New York's spiraling real-estate prices. As the century progressed and the wealthy moved away from homes in the older business streets, their comfortable houses were divided and divided again. At first only a few families might occupy the house, and the building would be maintained in good repair. But population pressure and land values continued to rise; the property had to produce more and more income. It was either torn down to make room for larger commercial buildings or converted into a tenement housing perhaps a dozen families.[26]

Having begun life as one-family dwellings—in a generation not yet given to pretentious scale in domestic life—these reconstructed tenements averaged but eighteen by thirty feet and were ordinarily three to four stories high. Little was spent on their remodeling or upkeep. In the third ward, indeed, just behind Trinity Church, one such building had no plaster on its walls; the stairs and roof were rotten with decay. Yet it housed seventy tenants, all Irish. In the fifth ward, near once

[25] Halliday, *Lost and Found*, pp. 190–195.
[26] N.Y.S. Assembly, "Report . . . Tenement Houses," pp. 10–12.

fashionable St. John's Park, state officials found another tenement in a state of almost total dilapidation, the rear "apparently abandoned to general filth and excrements." Twenty tenants still lived there. Such buildings were not atypical; investigators found no difficulty in unearthing even more-crowded and filthy examples of the reconstructed tenement.[27]

The second type of tenement common in mid-nineteenth-century New York was especially constructed to house large numbers of the poor. These had normally two or four apartments on each floor (depending on the building's width). The front room of the apartment opened on either the street or a back court; the inner bedroom was always dark and windowless. A twin building was often constructed at the rear of the first tenement. Reached through a narrow alley from the street, it was usually less than ten feet from the rear of the front building. Especially in the lower, commercial wards, where street frontage commanded high business rates, reformers frequently found rear lots filled with such newly constructed tenements. Filthy, foul-smelling, they were reached through a labyrinth of alleys or, ironically, glimpsed from the rear window of an elegant shop or hotel.[28]

Contemporaries agreed that the universal practice of letting cellar rooms was the most unhealthy aspect of New York's tenement problem. Such half-finished basements provided neither light nor adequate ventilation; their dampness encouraged not only rheumatism and respiratory disease, but—given the city's haphazard sanitary arrangements—threatened

[27] *Ibid.*, pp. 16–22.

[28] *Ibid.*, pp. 24–28; N.Y.S. Senate, *Report . . . Health Department*, pp. 30–31; New York Association for Improving the Condition of the Poor (hereinafter referred to as A.I.C.P.), *First Report . . . Sanitary Condition*, pp. 8–11; Cyrus Ramsay, *Annual Report of the City Inspector of the City of New York for the Year 1864* (New York, 1865), pp. 147–148.

occupants with typhoid, dysentery, and cholera. In damp weather, earthen and wooden walls would be beaded with drops of moisture seeping from drains, sewers, and privies. In 1842 the City Inspector complained that at least 1,459 cellars in New York were occupied, serving as homes for nearly seven thousand families. "Into some water is continually flowing from roofs and yards, and the small rooms are so crowded as to leave scarcely room to turn." Some had literally to be bailed out after each rain.[29]

New Yorkers' awareness of such conditions had come gradually. Since the War of 1812, a growing minority among the respectable had observed at first hand the misery in which so many of their fellow citizens existed. City missionaries, dispensary physicians, teachers in the city's public and industrial schools, Sunday school volunteers, the more conscientious occupants of the city inspector's office—all had visited the homes of the poor. As early as 1834, City Inspector Garrett Forbes had deplored the crowding and filth of the city's slums. Two years before, in 1832, New Yorkers, terrified by an impending cholera epidemic, had been dismayed by similar conditions. A decade later, in 1842, City Inspector and public health reformer John H. Griscom had appended a lengthy description of such disease-breeding conditions to his City Inspector's annual report of vital statistics. The annual reports of the New York City Tract Society, of the Protestant Episcopal City Mission Society, the Association for Improving the Condition of the Poor, and of the city's medical dispensaries referred frequently to the numbers of the poor and to their crowded and unhealthy living arrangements.

But it was not until the 1850's that New Yorkers generally awoke to the existence of such conditions. The cholera epi-

[29] Griscom, *Annual Report . . . 1842*, pp. 156, 162–165; N.Y.S. Senate, *Report . . . Health Department*, p. 115.

demics of 1849 and 1854, the depressions of 1855 and 1857, forced them to realize that large numbers of the poor lived in crowded, unhealthy slums, carefully segregated from the comfortable and well-to-do. In 1849, for example, immediately following a severe cholera epidemic, the city inspector pointed to the relation of cholera to the unsanitary, crowded tenements of the poor.[30] The following year, the newly formed American Medical Association, acting largely in response to the cholera epidemic of 1849, sponsored a study of urban disease incidence, a report widely commented upon in the city's press.[31] In 1850 the liberal Protestant *Independent* carried articles and editorials on juvenile vagrancy, cellar apartments, and the effect of tenement life on the public health.[32] Just three years later, the New York Association for Improving the Condition of the Poor, one of the city's newest and most active city missions, issued a lengthy census and discussion of tenement houses and circulated plans for model tenements among builders and capitalists. Its activities were widely publicized.[33]

By 1856, in the wake of one of New York's most severe depressions, the Panic of 1855 (a depression which, contemporaries felt, forced many of the respectable lower-middle-class into tenement apartments), public protest and awareness were sufficient to persuade the state legislature to appoint a select committee to examine tenement houses in New York and Brooklyn. (The committee reported with some surprise that they had found a large body of New Yorkers already

[30] White, *Annual Report . . . 1849*, pp. 505–506.

[31] American Medical Association, *First Report of the Committee on Public Hygiene* (Philadelphia, 1849).

[32] See, for example, New York *Independent*, II (January 17, 1850), 10, (January 24, 1850), 14, (February 7, 1850), 22, and (May 9, 1850), 76.

[33] A.I.C.P., *First Report . . . Sanitary Condition*.

informed about tenement problems and capable of assisting them in their investigation; [34] a growing number of reports and descriptions, the select committee discovered, had already forced a knowledge of the new slums and their inhabitants upon thoughtful New Yorkers.) No sooner had the legislative committee issued their report in 1857 than the second sharp depression of the decade struck New York. In 1859, the state legislature again appointed a special committee to survey the extent of the city's poverty, tenements, and disease. And again the press actively publicized their work.[35]

But the draft riots of 1863, more than any other single event, forced the well-to-do, the educated, and the articulate to recognize that they lived surrounded by great pockets of disease, misery, crime, and illiteracy, and that their city had changed radically since the beginning of the century. The draft riots proved the immediate stimulus to the formation of a citizen's committee to study poverty and tenement conditions in New York, and ultimately to the publication of an influential report on the public health. In combination with a threatened cholera epidemic in 1866, the riots led to the passage of New York's first major piece of welfare legislation, the Metropolitan Board of Health Act of 1866. The Tenement House Code—the first such code adopted for any United States city—was enacted into law the following year (1867). [36]

[34] N.Y.S. Assembly, "Report . . . Tenement Houses," pp. 3, 10.

[35] N.Y.S. Senate, *Report . . . Health Department.*

[36] The Citizens Association, the lobbying group most directly responsible for the reform in the city's health department, was founded in the months immediately following the Draft Riots. For the effect of these riots on respectable opinion, and especially on stimulating public health reform, see Gert H. Brieger, "Sanitary Reform in New York City: Stephen Smith and the Passage of the Metropolitan Health Bill," *Bulletin of the History of Medicine,* XL

The concern which led to the passage of this social legislation was, as we have indicated, not simply pragmatic and melioristic. In an age when moralism permeated every sphere of life and few barriers existed in the categories of conventional social thought between the physiological, the moral, and the social, it was easy for New Yorkers to see the tenement as the all-corrupting source of the city's problems. "The physical and moral," an earnest *Independent* editorialist explained in 1850, "are closely allied. The habit of living in squalor and filth engenders vice, and vice, on the other hand, finds a congenial home in the midst of physical impurities." [37] Reformers stressed the danger of licentiousness and prostitution developing in an environment where whole families, even boarders, slept in one room. (Such unnatural and unhealthful proximity was a medical as well as moral problem; the etiology of the venereal diseases was only a more explicit example of a more general relationship.) With children raised in close proximity to alcoholics and criminals, teachers and city missionaries asked, how could they long remain virtuous? [38]

(September–October, 1966), 407–429; Stephen Smith, "Riots and their Prevention," *Doctor in Medicine, and other Papers on Professional Subjects* (New York, 1872), pp. 188–195; Rosenberg, *Cholera Years*, pp. 187, 231.

[37] *Independent* (January 24, 1850), p. 14.

[38] See, for example, Smith, "Riots and their Prevention," p. 192; N.Y.S. Senate, *Report . . . Health Department*, p. 13. The distinction between that which we regard as pragmatic environmentalism and that which we dismiss as mere moralism is, in regard to the public health movement of the 1840's and 1850's, far more confusing than enlightening. Both styles of thought supplemented each other, interacting with the energies of pietism to motivate and broaden a concern with the human problems of the city. See Charles E. and Carroll S. Rosenberg, "Pietism and the Origins of the American Public Health Movement: A Note on John H. Griscom and Robert M. Hartley," *Journal of the History of Medicine*, XXIII (1968), 16–35.

City missionaries, physicians, and public officials spent a good deal of effort in the 1850's explaining to genteel Americans the ways in which slum life demoralized the poor, perpetuating its own ethos of immorality and hopelessness. Only the strongest of moral constitutions might hope to withstand the spiritual miasma of the tenements. High rents or temporary unemployment not infrequently forced families previously virtuous and hard-working into slum apartments. Here they struggled without a water supply, with primitive sanitary facilities, to maintain a clean and pious home. Gradually, however, surrounded by sickness, living in such debilitating circumstances, they fell ill. "Health failing them," the legislature's Select Committee on Tenement Houses reported, "want will follow; and then must come crowding rapidly upon them, neglect of home, neglect of children, uncleanliness, drunkenness and crime. This is no fancy sketch. . . . It is a stern reality, enacted every day in the midst of luxury and wealth." [39] Some seven years later a citizens' group gave dramatic emphasis to this report. Visiting a drunken mother living in a dismal rear court, the sanitary officer sympathetically asked why she drank. She replied simply, "If you lived in this place you would ask for whiskey instead of milk." [40]

The existence of such moral lesions in the social body led many Americans to denounce the immigrant as a bearer of Europe's social ills to America's idyllic shores. Others in the trying years before the Civil War began to fear for the continued viability of their free institutions; could popular democracy survive in the sordid environment of the new city?

[39] N.Y.S. Assembly, "Report . . . Tenement Houses," pp. 3–4, 8, 47, 52–53; Griscom, *Annual Report . . . 1842*, pp. 160–161, 175–181; Halliday, *Lost and Found*, pp. 27–31, 190, 198–199; and virtually every City Inspector's report in the 1850's and 1860's.

[40] New York State, Metropolitan Board of Health, *First Annual Report, 1866* (Albany, 1866), p. 135.

The majority chose, however, to reject neither the city nor the immigrant. While retaining a certain disdain for the alien poor, and a growing concern for the shape being assumed by their developing metropolis, New Yorkers still cast about for individualistic and moral factors with which to explain and order these new realities.

Most of these were traditional—drink, carelessness, original sin; but new emphases were coming into prominence. A new moral scapegoat had been found, for example, in the slum landlord. The tenant-house entrepreneur was a marginal figure economically, not infrequently the operator of a saloon or brothel in the tenement's basement. In origin he was frequently an immigrant himself, or a first-generation American; only rarely was he a member of the Protestant establishment that owned so great a proportion of the city's real estate. Most frequently he lived in a slum area himself. By focusing criticism upon this petty exploiter of his fellows, conservative New Yorkers were able to exonerate society generally from responsibility for the slum and at the same time transpose a widespread social blight into individual and hence comprehensible and remediable terms. City missionaries endorsed and documented the indictments of the city's slum landlords drawn up by mid-century public health advocates. "If they can get tenants into their buildings and get their pay, very little do they care whether the occupants live or die, if they only pay the rent for the time being." [41]

[41] Dr. Simon Bachelder, testimony, N.Y.S. Senate, *Report . . . Health Department*, p. 66; cf. extended testimony before the Select Committee to study tenement houses, especially N.Y.S. Assembly, "Report . . . Tenement Houses," pp. 10–12, 18–19. Fifteen years earlier the by-no-means-radical Lydia Maria Child commented bitterly upon the exploitation of New York's poor by slum landlords, a theme emphasized by most city missionaries during the 1850's and 1860's. Child, *Letters*, p. 20; *see* Chaps. 7 and 9, below. For an insightful

In the minds of many genuinely charitable New Yorkers, moreover, the immorality of the poor themselves was the moral counterpart of the landlord's greed in degrading the housing in which they lived. Even those New Yorkers most sympathetic to their plight tended to regard the city's poor as ignorant, stupid, and illiterate. The poor could not comprehend the need for cleanliness. They were unable to protect themselves from the tenement landlord, to find the strength and purpose to escape the city altogether—clearly the only lasting remedy for the problems of most tenement dwellers. The poor as moral dependents required the paternalistic attentions not only of private charity, but of the state as well. It was these views which sanctioned, even demanded, such social legislation as the acts establishing the Metropolitan Board of Health and the Tenement House Code of 1867.[42]

In the recognition of this new urban reality, the city missions had played an important role. Schemes for the improving of the public health and social welfare continued in

---

modern study of this pattern of transferring blame for a pattern of slum housing and low economic standards from the economy generally to the individual landholder, see Lawrence Friedman, *Government and Slum Housing: A Century of Frustration* (Chicago, 1968). Closely related to their castigation of the slum landlord was the reformers' demands for model tenements—from which they believed honest and respectable capitalists could construct and receive a 6 per cent profit. The city missions led the fight for such model tenements. *See* Chap. 9, below.

[42] For examples of this type of argument, see Griscom, *Annual Report . . . 1842*, pp. 175–180; A.I.C.P., *First Report . . . Sanitary Condition*, p. 5; Thomas K. Downing, *Annual Report of the City Inspector of the Number of Deaths and Interments in the City of New York during the Year 1852* (New York, 1853), pp. 287–288. Virtually every doctor testifying before the Senate Select Committee in 1859 demanded rigid tenant house legislation for these reasons. N.Y.S. Senate, *Report . . . Health Department*, pp. 5–6, 11, 13, 24–73, 85, 86–138.

this period to draw upon the knowledge and motivation of the city missionaries and their dedicated supporters. As the millennial hopes of the 1830's faded, the missions too had begun to change, to assume new—more limited and more pragmatic—forms. They found themselves casually and inevitably seeking new tactics with which to achieve a secular salvation for at least some of their fellow New Yorkers.

CHAPTER 7

The Missions in
the New City

New York's city missions underwent a fundamental transformation between the inaugurations of Martin Van Buren and Ulysses Grant. Their objectives, their programs, and their self-image changed strikingly in these decades. Such changes paralleled those undergone by New York City, which had grown to a world metropolis, a metropolis with social problems of a scale undreamed of in the century's first decades. The assumptions of New York's philanthropists changed as well. Despite a brief burst of religious enthusiasm during the 1857 revival, a more pessimistic moralism came to replace the deeply pietistic orientation of the 1830's. The millennium no longer beckoned in alluring proximity. Man, but partially perfected, was left to struggle with problems ever more secular and impersonal.

In the body of the chapter following, I have attempted to illustrate these institutional and attitudinal shifts in the history of two of the missions already discussed, the New York City Tract Society and the American Female Guardian Society. In the final two chapters I present two institutional variations upon the city mission theme, two mid-century products of this increasingly secular and pragmatic period. One is the Five Points House of Industry and the other the

New York Association for Improving the Condition of the Poor. The former was an organization financially dependent upon rural support; it sought—especially through the placing-out adoption system—to solve urban problems through a rejection of the city. The Association for Improving the Condition of the Poor was a formally secular, though highly moralistic offspring of the City Tract Society; it explicitly divorced itself from an explicitly religious base and saw its activities as exemplifying a newly "scientific philanthropy." Its history thus provides a useful framework for evaluating the transition between the evangelicalism of the city missions in the mid-1830's and the more melioristic, pragmatic mood which characterized their functional successors in the 1880's and 1890's.

[1] New York City Mission and Tract Society: 1837–1870

The evangelical impulse had determined the goals and methods of the New York City Tract Society throughout its early years. Even at the height of the 1837 Panic, the Society remained essentially pietistic in its expectations. It still sought primarily to convert all New Yorkers to "experimental" Protestantism. Nevertheless, the Society's missionary labors during the depression years had gradually sharpened its members' concern for New York's slum population. Society visitors had acted as agents for *ad hoc* ward-relief committees, and the Society's official reports had urged New Yorkers to use its visitors as experienced if unofficial almoners. From viewing their city as simply one geographic area in need of religious attention, the Society had begun to think of urban life as posing peculiar challenges.[1]

[1] N.Y.C.T.S., *Eleventh Annual Report for the Year 1837* (New York, 1837), p. 22; *Twelfth Annual Report for the Year 1838* (New

By the early 1840's, the minutes of the Society's executive committee had become filled almost completely with discussions of the needs of the poor, with debates as to the most efficient and economical means of distributing charity, and in recording attempts to seek out philanthropists willing to underwrite the Tract Society's expanding relief activities. In the spring of 1843, the Society's executive committee circulated a memorandum among their ward missionaries, asking for their suggestions "as to the most efficient mode of ameliorating the condition of the poor, and detecting the frauds of impostors." Within a month, the executive committee had decided that New York needed a new, city-wide organization to supervise the distribution of relief. The role of almoner to the city's poor was too great a task for a religious tract society to undertake, and still hope to fulfill its essentially evangelical goals.[2]

In July of 1843, therefore, the Tract Society's executive committee voted to establish a separate "Society for the Relief of the Worthy Poor." This organization—ultimately christened the New York Association for Improving the Condition

---

York, 1839), p. 28; *Thirteenth Annual Report for the Year 1839* (New York, 1840), p. 36; and *Fourteenth Annual Report for the Year 1840* (New York, 1841), pp. 16–17, 65.

[2] N.Y.C.T.S., "Minutes of the Missionaries' Weekly Meetings, April 1, and June 17, 1843." These minutes from February 24, 1838, to December 28, 1844, can no longer be located in the archives of the N.Y.C.T.S. However, in 1948, a verbatim copy of the notes was made by the N.Y.C.T.S. and sent to the Archives of the Community Service Society (the successor of the A.I.C.P.). This transcript is cited frequently in this section. For a modern discussion of the founding of the A.I.C.P., and a history of the N.Y.C.T.S., see Kenneth D. Miller and Ethel Prince Miller, *The People are the City* (New York, 1962), and Roy Lubove, "The New York Association For Improving the Condition of the Poor: The Formative Years," *New-York Historical Society Quarterly*, XLIII (1959), 307–27.

of the Poor—was organized, administered, and financed, by the managers and directors of the Tract Society.[3] Its purpose was to take from the parent Society the burden of caring for the poor the Tract Society visitors had found while acting as religious missionaries and to transfer this responsibility to the Association for Improving the Condition of the Poor.[4] In organizing a separate institution to deal with the temporal needs of the poor, therefore, the City Tract Society only re-affirmed a continued dedication to its original pietistic goals.

And indeed in the two or three years immediately follow-ing the establishment of the Association, the Tract Society returned to its original objectives and methods. The Society again concentrated on converting atheists, Roman Catholics, and Universalists; visitors appeared once more at respectable doors. The Society's annual reports boasted carefully tabu-lated lists, recording with pride the numbers of souls saved that year and the numbers of the unchurched brought into communion. The annual reports of the mid-1840's contain no mention of Society volunteers visiting the city's slums nor of charity distributed (though some visiting among the poor undoubtedly continued). They provide no analyses of

[3] See N.Y.C.T.S., "Minutes of the Missionaries' Weekly Meetings" from July, 1842, to December, 1844. The ties between the two organizations remained close throughout the pre-Civil War period. For instance, in 1860, the N.Y.C.T.S. wrote of the A.I.C.P.: "This institution and its parent the City Tract Society were proceeding hand in hand, seeking a common object, walking in the footsteps of Jesus." N.Y.C.T.S., *Thirty-fourth Annual Report for the Year 1860* (New York, 1861), p. 15. See also comments by tract visitors on their close working arrangements with A.I.C.P. volunteers. N.Y.C.T.S., *Nineteenth Annual Report for the Year 1845* (New York, 1846), pp. 27, 32; *Twentieth Annual Report for the Year 1846* (New York, 1847), pp. 18–19, 25–26; and *Twenty-ninth Annual Report for the Year 1855* (New York, 1856), pp. 29–30.

[4] For a more detailed treatment of the subsequent history of the A.I.C.P., see Chap. 9, below.

the causes or nature of poverty; such concerns had—the Society's managers felt—been safely delegated.

But during these very years the managers of the City Tract Society made a decision which was eventually to make their organization as temporally oriented as its secular arm, the Association for Improving the Condition of the Poor. In 1846 the Society's Board of Managers voted to emphasize the Society's religious work in the slums, even at the expense of missionary labors with other classes in society.[5] The need for this decision was obvious to contemporaries. Most important was an alarming increase in the number of immigrants—most of them destitute, unskilled, and Catholic—which followed America's returning prosperity and the European crop failures of the 1840's. These poverty-stricken immigrants as well as the infirm, the aged, the criminal never would, it seemed apparent, voluntarily attend one of the city's established churches. Religious New Yorkers concluded, that they must be sought out in their tenement homes, converted, and educated before they could be introduced to church membership. The City Tract Society was, it seemed clear to most of the city's clergy and philanthropists, the only organization equipped to perform such a task. Increasingly with the 1850's and 1860's, the Society became the emissary of New York Protestantism to the city's slum dwellers. Its annual reports and the reports of visitors and missionaries were again filled with accounts of missionary work among the tenements and shanties of the poor.

Paralleling these changes was a major structural alteration within the organization itself. This change followed from the executive committee's decision to hire salaried full-time workers to labor exclusively with the very poor and the immigrant. In the enthusiastic generation of its founding, the

[5] N.Y.C.T.S., *Twentieth Annual Report*, p. 18.

Society's zealous supporters had felt that all Christians must serve as missionaries, that all shared in the responsibility of converting their fellow citizens. By the 1860's, indeed by the late 1850's, pious New Yorkers, though loyal to the Society and its new goals, increasingly limited their commitment to a financial one. The Society's work was now performed by full-time, salaried, proto-professional workers. And these agents did not simply pray and exhort; they had become expert in such matters as job placement, wage scales, public health, and the coordination of the city's numerous charities. Indeed, throughout the Tract Society's history there was a clearly marked inverse relation between decreasing numbers of volunteer visitors and an increasing number of full-time, salaried workers.

The practice of hiring salaried missionaries had actually begun a number of years before the City Tract Society turned to work with the poor exclusively. In 1834, A. R. Wetmore had hired Samuel B. Halliday, then an active volunteer teacher in a black Sunday school, to act as the Society's first "city missionary." Halliday was to serve as a full-time assistant to Wetmore in his capacity as tract district chairman. (Wetmore's business responsibilities had prevented him from devoting as much time as he wished to the evangelization of his district.) Halliday supervised the work of the volunteer visitors; more importantly, he spent each day visiting and holding regular prayer meetings and Bible classes.[6] His success in increasing the number of converts in the district was immediately encouraging, and wealthy Tract

[6] N.Y.C.T.S., *Eighth Annual Report*, p. 24; *Eighteenth Annual Report for the Year 1844* (New York, 1850), p. 12; and "Report of the Committee Appointed to Study the Statements of Rev. Mr. Ortrom Concerning the Operations of the New York City Tract Society," 1840.

Society supporters soon pledged a sum great enough to hire a missionary for each district.[7]

These missionaries worked with New Yorkers of every social class. During the late 1840's and early 1850's, however, the Society's executive committee began to hire additional missionaries to work specifically with the city's poor. The numbers of these missionaries to the poor rose dramatically during the 1850's and 1860's. By the early 1860's, the Society employed thirty full-time salaried city missionaries, only nineteen of whom were regular ward missionaries (and thus dealing presumably with a cross section of the city's population). Three such missionaries worked with German-speaking slum dwellers; four others devoted themselves to the conversion of newly arrived English and Irish immigrants, and three were assigned to work in particularly forbidding slum areas.[8] All city missionaries, moreover, beginning in the early 1850's were also employed by the Association for Improving the Condition of the Poor to act as that Association's ward secretaries, supervising the distribution of charity in each of the Association's districts.[9]

As the number of professional tract agents increased, the

[7] Through the 1830's and most of the 1840's, the Society employed between fourteen and seventeen salaried missionaries (the number dependent upon the Society's fluctuating income during these difficult depression years).

[8] See, for example, N.Y.C.T.S., *Twenty-sixth Annual Report for the Year 1852* (New York, 1853), p. 7; *Twenty-eighth Annual Report for the Year 1854* (New York, 1855), p. 16; and *Twenty-ninth Annual Report*, pp. 47–50; New York City Mission and Tract Society, *Forty-third Annual Report for the Year 1869* (New York, 1870), p. 155. (In 1866 the Society changed its formal title to New York City Mission and Tract Society, hereinafter referred to as N.Y.C.M.T.S.)

[9] N.Y.C.T.S., *Thirty-fifth Annual Report for the Year 1861* (New York, 1862), pp. 37–38.

number of volunteer visitors declined. This decline began in the late 1850's and progressed rapidly during the early 1860's. It was clearly related to the Society's growing dependence upon "professional" help and its decision to work principally in slum areas. "There are localities in our city which are very repulsive, and which could not be reached by our ordinary procedure [i.e., volunteer visiting]," the Society explained in 1852.

They are crowded with men and women deeply sunk in immorality, yet possessing immortal spirits and hastening to final judgment. For their especial benefit three assistant missionaries have been employed, and the measure has called forth pleasing testimonials of approbation from neighboring churches.[10]

In 1870 the Society employed forty full-time salaried missionaries—but could claim only 31 volunteers.[11] The Tract Society by the late 1860's had acquired a professional staff and had in essence ceased to be a society administered and staffed by pious activists.

During the early 1850's the Tract Society officers began consciously to analyze the changed nature of their mission efforts. In 1853 Theodore L. Cuyler, a prominent clergyman and long-time supporter of the Tract Society and other city missions, pointed with satisfaction to the Society's newly specialized role as religious missionary to the city's tenement population.

There is a tendency and a temptation to provide a gospel for the rich in goodly sanctuaries, forgetting that Christ came to save the lowly. It is to counteract this tendency to pride and pomp and circumstance that this Society goes out on its mission of philan-

[10] N.Y.C.T.S., *Twenty-sixth Annual Report*, p. 16.
[11] N.Y.C.M.T.S., *Forty-fourth Annual Report for the Year 1870* (New York, 1871), p. 140.

thropy. . . . Its city missionaries preach at the doors, in the garrets, underneath the ground and to the outcast everywhere.[12]

In 1864, the Society, recognizing its new role as spiritual guardian of the urban poor, applied to the New York State legislature for a title more accurately reflecting these new responsibilities. It wished to change from the New York City Tract Society to the New York City Mission and Tract Society, because—spokesmen explained to supporters and New Yorkers generally—it was no longer simply an organization for the general distribution of tracts. Its new model had become the London City Mission Society, and its new object was to reach and convert the poor.[13] In 1869, when again seeking a new charter, the Society made the same point even more emphatically. "The objects of this corporation are to promote morality and religion among the poor and destitute of the City of New York." [14]

The methods of the City Mission and Tract Society changed with its objectives. In the 1840's the Society had still seen itself as an auxiliary of the city's churches seeking out converts and prospective members; by the 1850's the Society itself had become a church for the poor. This was

[12] Theodore L. Cuyler, "Sermon at the Twenty-seventh Anniversary Meeting of the N.Y.C.T.S.," cited in N.Y.C.T.S., *Twenty-seventh Annual Report for the Year 1853* (New York, 1854), pp. 10–11.

[13] N.Y.C.M.T.S., "Executive Committee Minutes, November 11, 1867." It was hardly a coincidence that the Reverend Frederick Clark, who proposed the name change, had just returned from a meeting of the London City Mission. Indeed during the late 1860's a number of the Society's officers visited England and Europe studying the institutions established by foreign philanthropists to aid the urban poor. N.Y.C.M.T.S., *Thirty-eighth Annual Report for the Year 1864* (New York, 1865), p. 12.

[14] N.Y.C.M.T.S., "Minutes of the Meetings of the Board of Trustees, December 15, 1869."

clearly a response to changing social conditions in the city and especially to its increasingly "compartmentalized" residential pattern. New York had always had its slums; but earlier in the century they had been within walking distance, often within sight, of prosperous residential areas and well-attended churches. With the 1840's and 1850's, as we have seen, the church-going and the wealthy moved uptown and their churches with them; few Protestant churches remained in the city's tenement districts. There seemed no alternative; the Society's managers felt called upon to provide New York's slums with churches and pastors.

Beginning in the late 1840's (about the same time that the executive committee voted to hire special city missionaries), the Society's annual reports mentioned the lack of regular churches convenient to the city's poorest districts.[15] By the early 1850's the Society began to act upon these observations. In 1852 the executive committee, in a radical departure from its formerly exclusive reliance upon a system of visiting the homes of prospective converts, voted to establish "mission stations" in churchless slum areas.[16] During the next ten years the Society established a total of eleven such mission stations and, as well, held scheduled prayer meetings and services in another twenty-five rented "halls." [17] These mission stations at first occupied a store front, loft, or tenement apartment in an area devoid of regular churches. Here the Society's ward missionary held regular prayer meetings and Sunday

[15] See, for example, N.Y.C.T.S., *Twenty-sixth Annual Report*, pp. 21–22; *Twenty-seventh Annual Report*, p. 16; and *Twenty-eighth Annual Report*, p. 10. This was a concern shared by most of New York's religious philanthropists. See, for example, an editorial in the A.F.G.S.'s *Advocate*, XXX (August 1, 1864), 178–179.

[16] N.Y.C.T.S., *Twenty-seventh Annual Report*, p. 16.

[17] N.Y.C.T.S., *Thirty-sixth Annual Report for the Year 1862* (New York, 1863), pp. 19–20.

and weekday services. Here, at specified times each day, the poor could see their own special "pastor," the Tract Society's ward missionary, for spiritual guidance and temporal aid. For it was the ward missionary who now acted as pastor of these new slum churches.[18]

Gradually the Society began to see the importance of placing these missions in more permanent and substantial buildings. In 1864, the Society, having raised $100,000 from the city's business community, initiated an ambitious building program.[19] Large church buildings rose up in slum neighborhoods housing not only a church proper but, like the later institutional churches, a number of other subsidiary areas: schools, libraries, meeting rooms, even coffee lounges. A few years later, the Society announced:

It is the aim of the Directors to give them [the poor] attractive mission stations and attractive preachers. They will make the mission station a centre of life, light and love; and religious services on the Sabbath, and moral and social entertainments through the week, will draw the people away from the evil influence of the saloons of frivolity, sensualism and vice, and save them and their children from destruction.[20]

Clearly these enlarged "stations" filled much the same role that the Protestant Episcopal City Mission Society had hoped

[18] N.Y.C.T.S., *Thirty-eighth Annual Report*, pp. 15–16; and *Thirty-ninth Annual Report for the Year 1865* (New York, 1866), pp. 25–29, 39; N.Y.C.M.T.S., *Forty-first Annual Report*, pp. 35–37. These ward missionaries, it should be noted, at the same time supervised the distribution of charity within their wards for the A.I.C.P.

[19] "Report of Director," N.Y.C.T.S., *Thirty-eighth Annual Report*, p. 20; N.Y.C.M.T.S., "Report of the Directors," *Fortieth Annual Report for the Year 1866* (New York, 1867), p. 21. On February 19, 1866, the State legislature granted the Society a new charter giving it the right to hold real estate, and thus to construct mission churches. N.Y.C.M.T.S., *Forty-first Annual Report*, p. 15.

[20] N.Y.C.M.T.S., *Forty-first Annual Report*, p. 18.

its mission churches would, that is, to be a church for the very poor. Indeed, the first mission station established by the Tract Society evolved, within the year, into a regular free church—the missionary of the district leaving the Society to become its first pastor. Another mission station, after ten years of operation, boasted 382 converts.[21] By the decade's end the Society decided to grant these now elaborate mission stations formal free church status. On December 15, 1869, the executive committee voted to establish regular "Christian congregations in the mission chapels." The stations had for fifteen years, the committee reported, and in some instances for even longer, regularly attracted considerable numbers of converts and a large congregation. They should have the right to organize as regular church congregations with baptism, communion, and—advised by the ward missionary—the right to admit members and elect officers.[22] The Society had come far from its origin as a simple tract-distributing organization; it was now a "mother of churches" for the poor.

With such deep institutional involvement in the spiritual life of the poor came inevitably a deepening concern for their physical needs. The Tract Society's annual reports for the late 1840's and 1850's again exhibited a growing interest in the environmental conditions of slum life. With the late 1840's the Board of Managers began to include in what were still essentially religious annual reports, articles on the wages paid women, on tenement conditions, and on the high cost of living.[23] In 1854, collaborating with other urban philan-

[21] N.Y.C.T.S., *Thirty-eighth Annual Report*, p. 33.
[22] N.Y.C.M.T.S., *City Mission Chapels, New York* (n.p., n.d.), leaflet, N.Y.C.T.S. Archives. From internal evidence, the leaflet appears to have been written during the 1870's.
[23] For examples of this type of article, see N.Y.C.T.S., *Twenty-second Annual Report for the Year 1848* (New York, 1849), pp. 26–

thropies but especially with the Association for Improving the Condition of the Poor, the Society helped found a home and industrial school for vagrant boys and a bath house for the poor of the Sixth Ward.[24] The Panics of 1855 and 1857 pressed visitors and missionaries into active relief work; by the 1860's, distributing money, food, and clothing had again become—as it was in the early 1840's—a recognized and important function of the Society's visitors and ward missionaries. Ward missionaries also appeared as expert witnesses before the various state legislative committees investigating health and housing in New York City;[25] lengthy attacks

---

27; *Twenty-sixth Annual Report*, pp. 20–21; and *Thirtieth Annual Report for the Year 1856* (New York, 1857), p. 20; N.Y.C.M.T.S., *Forty-first Annual Report*, pp. 35, 41. The "Minutes of the Executive Committee Meeting for November 5, 1854," for example, note that the Society was in correspondence with the American Geographical and Statistical Society concerning the possibility of having a census taken of the invalid population of American cities.

[24] N.Y.C.T.S., *Twenty-eighth Annual Report*, p. 18.

[25] As early as 1842 and 1843, the Society's missionaries worked closely with John H. Griscom, helping him prepare his City Inspector's *Annual Report . . . 1842* and his *Sanitary Condition of the Laboring Classes*. Not only did they prepare statements which Griscom included in his reports, but they provided him with detailed descriptions and statistics of cellar residences, then considered one of New York's principal public health problems. See, for example, Griscom, *Annual Report . . . 1842*, pp. 167–171, and *Sanitary Condition*, pp. 25–39. During the 1850's and 1860's, Samuel B. Halliday, the Society's first city missionary, was an active participant in the National Quarantine and Sanitary Convention which spearheaded and coordinated the public health movement during this period. In 1859, for instance, he was a delegate of the New York Sanitary Association to the Third National Quarantine and Sanitary Convention in New York City. The following year he was an active participant at the Fourth National Quarantine and Sanitary Convention held in Boston. He was a member of both the Committee on Plans for Tenement Houses and the Committee on Hours of Labor, and when he first rose to speak at the convention, he was introduced as "the American Chadwick, the American Sanitary Practitioner, who

upon tenement house conditions became a regular feature of the Society's annual report. In its 1864 *Annual Report* the Society urged:

We would have the tenement-house system revolutionized; we would have sanitary measures faithfully carried out for the protection of the people from disease and the promotion of health. We would that the honest, industrious, working poor were so housed that they might enjoy sunshine and pure air, and cherish in themselves and for their children the ideas of independence and self-respect.[26]

During the 1860's, the Tract Society began to undertake a number of other eclectic and highly concrete measures designed to improve living conditions in New York's slums. In 1868, the Tract Society's Board of Managers established their "Fresh Air Fund," a scheme allowing some among the slum poor to visit the country. The Fund was a product both of the city missionaries' familiarity with the oppressive tenement summer and the growing influence of public health ideas in city mission circles. The people's physical health had by the 1860's come to seem only a little less important than their spiritual health—indeed the distinction seemed an increasingly tenuous one. One way to improve health conditions was to establish summer resorts or camps where slum residents could escape for a day, a week, or perhaps for even longer periods each summer. Certain subscribers, the Society announced in 1868, had already given money so that a few families could

---

explores night and day, the purlieus of city life, and embodies in statistics the results of those observations." Third National Quarantine and Sanitary Convention, *Proceedings and Debates Held in the City of New York, April 27, 28, 29, and 30, 1859* (New York, 1859), p. 715; Fourth National Quarantine and Sanitary Convention, *Proceedings and Debates Held in the City of Boston, June 14, 15, and 16, 1860* (Boston, 1860), pp. 7, 59–61.

[26] N.Y.C.T.S., *Thirty-eighth Annual Report*, p. 22.

spend a day in New Jersey or Long Island. "At how little cost," the managers urged, "might there be an occasional treat of healthful enjoyment to those whose dreary and monotonous existence is scarce relieved by a bright scene or a merry hour through the livelong year!" Within a few years the Tract Society had organized a flourishing system of summer camps, the descendants of which still exist.[27]

The same year that the Society launched its Fresh Air Fund, two of its ward missionaries opened their mission stations at night to vagrants, providing destitute men with a cot to sleep on and one meal a day. The missionaries hoped in this way to exert some moral and religious influence over an ever-growing number of homeless men. But in a more immediate sense, they were simply reacting to the tremendous amount of human misery they found in New York in the years immediately following the Civil War. It seemed appalling that able-bodied men, many of them Civil War veterans, could not even afford a bed in one of the Five Points' crowded lodging houses. Soon a number of wealthy Tract Society supporters, made aware of the vagrant problem by the ward missionaries, subsidized the opening of two large residence halls to provide regular lodging for the city's vagrants.[28]

These same years saw the Society embark on two additional programs of temporal aid to the urban poor, born not of any overall moral design, but devised as simple expedients in the Society's daily struggle to aid the displaced and the unemployed. One was a plan to operate a chain of inexpensive

[27] N.Y.C.M.T.S., "Minutes, Meeting of Board of Directors, July 22, 1868"; and *Forty-second Annual Report for the Year 1868* (New York, 1869), pp. 43–44.

[28] N.Y.C.M.T.S., *Forty-second Annual Report*, pp. 16–17; "Executive Committee Minutes, November 4, 1867"; and *Forty-fourth Annual Report*, p. 46.

cafeterias for the laboring classes of New York. Complementing both the lodging halls and the cafeterias was a fourth meliorative program, the Society's Helping Hand Society. This was an employment agency which sought jobs for the women and children contacted by the tract missionaries during their regular visits.[29]

Yet not all New York's poor and newly arrived responded favorably to the Society's multiplying charities. Many felt that conversion to evangelical Protestantism remained its primary concern—its employment bureau and outdoor relief mere window dressing. And conversion remained into the 1860's an important goal—a goal not always secured. Many, visitors frequently complained, accepted tracts, but as quickly discarded them. Other visitors reported meeting derision and obscenity. Some even encountered physical violence. One missionary, for instance, reported being hit in the face by a man to whom he had offered a tract; another visitor wrote that a woman had threatened to burn her with scalding water if she again urged her not to pray to the Virgin Mary.[30]

Hostility between Protestant and Catholic, as well as a more elementary hostility of the poor to the moralism of the well-to-do, created much of the ill will the Society's visitors encountered. In 1860, the Society reported the reception given a new mission station which they had opened next to a beer garden in a German neighborhood.

When the mission station was opened for divine worship, they [at least some neighborhood residents] were greatly offended, and evinced their displeasure by throwing water into the open

[29] N.Y.C.M.T.S., *Forty-second Annual Report*, pp. 158–160; and *Forty-third Annual Report*, p. 21.

[30] N.Y.C.T.S., *Eleventh Annual Report*, pp. 57, 61, 64, 94–95; *Thirteenth Annual Report*, p. 66; and *Thirty-fifth Annual Report*, p. 36; N.Y.C.M.T.S., *Forty-second Annual Report*, p. 19.

windows, shouting, making noises in the hall, casting stones against the door, and other disorderly conduct; so that the aid of the police became necessary.[31]

The Society responded bitterly to such "papist" harassment. It criticized women who refused tracts as being "nurtured in the lap of popish superstition" and commented acidly about priests who forbade Catholics to read the Bible—or at least the Bibles they distributed. The Catholic press responded with equal vituperation. The *Freeman's Journal*, the official New York diocesan paper, called the New York City Tract Society "an organized vehicle of slander," asserting that it furthered its cause by "falsehood and misrepresentation . . . [and] humbug." [32]

Communications between Protestants and Catholics remained as difficult in 1860 as they had been in the millennial 1830's. Yet in most other respects the Tract Society had changed greatly during these thirty years. While the hope of converting the recipients of their temporal aid still lay behind much Tract Society work, it had become increasingly a rhetorical convention. Caring for the poor was becoming an end in itself; certainly it had become a meaningful and self-justifying object for a Christian philanthropic organization. This was a situation far closer to the benevolent world of 1800 than that of 1835. Summer outings, inexpensive cafeterias and lodging houses, an employment agency: all such activities demanded an involvement in day-to-day concerns which, while not actually replacing pious goals, did place heavy demands upon resources of time, emotional commitment, and—not least of all—financial resources. By the late

[31] N.Y.C.T.S., *Thirty-fourth Annual Report*, p. 40.

[32] N.Y.C.T.S., *Eleventh Annual Report*, pp. 77–78; and *Twelfth Annual Report*, pp. 19–21, 45, 52; *Freeman's Journal*, VIII (October 23, 1847), p. 132.

1860's, the Tract Society had ceased to anticipate an immediate arrival of the millennium; it had, indeed, ceased to hope or even work for the conversion of all New Yorkers. But it did attempt to care for many of New York's vagrants, to provide summer excursions for a growing number of slum families, to find jobs for the unemployed, and, in limited ways, to ameliorate some of the conditions of slum life. In this way the officers now hoped to save some of the poor.

The city's needs, and changes in religious temper, had gradually and on the whole unselfconsciously molded and changed the highly flexible city mission institution. The pious founders of the New York Religious Tract Society in 1812 and the zealous evangelicals who supported the Tract Society in the late 1820's and early 1830's would have had some difficulty in understanding and completely accepting this new pragmatic and melioristic shape their organization had assumed. By 1870 the New York City Mission and Tract Society had acquired a new title, new objectives, and new methods.

[2] American Female Guardian Society: 1837–1870

The history of the American Female Moral Reform Society demonstrates, perhaps even more clearly than that of the New York City Tract Society, an increasing and ultimately absorbing concern for the day-to-day problems of the urban poor.

The Moral Reform Society, it will be recalled, had been founded in the early 1830's as a zealous—and in some ways feminist—movement to end sexual transgressions and hasten the millennium; by the 1860's, the Society, renamed the American Female Guardian Society, had become a shelter for indigent women, an employment agency, and an educator of slum women and children. Instead of filling its publications with exhortations to moral and spiritual perfection, it now published analyses of city inspectors' reports on health and housing, articles concerning milk adulteration, and discussions of proper diet for the working poor. Increasingly knowledgeable in regard to the problems of slum life, the Society's managers embarked upon a highly eclectic "social service" program: they operated industrial schools for ill-clad and illiterate children; they rented sewing machines to unemployed seamstresses; they even encouraged working women to organize and raise wages.

This change came slowly. In the years between 1837 and the late 1840's, pragmatic benevolence still remained secondary to the Society's traditional moral reform goals; enforcement of the Seventh Commandment was still the Society's primary aim. Despite a growing involvement by its New York workers with the temporal needs of their city's slum dwellers, the Society's national leadership remained as staunchly evangelical as it had been in 1835 or 1836; quarterly and annual meetings still centered on the problems of achieving true sexual morality. The *Advocate of Moral Reform*'s editors continually warned their largely rural readship against novel reading, the theater, and dancing. They urged mothers to instruct their children in matters of sexual morality and emphasized the dangers of promiscuity. Officers and members still sought the salvation of rural areas through the distribution of moral reform literature.[33] Male as well as female moral reform societies increased in number, and the

[33] American Female Moral Reform Society (hereinafter referred to as (A.F.M.R.S.), "Quarterly Meeting Minutes, July, 1839"; N.Y.F.M.R.S., "Executive Committee Minutes, October 24, 1838"; A.F.M.R.S., *Thirteenth Annual Report for the Year 1847* (New York, 1847), pp. 4–5; American Female Guardian Society (the A.F.M.R.S. adopted this name in 1849; as indicated above, it is

Society launched a vigorous lobbying campaign to secure the passage of a bill making seduction a felony.[34]

Even the New York Female Moral Reform Society, although more aware of urban poverty and unemployment than its rural counterparts, nevertheless devoted most of its time and energy—at least as late as 1845 or 1847—to the struggle against licentiousness. A few hardy members continued to visit brothels and prisons.[35] The executive committee worked diligently to secure the appointment of female wardens in the women's wings of all state and city prisons. (It was hoped that such matrons would both protect the virtue of female convicts and exert a moral influence over them.) [36] The committee's minutes continued to record cases in which the Society helped women bring suit against their alleged seducers, and as late as 1845 and 1846, committee members still sought to expose employment agencies suspected of being involved in the white slave trade.[37] With the

---

referred to herein as A.F.G.S.), *Sixteenth Annual Report for the Year 1850* (New York, 1850), pp. 8–9; *Advocate*, IV (April, 1838), 53.

[34] *Advocate*, IV (January 15, 1838), 16; A.F.M.R.S., *Twelfth Annual Report for the Year 1846* (New York, 1846), p. 1; and "Executive Committee Minutes, October 24, 1838."

[35] *Advocate*, IV (January 15, 1838), 15; A.F.M.R.S., "Executive Committee Minutes, March 1, 1838, and April 22, 1845"; and "Board of Managers, Minutes, June 2, 1847."

[36] A.F.M.R.S., "Executive Committee Minutes, September 10, 1840, September 15, 1840, and November 4, 1840"; A.F.G.S., *Wrecks and Rescues, by an Early Member of the Board of Managers of the American Female Guardian Society* (New York, 1859), pp. 196–210; S. R. I. Bennett, *Wrought Gold* (New York, 1875), p. 28.

[37] It was the New York Society's policy to aid all seemingly "worthy" seduced women who contacted them to bring suit against the alleged seducer. See A.F.M.R.S., "Executive Committee Minutes, 1843–44," *passim;* and "Executive Committee Minutes, February 12, 1845, and July 8, 1846."

help of their rural auxiliaries, the Society lobbied relentlessly for their antiseduction measure, and in 1848 finally achieved a hard-fought victory.[38]

Yet this antiseduction bill, though hailed by the Society's officers as an achievement of lasting significance, marked the end rather than a heightening of the Society's older millennial enthusiasm. The Moral Reform Society did not pursue its victory, but instead shifted its aims and emphasis. The same year, 1848, that the Society secured the passage of an antiseduction bill, it also opened a "Home for the Friendless and House of Industry" in New York City. The Home was both a shelter for destitute women and children and a center where they might be taught skills and placed in secure jobs or homes—though preferably in a rural community.

The idea of opening a shelter and of placing women and children in rural homes had had a long germinal period. As we have already seen, the officers of the New York Female Moral Reform Society had begun in the late 1830's—especially in the years following the Panic of 1837—to distribute temporal charity and to concern themselves with the material problems of the poor. This work had been developed originally in the hope of preventing indigent women from turning to prostitution and was thus considered by the Society's managers as but one aspect of their crusade for moral prophylaxis. But the ladies were motivated as well by a real concern for the sufferings of the slum poor they met while distributing tracts. In 1837, the Reform Society opened a "register,"

[38] A.F.M.R.S., "Executive Committee Minutes, January 5, 1842, February 18, 1842, April 25, 1844, and January 8, 1845"; *Eleventh Annual Report for the Year 1845* (New York, 1845), p. 3; and *Fourteenth Annual Report for the Year 1848* (New York, 1848), p. 12.

or employment agency, in an effort to find jobs for needy yet morally upright females. Two years later, the Society's visiting committee began to distribute food and clothing regularly with its tracts. That same year they hired Samuel B. Halliday to visit and preach at the Five Points and other slums. Gradually Halliday and the visiting committee began to seek homes and jobs for the destitute women and children they encountered. (Appeals were made in the pages of the *Advocate of Moral Reform* as well as informally among urban members.) The depression of the 1830's and 1840's, by increasing the distress felt by New York's poor, spurred their efforts.

As knowledge of the Society's newly assumed functions spread, the Society was overwhelmed with applicants for employment. In 1843–1844 the Register received 633 applications for work, the next year 1,415. In this latter year, the visiting committee also distributed 1,500 garments and 249 pieces of bedding along with its moral reform and temperance tracts. The Society enlisted its rural auxiliaries in this new work; they contributed food, money, and clothing, and sought homes for adults and children.[39] The American Female Moral Reform Society had, it would seem, become deeply and irrevocably committed to work with the urban poor.

At the same time—the late 1830's and early 1840's—members of the New York executive and visiting committees began to take into their own homes—or to board informally at their own expense—particularly destitute women and children. They hoped that appeals in the *Advocate of Moral*

[39] A.F.M.R.S., *Tenth Annual Report for the Year 1844* (New York, 1844), pp. 4–8; *Eleventh Annual Report*, p. 5; and *Twelfth Annual Report*, pp. 6–10.

Reform might find jobs and homes for these unfortunates.[40] The depression, however, multiplied the numbers of such homeless dependents far beyond the capacities of a few private individuals. In 1842, as a consequence, the executive committee discussed the possibility of establishing a permanent home where the unemployed and homeless could be taught new skills and be sheltered until jobs and homes could be found for them.[41] But even after the depression had lifted, funds were hard to raise. Although not giving up hope of building a permanent shelter, the New York Female Moral Reform Society decided to open a temporary "Home for the Friendless and House of Industry." [42]

Opened in July of 1847 on First Avenue at Second Street, the "Home" contained a large workroom as well as dormitories for women and children. Its "inmates" were as a group basically similar to those already coming to the Register: widows, mothers with dependent children, and young girls entering the job market. While still planning their home, the Society's managers had reported to the New York *Evangelist* that it's efforts would be directed largely toward aiding the city's unemployed women. Particular attention would be

[40] A.F.M.R.S., "Executive Committee Minutes, December 1, 1841, and December 8, 1841"; *Advocate*, IV (March 15, 1838), 46; A.F.M.R.S., *Eleventh Annual Report*, pp. 5–9; Halliday, "History of the Home for the Friendless," in *The Little Street Sweeper; or, Life Among the Poor* (New York, 1859), p. 238.

[41] A.F.M.R.S., "Executive Committee Minutes, January 5, 1842." The New York officers were clearly influenced in their decision to open a Home by the example of the London Society for the Protection of Young Females, which sent a brochure and corresponded with the New York Executive Committee, "Minutes, July 13, 1842, and of 1844," *passim.*

[42] A.F.M.R.S., "Executive Committee Minutes, December 17, 1845, November 4, 1846, November 18, 1846, June 2, June 23, and June 30, 1847."

paid to recent arrivals from the country who, despite high expectations, had been unable to find work and were thus quickly reduced to destitution. The Society claimed in 1846 that there were thousands of such unemployed women in New York.[43]

Before work could be sought for such needy women, they frequently had to be equipped with new skills. Adults were taught sewing, hatbox-making, basket weaving, and other simple crafts in the Society's workshops. Children, often illiterate, were instructed in basic reading and writing, and both women and children were of course instilled with the basic tenets of evangelical religion and social morality. Appeals for jobs appeared regularly in the *Advocate of Moral Reform*, especially for positions in the country where mothers could bring their young children. The ladies assured rural subscribers that those rescued from the slums would happily work for quite "moderate" wages.[44]

During 1847–1848, while still in their temporary home, the Society gave shelter to 334 adults and 271 children. Homes were found for 204. The next year the Society admitted 407 adults and 237 children. Two hundred and ninety-eight women found jobs; 144 children were placed in foster homes or apprenticed.[45] In 1849, the Society petitioned the State legislature and won an important change in its charter, one which formally sanctioned their placing of destitute children

[43] A.F.M.R.S., "Executive Committee Minutes, July, August, September, 1847," *passim;* and *Twelfth Annual Report,* pp. 1–2.

[44] A.F.M.R.S., "Executive Committee Minutes, November 10, 1847"; *Thirteenth Annual Report,* p. 4; and *Fourteenth Annual Report,* p. 4; Northrup, *Record,* pp. 31–32; A.F.G.S., *Fifteenth Annual Report for the Year 1849* (New York, 1849), pp. 15–18; and *Seventeenth Annual Report for the Year 1851* (New York, 1851), p. 4.

[45] A.F.M.R.S., "Executive Committee Minutes, December, 1847, and January 5, 1848"; A.F.G.S., *Fifteenth Annual Report,* p. 13.

—with the consent of the child's natural parents—in rural foster homes.[46]

The previous year, the Society, pressed for space by an ever-expanding number of applicants, had finally been able to purchase five lots on Fifth Avenue between Twenty-ninth and Thirtieth Streets—in the mid-1840's still almost a suburban location. In December of 1848, the building was completed and the following spring received its first occupants. The new Home and House of Industry was four stories high and contained dormitories, a workroom, chapel, schoolrooms, nursery, the business offices of the Society, and editorial offices for the *Advocate*.[47] Between the spring of 1849 and 1855, the Society sheltered and trained 2,140 women and 1,537 children. Another fifteen hundred New Yorkers found jobs through their employment service; 739 children were apprenticed or placed in foster homes.[48]

The ladies hoped in constructing this substantial building to provide only a temporary refuge for the destitute and vagrant until they found their way to rural and Protestant homes. This practice of finding rural homes for dependent city children and adult women was known to contemporaries as the placing-out system, and by the mid-1850's it had become enormously popular among American philanthropists. The Female Moral Reform Society was one of the first Amer-

[46] "An Act to Incorporate the American Female Guardian Society Passed April 6, 1849," reprinted A.F.G.S., *Fifteenth Annual Report*, inside front cover.

[47] A.F.G.S., "Executive Committee Minutes, May 9, 1848, and December 19, 1848"; A.F.M.R.S., *Fourteenth Annual Report*, p. 4. For details concerning the financing of the House, see A.F.G.S., *Fifteenth Annual Report*, p. 12. Halliday in "Home for the Friendless," pp. 241–242, gives a detailed description of the size and layout of the Home.

[48] Each annual report contains statistics for the Home and the employment register.

ican organizations to develop this adoption scheme, but it was not alone in employing it. Charles Loring Brace of the Children's Aid Society, Louis Pease of the Five Points House of Industry, the managers of the Five Points Mission, the Juvenile Asylum, and many similar philanthropic organizations in New York and other eastern cities relied upon the placing-out system. Several of these societies would sometimes cooperate in sending out a "caravan" of vagrant children.[49]

The Moral Reform Society had the advantage of being able to call upon its far-flung network of auxiliary societies in seeking homes for women and dependent children. Beginning in the early 1840's, as we have seen, these local groups had been asked to find homes for vagrant women and children; by 1847, this had become one of the normal functions of these rural subsidiaries. The annual reports regularly carried lengthy appendices of stories and letters concerning homeless or neglected children. (The reports were printed in large editions for fund-raising and promotional purposes.) Increasingly, as well, the columns of the *Advocate* were filled with similar tales of starving, mistreated children desperately in need of loving Protestant homes;[50] the Society had already

[49] Charles Loring Brace, *Dangerous Classes of New York, and Twenty Years' Work Among Them* (New York, 1872); Emma Brace, *The Life of Charles Loring Brace Chiefly Told in His Own Letters* (New York, 1894); Miriam Z. Langsam, *Children West. A History of the Placing-Out System of the New York Children's Aid Society* (Madison, Wis., 1964); Carroll S. Rosenberg, "Protestants and Five Pointers: A History of the Five Points House of Industry," *New-York Historical Society Quarterly*, XLVIII (October, 1964), 327–347.

[50] A.F.M.R.S., "Executive Committee Minutes, May 5, 1847, January 25, April 26, 1848, October 24, November 14, 1849"; A.F.G.S., *Seventeenth Annual Report*, pp. 8–10; and *Nineteenth Annual Report*, pp. 12–19.

composed a standard form to be signed by any family taking a child from the Home:

This may certify, that I have this day, ————, received into my family, J——— N———, from the Managers of the "Home for the Friendless" and that I hereby engage to train this child with a view to her present and future well-being; to regard her interests, mental, moral, and physical and so educate her in these respects that she may become a blessing to herself and to others. I also engage to inform the Managers annually or semi-annually respecting the welfare of the child.

(signed)————[51]

Each child adopted would—hopefully—be rescued from the physical and moral evils of the city, each started upon the road to a productive and Christian life.[52]

[51] This form appeared for the first time in the Society's *Fourteenth Annual Report*, p. 6, and appeared in each subsequent annual report. Legal guardianship rested with the Society until the family formally adopted the child. The Society attempted to send an investigator to visit the child each year, either a member of the official Visiting Committee, or, if that were not possible, then a member of a nearby auxiliary. The "Children's Secretary" in New York City was also expected to correspond with the family and to keep a complete record of each child who passed through the Home. The Society's Executive Committee was not unaware of the dangers inherent in such a loosely organized system and not infrequently discussed cases where children were mistreated by the families caring for them. See, for example, A.F.G.S., "Executive Committee Meeting Minutes, February 19, May 21, September 9, October 1, 1851." E. C. Ray in *John Bancroft Devins, A True Greatheart* (New York, 1912), describes the hardship and emotional deprivation experienced by at least one child apprenticed by the Society at mid-century to a farm family; this situation was presumably not uncommon.

[52] The Society by developing the placing-out system emphasized its commitment to the family as the only satisfactory environment for raising a moral and Christian child. The conflict as the Society saw it was not between the institution and the family but between the undesirable slum family (often immigrant and Roman Catholic)

In opening their Home for the Friendless, in seeking to train women for new trades, in finding homes for the destitute, the New York executive committee had shifted away from its original millennial objectives and committed both the New York society and its rural auxiliaries to a highly eclectic and expensive program of meliorism in dealing with the problems of the urban poor. In effecting and justifying this radical change in their organization's aims and activities, the ladies had, during the 1840's, gradually and imperceptibly redefined the moral objectives of the Society as well as its methods of operation.

Throughout its early years and indeed into the 1840's, the Society had thought of moral reform exclusively in terms of sexual morality, of observing the Seventh Commandment. Geographic location or economic status were of little significance; only the soul's relation to God mattered. And in the Society's early years, America's rural communities were a principal field of exertion. The opening of a shelter and workroom implied a distinct—if unselfconscious—shift from this early understanding of moral reform. Yet it was no sudden break, but one which came only after a decade of work with the urban poor. The Society had originally under-

---

and the farm family (always Protestant). "The Society," its managers announced at the commencement of their placing-out program, "would in no case encourage the sundering of parental ties, unless a determined course of vice or such extreme destitution as might prompt to it, is known to exist." A.F.M.R.S., *Thirteenth Annual Report*, p. 12. A few years later in response to a letter urging them to consider adopting a cottage system in their Home, the managers reasserted their basic assumption that the family and not an institution was the proper environment for a young child. Children, the ladies responded, remained in their Home for as short a time as possible; their Home was only a means of facilitating the removal of children from undesirable homes and placing them in desirable ones. *Advocate*, XXX (October 1, 1864), 229.

taken these secular tasks in an effort to save destitute women and girls from a life of prostitution. Their program was thus a kind of preventive moral reform. Increasingly, however, workers and officers came to see tenement life as a moral evil in itself, not simply as a factor promoting sexual license. Slum life brought with it constant threats not only to sexual morality, but to every aspect of an upright Christian life. Filth, laziness, begging, and illiteracy were—like sexual license—inextricably related to the misery which accompanied tenement life. The more deeply involved in the life of the slum dweller the Society became, the more its workers tended to think of moral reform in terms of the prevention of this pervasive moral degeneration rather than exclusively in terms of sexual misconduct.

This redefining of moral reform was a gradual though steady process—yet one never formally announced. It is, however, apparent in the Society's changed mission activities and in the terminology it employed in discussing moral decay and moral reform. The first explicit indication of this change occurred in 1845 when the Moral Reform Society announced in the *Advocate* that its first great aim, the purification of American society, had been largely accomplished. The promiscuity and lewdness acceptable ten or fifteen years earlier in circles ostensibly Christian, the ladies reported with satisfaction, was now unthinkable.[53] The Society was ready to assume new responsibilities. Its members still maintained, however, a simultaneous commitment to both pietistic and melioristic programs, for example, by lobbying in support of an antiseduction bill and by raising contributions for their Home for the Friendless. The new charter requested and obtained by the Society in 1849 clearly reflects this same mixture of aims and methods. "The object and business" of the

[53] A.F.M.R.S., *Tenth Annual Report*, p. 9.

American Female Moral Reform Society, the charter stated, "shall be, by the publication of books, papers and tracts, and by other moral and religious means, to prevent vice and moral degeneration and," it added, "to establish and maintain Houses of Industry and Homes for the Friendless, destitute or unprotected females, and for friendless or unprotected children." [54] In 1851, the Society's managers recalled with a natural if convenient inaccuracy that:

one of its chief aims from the beginning to the present time, has been to reach, by moral and Christian influences, that class in society peculiarly exposed to moral and physical degradation and want, viz.: young females and children who have been by untoward circumstances placed upon the list of the homeless and friendless. [55]

Thus by 1851, the objects of moral reform had been defined in largely environmental terms. The success of the Society's pious crusade now hinged not simply upon an individual's religious conversion, but upon his social and economic elevation as well. Prayer was still an important instrument in the crusade, for none could rise spiritually or economically without Christian faith. But jobs, education, and vocational training had become essential tactical devices. This was no longer the cause of John McDowall.

This development can be seen with particular clarity in the Society's increasing emphasis upon work with children, in contrast to their original concern for the salvation of adult females. In 1855–1856, the Society's managers reversed the policy of their home by admitting children in preference to adults; beginning that year the managers admitted only the most destitute and helpless of adult females. Three-quarters

[54] "Act to Incorporate the American Female Guardian Society."
[55] Reported in the *Independent*, III (May 10, 1851), 77.

of the Home's inmates in 1855 were children, a percentage which remained constant into the 1870's.[56] Adults were certainly more difficult than children to place in rural homes—and their rescue always more problematical.[57] More significantly, however, within the complex of social assumptions shared by the Society's managers, and their rural supporters, saving young children had a peculiar importance.

By the time he reached maturity, the Society had come to believe, the slum resident was irretrievably warped; even a child removed from the slum at ten or eleven years of age would never be able to achieve his full moral, or even educational, potential. The slum was a spiritually disfiguring experience. The only possibility of escape lay in physical removal to the pure—and Protestant—air of the countryside while the child was still an impressionable preadolescent. This was clearly the rationale behind the adoption of the Society's placing-out system. "How shall we save the children," the Society's officers asked in 1859, "how bridge the social chasm into which the parents have fallen, and where their hapless offspring must soon likewise perish unless rescued by Christian hands?"[58] Each passing year made a child's reform less likely; by adolescence the prospect was almost hopeless—at least while the child remained in the city. In the country, however, subjected to a wholesome Christian atmosphere, even hardened street boys might soon be converted not only to evangelical religion, but to a rural, prudent, and productive style of life. By the simple process of removing slum

[56] A.F.G.S., *Twenty-second Annual Report for the Year 1856* (New York, 1856), p. 10. For statistics for subsequent years, see the annual reports for those years.

[57] See, for example, complaints about the difficulty of working with adult women. A.F.G.S., *Fifteenth Annual Report*, pp. 12–13.

[58] A.F.G.S., *Twenty-fifth Annual Report for the Year 1859* (New York, 1859), p. 3.

children from the city, the Society felt assured, urban poverty and its accompanying moral depravity might largely be eliminated.[59] Indeed, a child's escape from the tenement was often imperative for physical as well as spiritual reasons. Infant mortality rates had begun to shock concerned New Yorkers—as had the slum child's precocity in vice.

Thus, between 1848 and the Civil War years, the managers of the Society refused to accept any child for admission to the Home unless his parents or guardians were willing for him to be placed in a rural, Protestant home.[60] Nor were the managers content to leave the fate of the city's slum children to chance or to the random persuasion of visiting committee members. In 1849, the officers of the American Female Moral Reform Society combined with those of the New York Association for Improving the Condition of the Poor, the New York City Tract Society, and the Juvenile Asylum to petition the state legislature for the passage of a truancy and vagrancy act.[61]

The poor themselves did not always share the Society's

[59] Editorials and vignettes depicting the happy and moral life led by children placed in rural homes from the mid-1850's into the 1870's characterized every issue of the *Advocate* and each annual report. They clearly indicate that the Society's officers held a very stylized and negative view of the city and of the moral effect of slum conditions upon the individual.

[60] The executive committee established this policy shortly after they opened their Home in the fall of 1848. A.F.M.R.S., "Executive Committee Minutes, October 25, 1848, and April 4, 1849."

[61] The proposed act (a clear example of the Society's attitude toward the slum poor) read in part: "whereby dissipated and vicious parents by habitually neglecting due care and provision for their offspring, shall thus forfeit their natural claim to them and whereby such children shall be removed from them and placed under better influences, till the claim of the parent shall be re-established by continued sobriety, industry and general good conduct." A.F.G.S., *Twentieth Annual Report for the Year 1854* (New York, 1854), p. 8.

view of their hopelessly corrupted and corrupting condition. Many resented the Society's virtual requirement that they must surrender their children to the placing-out system before receiving temporal assistance. None were more adamant in their condemnation of the Society than the city's Catholic hierarchy. The *Freeman's Journal* accused the Society of soliciting funds from Catholic merchants, yet at the same time of withholding food from destitute Catholic families who refused to attend the Society's Bible and prayer meetings. Catholic girls when inmates of the Society's Home, the *Journal* asserted, were not permitted to see priests, even when ill and near death. Most alarming to Catholics was the placing-out system. The American Female Guardian Society and other similar Protestant charities—with the aid of the new vagrancy law—the editor of the *Journal* asserted, literally stole Catholic children and spirited them out of the city. "They [such children] are the captives of a terrible servitude—the redemption of them from bondage is the noblest work for Catholic charity. There are multiplied societies, seizing them in the name of charity and of religion, and carrying them away to be brought up aliens to the Catholic faith." [62]

But although the rhetoric of the *Advocate* implied a continuation of the Society's rejection of the city (and a continued rejection of the Society by many in the city), the day-to-day activities of the Society and its approach to urban problems began to undergo yet another change during the late 1850's. This change would ultimately result in a more accepting attitude toward the city and the slum. In 1855 and again in 1857, New York City experienced severe financial

[62] *Freeman's Journal*, VIII (February 5, and March 4, 1848), 252, 284; XIX (April 16, 1859); *Advocate*, XXX (January 1, and August 16, 1864), 74, 192.

panics. These were accompanied by poor harvests and high food prices. Faced for the second and third times within a decade with widespread unemployment and destitution, the Society's officers and workers came gradually to the conclusion that the solution to urban poverty could not be found in institutionalizing or in sending the indigent from the city. A change of scene might reform some among the new generation, but it offered (or so it began to seem to Society workers after three Panics) no real solution to the overwhelming social disorganization of the slum and the vast and growing numbers degraded by its influence. The poor would have to be aided within the city.

At no time, indeed, had the Society ever relied upon the placing-out system to the complete exclusion of other, more melioristic solutions to urban poverty. In 1849, for example, when the Society accepted 407 destitute women in the Home, its register received over 2,000 applications for work. That same year members of the visiting committees busily distributed food and clothing with their tracts and Bibles.[63] Indeed, with the mid-1850's, the Society had begun to give piece work in the Home's workshops to particularly needy slum residents who had applied at the register but could not immediately be placed in jobs or rural homes. By 1859, almost twelve hundred such women were at one time or another employed in this workshop (while the supervisors, of course, read to them from the Bible).[64] And each year the

[63] A.F.G.S., *Fifteenth Annual Report*, pp. 9, 13. The Executive Committee Minutes for the 1850's are filled with accounts of relief given by members of the Society's active visiting committee to slum families.

[64] A.F.M.R.S., "Executive Committee Minutes, September 24, 1845"; A.F.G.S., *Fifteenth Annual Report*, p. 9; *Sixteenth Annual Report*, p. 95; and *Twenty-fifth Annual Report for the Year 1859* (New York, 1859), pp. 8–9; Halliday, *Little Street Sweeper*, pp. 241–242.

job register received an ever-greater number of applicants for both work and immediate relief; in the early 1860's an average of from one to three hundred applications daily was reported.[65] In the face of this need, the visiting committee increased its membership and the amount of charity it distributed, working closely with the visitors of the Association for Improving the Condition of the Poor.[66]

Such work drew the Society into increased contact with slum conditions and its workers and managers into more systematic plans and programs for ameliorating the misery they encountered. In 1859, for example, the officers of the Society instituted a program of selling sewing machines on reasonable installment terms to New York seamstresses. The Society's managers had noted that the incipient mechanization of the ready-made clothing industry had already begun to affect New York's working women. Most of the tasks in the needle trades were still done at home on a piecework basis; increasingly, however, shop managers would only let out work to women who owned sewing machines. Other entrepreneurs forced their piece workers to rent machines at exorbitant daily rates. It was to remedy such injustice that the Society decided to buy and resell machines at low rates; this was not an ideological decision, but a natural and eminently practical attempt to solve a discrete social problem.[67]

The Society's industrial schools played an even more sig-

[65] A.F.G.S., *Twenty-seventh Annual Report for the Year 1861* (New York, 1861), p. 26. For employment agency statistics, see the Society's annual reports.

[66] A.F.G.S., *Twenty-fifth Annual Report*, pp. 9–10; *Twenty-eighth Annual Report for the Year 1862* (New York, 1862), p. 26; and *Twenty-ninth Annual Report for the Year 1863* (New York, 1863), pp. 18–19.

[67] A.F.G.S., *Twenty-sixth Annual Report for the Year 1860* (New York, 1860), pp. 18–19.

nificant role in its increasingly melioristic program. These schools were established to provide rudimentary education and industrial training for children too ill-clothed, too ill-educated, and insufficiently motivated to enter the public school system; such children were the "hard-core" poor of the 1850's. The schools sought to prepare these charges for either jobs or the public schools by teaching reading, writing, and some crude skills. The ladies' attitude toward their students and toward the function of the industrial school system is clearly seen in the comment of an industrial school-teacher on preparing students for admission to the public school system. "It would," she wrote, "be pleasant to retain the children with us when they become our best scholars, but the objects of the school can be better secured by advancing them to the Ward schools, and receiving others to fill their places who need also to be humanized, decently clad and fitted to receive like benefits." [68] The ladies hoped, as well, to bring a moral and religious influence into lives otherwise dismayingly "heathen." "As the Sabbath-school is the nursery of the church," they wrote, "so are these to some extent, the nursery of the Sabbath-school." [69]

It is apparent from the Society's discussions of their industrial schools that they thought of them as a necessary compromise between doing nothing and the more thoroughgoing —if often unrealizable—solution offered by the placing-out

[68] A.F.G.S., *Twenty-eighth Annual Report*, p. 19.
[69] A.F.G.S., *Twenty-ninth Annual Report*, p. 14. For descriptions of school routine, see A.F.G.S., *Thirty-fourth Annual Report for the Year 1868* (New York, 1868), p. 28; see also "Extracts from the First Report of the First Home Industrial School," printed in S. R. I. Bennett, *Woman's Work Among the Lowly. Memorial Volume of the First Forty Years of the American Female Guardian Society and Home for the Friendless* (2d ed.; New York, 1880), p. 200.

system.[70] The group of children affected was essentially the same. The ultimate end was similar as well—to return the outcast, degraded, slum child to society.[71] But while one emphasized flight from the city, the other implied a commitment to work in the worst of the city's slums. For years, the Society employed both methods in its war against the moral blight of tenement life.

The idea of an industrial school had come partially from the example of the London "ragged schools" of the period, partially from the example of a small industrial school run by a group of women on Avenue D in Manhattan. During the winter of 1853–1854, the Society opened its first industrial school, located at the Home itself. That spring, the Society could boast a registration of 105 and an average attendance of between fifty and sixty. The first school was limited to girls, a reflection of the Society's traditions and stated aims.[72] Three years later, the managers assumed the responsibility for a second industrial school located on West Forty-first Street when the school's founders, a group of concerned church ladies, requested them to do so. In 1861, the Society opened two additional schools, one of which was for boys. In 1868, the Society's schools boasted a total registration of 2,941. The

[70] The ladies early found immigrant families, especially Catholic immigrant families, no matter how destitute, staunchly unwilling to surrender their children to the Home and placement in distant Protestant families. The children they received were either vagrants or the children of widowed or deserted women who simply could no longer provide for them.

[71] See, for example, comments in A.F.G.S., *Twenty-seventh Annual Report for the Year 1861* (New York, 1861), p. 19; and *Thirty-fifth Annual Report for the Year 1869* (New York, 1869), pp. 13–14.

[72] A.F.G.S., "Executive Committee Minutes, February 11, September 8, March 1, March 8, June 27, 1854"; *Twentieth Annual Report*, pp. 8–12; *Golden Jubilee*, pp. 39–40; and *Twentieth Annual Report*, p. 14.

managers hastened to add, however, that with "a class so migratory and irregular in their habits," average attendance was usually one-third of total registration; a year later average daily attendance was 823.[73]

A principal function of the industrial schools had been from the beginning to feed and clothe as well as to educate. The clothing, bedding, and shoes made by the school children as part of their industrial training were distributed to their families, as was much additional clothing and food donated by the Society's rural auxiliaries. The teachers soon began to visit their scholars at home—and improved such opportunities by instructing and reproving wayward parents. By 1863, indeed, the efforts of the visiting committees as well as those of the industrial schoolteachers had become almost monopolized by the needs of the industrial school children's families.[74] The Society's efforts were now concerned almost exclusively with the slum child and his family (practically speaking, with those children and families socialized enough to make an appearance at the Society's industrial schools). A limited institutional program had once again evolved in an increasingly narrow and pragmatic direction.

The development of these two institutions, the New York City Tract Society and the American Female Guardian Society, was typical; other city missions, such, for example, as the reconstituted Protestant Episcopal City Mission Society, also drifted gradually in the direction of a melioristic—though still moralistic—concern with the inhabitants of their city's tenements. Similarly, individual churches throughout the city be-

[73] A.F.G.S., *Twenty-eighth Annual Report*, pp. 18–24; and *Thirty-first Annual Report for the Year 1865* (New York, 1865), p. 15; Northrup, *Record*, p. 38.

[74] A.F.G.S., *Twenty-ninth Annual Report*, p. 16; *Thirty-first Annual Report*, p. 33; and *Thirty-fourth Annual Report*, p. 15; *Advocate*, XXXI (March 1, 1865), 53; XXXV (June 1, 1869), 124.

gan in these same years to develop ambitious programs of local social service—establishing precedents for the institutional churches of later generations. Middle-class, church-going New Yorkers had become increasingly aware of the needs of their city's slums, while the habit of pious activism made this awareness a call to church action.

CHAPTER 8

The Five Points
House of Industry

By 1850 the city had, as we have seen, become a very real and very threatening part of American life. With each census the percentage of Americans living in cities grew, and with this growth seemed to come a corresponding increase in poverty, crime, illiteracy, and irreligion. Yet it was neither census figures nor police reports which made Americans conscious of this change. Statistics have little emotional meaning for ordinary men. Men are moved by incident and example, and New York's Five Points dramatized to many the evil which the growth of cities seemed inevitably to create.

The Five Points House of Industry, founded with much publicity and assurance in 1854, soon became one of New York's best known and most influential city missions. The circumstances of its founding and subsequent development throw a good deal of light upon the new influences reshaping the city mission movement during the 1850's and 1860's—and on the influence exerted by the city mission movement upon American social thought and philanthropy generally.

The Five Points House was itself a product of the city mission movement. It was founded not as a pietistic expression of the Second Great Awakening, but specifically to save the urban poor—whose spiritual and temporal condition the early city missions had done so much to publicize. The Five Points House was thus inspired not by the millennial aims which had shaped the American Female Guardian Society or the New York City Tract Society, but by the more limited goal of saving the residents of New York's worst slum.

In its choice of mission field, the Five Points House revealed not only Americans' growing awareness of the problems posed by urban poverty, but also the horror felt by largely rural Americans at the growth of urban slums populated increasingly by immigrants—alien in both religion and personal morality. The Five Points House's founders chose the Five Points as their mission field for very much the same reasons that, a generation earlier, the founders of the Female Moral Reform Society chose prostitution and licentiousness —it was for them a most grievous example of the evil afflicting American society. Significantly, in the twenty years between 1834 and 1854, the evil had lost its transcendent spiritual essence and become a social and economic problem, though with markedly moral overtones.

And the history of the Five Points House of Industry demonstrates other aspects of this later city mission movement. The founders and workers of the Five Points House experimented with almost every method of aiding the city's poor—temperance, institutionalization, workshops, the placing-out system. Finally, like the New York City Tract Society and the American Female Guardian Society, overwhelmed by the numbers and the needs of the urban poor, the Five Points House adopted an eclectic and melioristic program of aiding the city's tenement dwellers. The history of the Five Points House is thus in many ways a paradigm of the city mission movement as it developed during the years between 1850 and 1870.

[1]

The idea of establishing a permanent chapel and a resident minister at the Five Points came first from a group of devout and respectable New York women. These ladies, members of the Ladies Home Missionary Society of the Methodist Episcopal Church, had since 1843 worked among New York's immigrants and slum dwellers, seeking to bring them to God. They besieged incoming immigrant ships with tracts and Bibles, founded chapels among the German ragpickers of Bloomingdale, and established Sunday schools and Bible classes in the city's dingiest neighborhoods. In 1848 they turned to the spiritual needs of the Five Points and within two years had secured a Board of Trustees from among New York's most prominent merchants and men of wealth. Among them were Anson G. Phelps, William B. Skidmore, and Daniel Drew. In 1850 the Five Points Mission was officially incorporated.[1]

In May of that year their first missionary, Louis M. Pease, arrived at the Five Points. With the ladies' help he established a mission chapel in a small room at the corner of Little Water and Cross Streets, diagonally across from the "Old Brewery," the city's most notorious slum. From this central location Pease and his sponsors spread out over the Five Points, holding prayer meetings, distributing tracts, comforting the sick

[1] *Christian Advocate and Journal,* XXVII (January 15, 1852), 10; (April 22, 1852), 67; XXVIII (May 19, 1853), 78; William F. Barnard, *Forty Years at the Five Points* (New York, 1853), pp. 10–11; The Ladies of the Five Points Mission, *The Old Brewery and the New Mission House at the Five Points* (New York, 1854), pp. 36–37; Louis Pease, "Five Points Mission," *Monthly Record of the Five Points House of Industry,* I (August, 1857), 114–116. This chapter has appeared in a somewhat different form in the *New-York Historical Society Quarterly,* XLVIII (October, 1964), 327–347.

and destitute. Soon they were able to number 45 persons in their weekly Methodist classes and 70 children in their Sunday school. Two hundred attended Sunday services in their crowded and ill-equipped room. Encouraged, the ladies decided after a few months to open a charity day school—children who spent six days of the week in street gangs, sweeping street corners for pennies, or begging their meals, could not be expected to reform their ways after one Sunday morning. By the winter of 1850–1851 one hundred children were in daily attendance at the ladies' school, and two full-time teachers were employed.[2]

As Pease and the Methodist ladies worked at the Five Points, they came increasingly to accept two principal factors as causes of the poverty and misery surrounding them. The first was intemperance, the second, unemployment. Even children, the ladies reported in distressed tones, came to classes intoxicated; attempts to find positions for men and women were frustrated when they arrived at their jobs too drunk to work. Resolutely the Society organized weekly temperance meetings, distributed temperance tracts on street corners, and urged all who attended Sunday services to sign the pledge. Pease frequently invited temperance advocates to speak at the mission house and insisted that all his charges attend these "Band of Hope" meetings. School children were sent home with temperance pledges in their pockets and temperance hymns on their lips.[3]

[2] Ladies of the Five Points Mission, *Old Brewery*, pp. 37–39; Pease, "Five Points Mission," *Christian Advocate*, XXVI (February 13, 1851), 28; XXVII (January 29, 1852), 19. Timothy L. Smith puts the work of the ladies in the context of Methodist perfectionism in *Revivalism and Social Reform, in Mid-nineteenth Century America* (New York, 1957), pp. 169–171.

[3] W. S., "First Fruits," *Monthly Record*, II (1858), 85; Thomas S. Eells, "Leaves from My Journal," *The New Charitable Monthly or*

But as the summer wore on, the Methodist workers became increasingly convinced that exhortation and prayer meetings had little effect upon the filth and wasted lives at the Five Points. Daily experiences—visits to the poor, conversations with the parents of school children—showed them that drunkenness, crime, and prostitution were not simply willed acts of immorality but might also be responses to the want and despair of slum life. Indeed, Pease soon decided that prayer and good example could neither win the confidence of the poor nor aid them in efforts to reform. The poor needed regular jobs before they could be expected to profit from lectures on morality.[4]

Within two months of his arrival, Pease persuaded a local textile manufacturer to provide him with piecework for the neighborhood women, and then, not unlike the Female Moral Reform Society, converted his evening prayer room into a sewing shop by day. All who came were given work provided that they were sober on arrival, agreed to sign a temperance pledge, and promised to lead moral, respectable lives. Within a week 40 women were busily engaged at the mission. With the hardships and unemployment of winter, Pease became increasingly involved with his workshop. He sought not only to provide charity in return for a job done, and thus to lift the morale of the poor and test their good intentions, but also to teach the adults of the neighborhood useful trades to prepare them for outside jobs. By February, 1851, he could report that 60 adults had obtained regular employment as a

---

"*What is Done for the Poor*," I (March, 1855), 40–42; "A Story for Today," *New Charitable Monthly*, I (February, 1855), 22–28.

[4] Pease, "Five Points Mission," *Christian Advocate*, XXVI (February 13, 1851); Pease, "Calls upon our Neighbors," *Monthly Record*, I (June, 1857), 56–62; Henry M. Hudson, "The Five Points House of Industry," *Monthly Record*, II (1858), 17, 32, 67.

result of his training while another 42 were still at his mission, learning such simple trades as sewing, baking, and cobbling.[5]

But jobs were not an end in themselves. The purpose of the missionary work of Pease and his sponsors had always been the ultimate religious and moral reformation of the poor. Displaying an interesting mélange of pietistic, moralistic, and melioristic values, Pease and his associates insisted that jobs were an essential, but only a preliminary, means. Before they could hope to effect the eternal salvation of their charges, the workers at the Five Points House had first to instill self-respect, to provide an honest alternative to crime, and to enable families to find homes away from the corruptions of the Five Points. Pease contended, in what was perhaps an unconscious secularization of traditional Calvinism, that all men were born with certain "infirmities." Early moral training, virtuous associates, and religious habits would inhibit these evil inclinations. "An individual who leads a comfortable life in the ways of virtue, will not once in ten thousand cases turn a thief, a sot, or a harlot; because, deep as the moral corruption may be, the mind is generally strong enough to keep the passions within the bounds of obvious and immediate interest." But "our outcast poor" did not have this early moral training, and far from having good associates, were surrounded by every temptation. It was natural, therefore, that Pease would want to supervise not only the working hours of his charges, but their home life as well; like the Female Moral Reform Society he saw poverty, intemperance, immorality, and unemployment as interrelated problems and the poor most often as the weak and incompetent of society. There was no hope, Pease concluded only a few years after the Moral

[5] Pease, "Five Points Mission," *Monthly Record,* I (August, 1857), 116–117.

Reform Society had reached the same decision, of effecting moral reformation in any family that remained subject to the depraved influence of Five Points companions. Accordingly, he rented a house in August at 3 Little Water Street—next to the Methodist chapel—moved his own family there and required that all who sought a place in his workshop leave their homes and live with him. In return he would find them jobs and a good home with some Protestant family. In February, 1851, Pease expanded his operations and rented an adjoining building. Between May of that year and January, 1852, he provided shelter and work for some three hundred persons.[6]

Although he received support from the Ladies' Missionary Society, Pease had from the beginning borne complete financial responsibility for his combined workshop and home for inebriates. By the second winter, with the number of applicants for help increasing, Pease found that he could no longer expand his operations without outside assistance. It had also become apparent to Pease and the ladies that one man could not supervise a workshop and day school and minister as well to the spiritual needs of a community of several thousand. In May, 1851, they reorganized their work. Pease, with the financial assistance of the National Temperance Society, confined his activities to supervising his workshop and school (to be known as the Industrial Temperance Home). The ladies applied to the Bishop of New York for a minister to assume Pease's religious duties at their Methodist chapel. Thus the relationship between Pease and the Methodist ladies ended.

[6] Pease, "Thy Weak Brother," *New Charitable Monthly*, I (June, 1855), 81–85; Pease, "Address of the Reverend L. M. Pease to the Trustees of the Five Points House of Industry," *Act of Incorporation, By-Laws and Address of the Trustees and Superintendent* (New York, 1854), pp. 5–7.

After May, 1851, there were two separate missions at the Five Points, the Methodists' Five Points Mission and Louis Pease's workshop and home.[7]

Until June 1852, relations between Pease's home for inebriates and the Five Points Mission continued to be amicable, and the two institutions worked closely together. Between June and November, 1852, however, relations must have become strained, for on November 12 the board of trustees of the Mission announced in the New York *Daily Times* that Mr. Pease was not connected with the Mission and had not been for the past 18 months. On November 18 the Mission complained in the *Christian Advocate* that Pease had been slandering its work. Within the year the dispute had hardened into an open breach. The Ladies Home Missionary Society called Pease an infidel, a socialist, a communist, and a Fourierist, while Pease charged the ladies with sectarian bias. It is difficult to discover the real cause of the rift since both parties later claimed that it occurred when Pease left the Mission in 1851, although it clearly did not occur until much later. It probably originated in the competition between the two missions for financial support. And since both organizations were simultaneously expanding their operations, rivalry might also account for the conflict.[8]

The next few years were difficult ones for Pease. Within a year of establishing his independent mission he was again

[7] Imogen Mercein, "Ladies Home Missionary Society," *Christian Advocate*, XXVI (June 5, 1851), 91; Pease, "Efforts at the Five Points," *Christian Advocate*, XXVII (Janaury 29, 1852), 19.

[8] Pease, "Efforts at the Five Points," *Christian Advocate*, XXVII (June 17, 1852), 99; XXVIII (December 8, 1853), 194; XXX (February 22, 1855), 30; Pease, Letter to the Editor, New-York *Daily Times*, December 20, 21, 1852; Hudson, "Five Points House," p. 36.

without financial support. The Temperance Alliance had replaced the National Temperance Society, and under its new constitution the Alliance was not free to support such undertakings.[9] For the next three years Pease was forced to assume personal responsibility for financing his small mission. Fortunately, he was able to call upon the financial resources of the Church of the Ascension, and of its minister, the Reverend G. T. Bedell. From 1850 until 1865 the vestry of this fashionable Episcopal church supported the Five Points Day School, and in 1854 the vestrymen persuaded a group of prominent New York businessmen to act as a board of trustees for Pease's mission. In April of that year, the Five Points House of industry was incorporated.[10]

When seeking legislative incorporation in 1854, Pease stated the threefold aims of his proposed corporation: to aid the destitute to support themselves by helping them to secure employment, to care for children and others unable to provide for themselves, and, finally, "to imbue the objects of its care with pure principles of Christianity." Such intentions implied a highly eclectic approach to a solution of the problems of urban life, encompassing both religious and temporal measures and including every possible category of the unfortunate: the criminal, the alcoholic, the unemployed, the unwanted child, and the handicapped adult. His mission was, as Pease put it in 1855,

expressly designed to lend strength and support to infirmity of every kind, by a variety of methods, and while educating and

[9] Pease, "Address to Trustees," *Act of Incorporation,* pp. 6–7; Barnard, *Forty Years at the Five Points,* p. 15.
[10] "Certificate of Incorporation of the Five Points House of Industry, March, 1854," manuscript copy, Five Points House Archives, New York City.

patronising the children, extending a strong and friendly arm to the parents also. The complexity of our social existence cannot be evaded, and we claim it as an evident truth, that in so far as a system of benevolence ignores or neglects any of the parts of social man, its work is perverted and wasted.[11]

Yet no single mission could have helped everyone in need at the Five Points. Each day and each admission forced Pease, and after 1857 his successors, to decide which of those among the increasing number of applicants were to be helped. With these decisions came inevitable compromise and change.

Between 1850 and 1854, in the years before its incorporation, the Five Points House had provided lodgings and found jobs for approximately two thousand persons. Many were children, but men and women also came to the Five Points House to learn trades or to find positions as domestics, clerks, and farm hands.[12]

With incorporation, expansion, and increasing experience, however, came a reappraisal of the House's policies. Gradually Pease and his successor, Benjamin R. Barlow, who took over when Pease resigned in 1857, began to work more and more exclusively with children. While over two-thirds of the inmates of the House were adults in the year 1854–1855 (778 to 426), by 1863 this ratio was completely reversed: two-

[11] *Ibid.*; Pease, "Thy Weak Brother," p. 83.

[12] In 1854, for instance, Pease employed 2 men and 30 women at sewing, 16 girls at basket-weaving, 3 men and 10 boys at shoemaking, and 25 men at an Eastchester, New York, farm which had been donated to the mission. Much of the House's expenses were met by the proceeds of work done on the premises. Between July, 1850, and March, 1854, $26,684 was realized from such sales—more than half the total expenditures for the period ($49,000). Five Points House of Industry, *First Annual Report, April, 1854* (New York, 1854); Five Points House of Industry, "Second Annual Report, April, 1855," *New Charitable Monthly*, I (May, 1855), 57–64.

thirds of the House's beneficiaries were children under sixteen. By 1865 this proportion had increased to four-fifths.[13]

The House had changed. Founded as a workshop and employment agency, it had within a half dozen years become a nursery, a school, and an adoption agency. For homeless children the House provided a day school, hot meals, and free clothing. The center of all this activity was Pease's rapidly growing school. From the 772 children enrolled in 1855, attendance rose to 1,200 in 1856, and by 1859 to 2,317. In the period 1855–1865, 15,593 children attended the Five Points school. By 1861, $1,600 annually was expended for teachers' salaries and another $6,380 in supplying the children with hot meals.[14]

The goal of the superintendent of the Five Points House was not simply to shelter and educate these children until they were old enough to enter the city's labor market. The hope, whenever possible, was to remove them from the city completely, to find them homes—or at least jobs—with rural Protestant families. Profiting by the examples of the American Female Guardian Society and the Children's Aid Society, the House of Industry developed a carefully organized program encouraging rural families to adopt these city children. The trustees established local committees in rural areas where children were likely to be adopted. The committees emphasized

[13] Five Points House of Industry, "Second Annual Report"; Five Points House of Industry, "Report of Trustees, March 1, 1856, and March 1, 1857," *Monthly Record*, II (March, 1859), 248–250; III (May, 1859), 7–9; V (August, 1861), 13; VII (May, 1863), 6–7, 34–37; VIII (December, 1865), 116.

[14] *Monthly Record*, III (March, 1860), 280–281; V (December, 1861), 171; VI (June, 1862), 38; (August, 1862), 86; VII (May, 1863), 6–7; VIII (December, 1865), 116. Still, in 1863, as Barlow pointed out, there were sixty thousand children of school age in the city not attending any school—over five thousand of them in the neighborhood of the Five Points alone.

equally the duty of caring for such waifs and the advantage of having an extra pair of hands for farm and domestic work. Each issue of the mission's monthly magazine featured stories, written with elaborate pathos, of orphans and beggars desperately in need of a loving home with some fine Protestant mother. So successful were these pleas that the House rarely had to resort to the methods of the Children's Aid Society, which sent "caravans" of children from town to town until all were either adopted or employed. For the most part, those interested in adopting a child through the House of Industry had to come in person to choose him. It was not until the winter of 1861 that their rural supporters failed the House in this regard. That year Barlow had to send 17 children west in a caravan together with children from the Five Points Mission and the Children's Aid Society.[15]

Why did the House turn increasingly to work with children? Two factors explain at least part of this change. The first was the depression of 1855, which undermined the assumption of many New Yorkers that their city's economy could absorb all the unskilled thousands who arrived annually in search of employment. The second factor was the failure of Protestant missionaries to make any appreciable number of converts among the Five Points' predominantly Irish Catholic population.

In the late summer and early fall of 1854, the New York business community noticed the first faint symptoms of a financial panic; by that winter the city was in the depths of

[15] *Monthly Record*, II (February, 1859), 225–226; Barnard, *Forty Years at the Five Points*, p. 21; Admission Ledger, entry for July, 1862, pp. 751–752, Five Points House Archives. For a survey of how children "placed out" were treated, see Samuel Halliday, *Monthly Record*, VIII (April, 1866), 206.

a major depression. Declining industrial activity, business frauds, and unsound speculation had combined with a prolonged drought and crop failures to precipitate strikes and riots, a stock market panic, and a run on the city's banks.[16] By early December, twenty thousand families had already applied for relief to New York's chronically crowded almshouse. Many private charities had exhausted their resources, and the poor harvest brought high food prices and even scarcity. Relief committees were organized in 12 of the city's 22 wards to distribute clothing and fuel and to organize soup kitchens. The committees received contributions from individuals and businesses throughout the city, from the English Opera playing at Niblo's, from Barnum's Museum, and even from Lundenmuller's lowly beer garden.[17]

The newly incorporated Five Points House mobilized all its resources. During the first three weeks of January, 1856, the House fed some nine thousand persons in addition to its own residents. In the four winter months from November, 1855, through February, 1856, Pease distributed forty thousand meals and twenty-eight thousand articles of clothing, as well as substantial quantities of fuel, medicine, and groceries. At the same time he received 254 persons into the House, cared

[16] Federal Reserve Bank of New York, *Index of Estimated Cost of Living in the U.S., April, 1955;* Federal Reserve Bank of New York, *Index of Wholesale Prices in U.S., July, 1951;* A.I.C.P., *Twelfth Annual Report, 1855* (New York, 1855), pp. 13–36.

[17] A.I.C.P., "Minutes, Board of Directors, January 8, February 12, March 12, and April 9, 1855," manuscript copy, Community Service Society Archives; and *Twelfth Annual Report,* pp. 24–25; Allan Nevins and Milton Halsey Thomas, eds., *The Diary of George Templeton Strong* (4 vols.; New York, 1952), II, 208–209; "What is Done for the Poor," *New Charitable Monthly,* I (January, 1855), 1–8; New-York *Daily Tribune,* November 8, 1854, January 1 and 5, 1855.

for 300 children in the schools, and employed 250 adults in the workshop.[18]

While New York philanthropists were encouraged by their achievements in helping the unemployed and in staving off class violence, their optimism did not outlast the depression winter. By the summer and fall of 1856, as reformers and missionaries took stock of their experiences, pessimism began to replace the buoyancy and optimism characteristic of reform writing during the preceding decade. To many New York philanthropists, indeed, it seemed as if their years of work to find jobs for the poor, to prevent pauperism, and to introduce "scientific principles" into philanthropy had been swept away in the bitter winter. Beneath the commercial and physical growth of their city they now discerned increasing poverty—poverty which for many would prove chronic and irremediable. It seemed to Pease and to many others associated with New York's missions that the city could never provide steady employment to all who sought jobs there. On the contrary, every winter would find a growing number, even of hardworking and thrifty workmen, thrown upon the dole and the good will of the benevolent. Whereas previously these philanthropists had looked forward to the day when public health reform, the Maine Law,[19] and personal exhortation would wipe the curse of poverty from the city, they now admitted that the combination of individual incompetence and a seasonal labor market would keep many men and women dependent upon the city's almhouse and upon the charity of private organizations. So long as immigrants and farmers'

[18] "Five Points House of Industry," *New Charitable Monthly*, I (February, 1855), 28–31, 44–45; Five Points House of Industry, "Second Annual Report," pp. 57–64.

[19] In 1846 the Maine legislature had passed the first prohibition law in the United States. The term "Maine Law" became synonymous with prohibition.

children kept flocking to the city, many of them would inevitably find only cold, hunger, and misery. The winter of 1855 seemed but an acute phase of a chronic phenomenon.[20]

Pease, and indeed a majority of New Yorkers, believed that the only permanent solution to this problem of unemployment lay in somehow transferring the poor from the city to the countryside, where, they assumed, there would always be work for the willing. Poverty in a country as rich in resources and as underpopulated as the United States was unnatural. It resulted, Pease maintained, from an improper distribution of the labor force: too great a proportion of the nation's manpower had been trapped through ignorance or folly in the city's slums. This, Pease felt, was the lesson the House had learned in 1855.[21]

During these months of suffering and want, everyone connected with the Five Points House had attempted to find jobs or homes in the country for all who came seeking aid. The trustees blanketed neighboring communities in Westchester County, New Jersey, and Long Island with circulars describing the sufferings of the poor in New York. They pleaded with all who could to hire some of the city's unemployed, or at least to offer them board and room in return for farm or domestic labor. As a result, during December alone, the

[20] Pease, "Periodical Destitution in the City," *New Charitable Monthly*, I (March, 1855), 33–38; A.I.C.P., *Annual Reports* for 1854, 1855. See also Pease's articles, "What Shall Be Done for Our Poor," *Monthly Record*, I (November, 1857), 170; "The Question Before Us," "Emigrant Employment Society," "The Reverses of Labor—Public Employment," *New Charitable Monthly*, I (January, 1855), 17–18, 36–38, 49–50.

[21] Pease, "Periodical Destitution," pp. 33–34; Pease, "The Reverses of Labor," pp. 49–50. Nor did the attitude change. Three successive superintendents dotted their monthly magazine with articles warning would-be immigrants to the city of the dangers and misery of urban life.

House received hundreds of requests for domestics and children. It was forced, indeed, to advertise for unemployed women to come to the mission to fill places in the country. By January Pease was sending sixty New Yorkers a week to positions in rural communities. And by 1857 the House had announced that it would refuse aid to any adults who would not agree to leave the city if jobs could be found for them elsewhere.[22]

But the Five Points House was more than a workshop or an employment agency. It was an outpost of Protestantism among the infidel and, especially, among the Roman Catholic. One of Pease's objects, like that of all New York's numerous city missionaries, was the conversion of the poor—conversion, of course, to the evangelical Protestantism espoused by the Methodists, Presbyterians, and low church Episcopalians who supported the mission movement. (Unitarians, Universalists, and Catholics, no matter how devout, were almost certainly damned.) No Five Pointer, no matter how clean, thrifty, or moral, could be considered saved until he had personally experienced Christ's saving grace.

The winter of 1854–1855 was a pointed lesson in the futility of attempts to help individuals earn a secure livelihood in the city; each day of the House's existence underlined the dispiriting conviction that the religious conversion of the Five Pointers was a goal even more illusory than that of finding them jobs. Despite the temperance sermons and prayer meetings, the moral and religious climate of the Five Points remained unchanged. Apartments were still filled with the drunken and the criminal. Most discouraging of all was the fact that Sunday and weekday services were attended only by

22 "What is to be Done for the Poor," *New Charitable Monthly*, I (January, 1855), 8–10.

a few native-born Protestants and by the mission's school children.[23]

The predominantly Irish Catholic population of the Five Points, having resisted centuries of British efforts to wean them from their traditional beliefs, viewed with hostility and resentment the appeals of these new-world Protestants. With instinctive unity of purpose they boycotted "Old Pease's School" and all who attended it. They refused tracts and Bibles and ignored the House's temperance meetings, prayer sessions, and Sunday services.[24] Irish parents seemed to view almost any alternative as preferable to that of placing their children with the Five Points House of Industry. The Catholic children in Pease's school came apparently from the area's most economically depressed homes. They were the vagrant street children of the police commissioners' reports—children of destitute widows, of alcoholics, from broken or violence-filled homes. Some children came on their own or through misunderstandings, for a number of law suits were brought against Pease (and against the other city missions) by aggrieved parents claiming their children had been clandestinely removed from the city and placed, against their parents' wishes, in distant (and Protestant) foster homes.

The House's superintendents were not equipped to deal sympathetically with so recalcitrant a flock. They had been raised to view the Church of Rome as the "harlot" of *Revelations*, and Catholic theology and liturgy as a collection of medieval superstitions. In attempting to win these new immi-

[23] Pease, "Our Mission Work," *Monthly Record*, I (September, 1857), 125–134.

[24] B. N., "Sabbath Scenes," *Monthly Record*, II (September, 1858), 109–116; III (September, 1859), 110; VII (February, 1864), 259–260; "Bible Reader's Report," VIII (December, 1865), 125–126.

grants to Protestantism, they criticized their priests, scoffed at the Sacraments, and particularly derided the Mass and the Eucharist. This was hardly the way to win converts, and those deserting the Church of Rome were few indeed. With repeated failure the workers at the House became increasingly bitter and pessimistic. With ever greater frequency the House's *Monthly Record* carried articles and editorials, critical of the Catholic Church, which attributed the intemperance, filth, and irreligion of the poor to the doctrines and practices of Catholicism. By the 1860's the workers at the House had accepted the fact that hopes of converting adults to Protestantism were doomed to failure. "We have," as one editorialist put it, "long ceased to expect any marked results of our labors among this class of people."

The adults of the neighborhood are mostly Catholics, and have no disposition to enter a Protestant place of worship, even had they decent garments in which to appear. Our expectations of great results among this class are not as strong as they were three years since. . . . They seem inaccessible to any good influence, and it is only by removal and a change of circumstances, that we have much hope of seeing these barriers broken down, and a willingness manifest to listen to the truths of the Gospel.[25]

By the 1860's the Five Points House had limited its efforts largely to the "accessible," to the few industrious Protestants of the Points, and, in particular, to the children. If the House of Industry could not save those confirmed in sin, it might deter their children from following a similar course.

[25] Pease, "Who are Our Inmates," *Monthly Record*, I (February, 1858), 252–255; Barlow, V (August, 1861), 73; Pease, "Dance House of the Five Points," I (October, 1857), 147–153; Archibald Russell, "Presidential Address, Ninth Annual Meeting, April, 1862," VI (June, 1862), 38; Halliday, VIII (August, 1865), 56.

[2]

Yet despite their emphasis both in theory and in practice upon work with children, the superintendents of the House of Industry could not so limit themselves. As the mission's Bible readers and teachers visited the tenements of the Five Points to gather their charges for school, they encountered families without food or fuel, mothers sick and without medicines, houses filthy and poorly ventilated. When possible, they offered immediate assistance—loaves of bread, tea, medicines. By the 1860's the House was providing four thousand hot meals a week to adults resident in the Five Points, and was operating a medical dispensary with the help of philanthropic physicians. Since few tenements had the luxury of running water, the House enlarged its bathing facilities so that every Five Pointer could bathe if he so desired. Superintendent Halliday, so long an advocate of temporal charity and public health and tenement-house reform, succeeded Barlow in 1864. He immediately organized detailed surveys of housing conditions and proposed specific housing and public-health legislation based on these surveys.[26]

The Five Points House, like the Female Moral Reform Society, could not long rely on flight as a solution to urban problems. In daily residence at the Five Points, workers at the House began increasingly to think in environmental terms —to see the poverty of their motley flock as something more than simply the result of drunkenness, incompetence, or immorality.

[26] *Monthly Record*, III (March, 1860), 58–61; IV (May, 1862), 12–17; (August, 1862), 90–91; VII (February, 1864), 263–265; VIII (September, 1864), 74–75; (December, 1864), 119–121; IX (November, 1865), 101–102.

But these traditionally accepted causes of poverty could hardly be discounted; they were too much a part of the assumptions about individual responsibility which the mission workers and their supporters had grown up believing. Both the ideas and the practices of the Five Points House reflected a workable eclecticism, a willingness to adopt both temporal and spiritual means to alleviate poverty, and to assume both moral and environmental causes for the misery they sought to combat. If their position was in some respects inconsistent, the inconsistency never became apparent to the generation which founded and staffed the Five Points House of Industry.

CHAPTER 9

New York Association for Improving the Condition of the Poor

As the depression of the late 1830's lingered on into the mid-1840's, not a few articulate New Yorkers began to fear that many of the city's workingmen would never again find regular employment, that the creation of a permanent pauper class in America was almost inevitable. It was during these years and in response to such ominous premonitions that New Yorkers already concerned with city mission work organized the New York Association for Improving the Condition of the Poor.[1]

This organization has been the subject of some interest to social historians; scholars concerned with the evolution of American social work and class relationships have seen the

[1] A.I.C.P., *Address to the Public, Constitution and By-Laws of the Association for the Improvement of the Poor* (New York, 1844), p. 36; and *First Annual Report of the New-York Association for the Improvement of the Condition of the Poor for the Year 1845* (New York, 1845), p. 14. For a modern account of the founding of the A.I.C.P., see Lubove, "New York Association for Improving the Condition of the Poor." Lubove seems unaware of the Association's relation to the city mission movement and in particular to the New York City Tract Society, seeing the A.I.C.P. as a "secular" response by New Yorkers to their city's growing poverty.

Association as a crucially important proto-social welfare organization.[2] But to view the Association solely from the perspective of the late nineteenth century—to see it solely as a pragmatic social innovation—is to ignore much of its history. For it was the product as well of the gradual secularization of a two-generations-long city mission effort.

Founded by the New Yor City Tract Society in 1843, the Association for Improving the Condition of the Poor was essentially a hybrid organization. Although largely modeled after existing city missions, it had an avowedly secular goal—the moral and economic rehabilitation of the poor by means of the "scientific" distribution of charity. The leaders and workers for the Association clearly shared the pious commitment of their parent organization; indeed they had begun their charity work in its evangelical ranks. And though the Association's object was not formally the eternal salvation of men's souls, the moral and psychological views of poverty its leaders entertained were identical with those expressed by New York's city mission spokesmen.

For the first generation of the Association's existence, moreover, it maintained the closest of ties with the New York City Tract Society. Institutionally and intellectually, the two societies found themselves in close and natural agreement. Each viewed the distribution of temporal aid in much the same way; it was always a means, not an end. As the Tract Society had since the 1830's distributed temporal assistance in an

---

[2] Lubove, "New York Association for Improving the Condition of the Poor"; Robert H. Bremner, *From the Depths* (New York, 1956); Frank D. Watson, *The Charity Organization Movement in the United States* (New York, 1922); Rosen, *Public Health;* W. H. Tolman, "Half-Century of Improved Housing Effort by the New York Association for Improving the Condition of the Poor," *Yale Review* V (1896–1897), 290.

effort to facilitate the conversion of the poor, so the Association—product of an increasingly pragmatic and moralistic age —used financial aid in hopes of inducing a somewhat more secular grace in the shape of moral and economic regeneration. (Indeed it was the Tract Society's ward missionaries who supervised the Association's distribution of charity.) Even the Association's relatively pragmatic involvement with matters of public health and medical care mirrored and parallelled interests already well established in city mission circles.

Nor, as we have seen, was the City Tract Society able to return to an exclusively spiritual orientation. Within a decade of the Association's founding, its parent organization was again deeply involved in the distribution of charity and the amelioration of slum conditions. Through the 1860's and indeed almost until the century's end, the City Tract Society and the Association worked hand in hand, united in their desire to make the poor self-respecting, economically stable, church-going members of society.

[1]

In July of 1843, at the depth of the lengthy depression, four of the New York City Tract Society's wealthiest managers—A. R. Wetmore, James Brown, Robert Minturn, and James Boorman—drew up a constitution for a proposed "Society for the Relief of the Worthy Poor." They submitted the draft to the Tract Society's executive committee, which promptly voted affirmatively. The executive committee hoped that this new organization would free their still evangelical Society from the increasingly onerous burden of distributing charity and might, ultimately, even reduce the amount of destitution in the city. The Tract Society immediately hired a professional agent and dispatched him on a tour of other eastern cities; perhaps he might garner useful ideas from their means of distributing relief.

For the next year and a half—from July, 1843, through December, 1844—the new organization remained the experimental brainchild of a number of the City Tract Society's wealthy supporters. Its founders made no immediate public announcement of its formation or request for contributions; the managers of the New York City Tract Society, at their own weekly meetings, actually directed and managed the new society. (Its affairs sometimes occupied the entire weekly executive committee meeting.) The Association recruited its members and financial support exclusively through the City Tract Society. It was indeed almost two years before its founders felt that their neonate had developed a membership and financial base adequate to an independent existence.[3]

At the end of 1844, the New York Association for Improving the Condition of the Poor—the final form reached in the evolution of the Society's title—issued its first "Address to the Public." The following year, the Association's members elected officers and a Board of Managers, and published their first report.[4]

Adopting the Tract Society's system of city-wide organization, the New York Association for Improving the Condition of the Poor, like its parent society, divided the island into seventeen districts, corresponding to its political wards. The districts were then subdivided into smaller districts, each the responsibility of a five-man advisory committee. These local committees were again to divide their assigned territory into sections containing, ideally, some twenty-five poor families.

[3] For material describing the actual formation of the Association and its early relationship to the N.Y.C.T.S., see N.Y.C.T.S., "Minutes of the Missionaries' Weekly Meetings, February 24, 1838, to December 28, 1844."

[4] A.I.C.P., *Address to the Public;* and *First Annual Report, passim.*

It was the task of the district committee to recruit a requisite number of concerned volunteers to work with each twenty-five-family unit. (Throughout its early history, however, the Association was forced to work with a roughly sixty-family-to-one-visitor ratio.) No one connected with the Association —either as worker or contributor—was to aid any needy person directly; applicants for relief were referred to the visitor for the area in which he lived. The heart of the visitor's work, therefore, lay in investigating each of his needy families and deciding upon the true origin of its plight; were its members victims of unavoidable misfortune or of their own moral inadequacy? The visitor was supposed, as well, to familiarize himself with the city's numerous charitable organizations; if the needs of a particular family seemed appropriate to the purview of a particular agency, it was the visitor's duty to act as liaison between that charity and its would-be object.[5]

In 1844, during its first year of independent operation, the Association extended its activities from the Battery to Fortieth Street (an area corresponding to sixteen of the city's seventeen wards). The territory was divided into 236 sections, each with its own visitors; within a year, the Association was able to add forty-two new visitors—and thus new sections—to its organization. At the same time it devised a number of practical ways in which to aid the poor more efficiently. It loaned coal stoves, for example, to families too poor to have any place to burn their coal, and devised a program for the orderly collection and distribution of used clothing and of what was then called "cold vittels," scraps from the tables of hotels and private homes.[6]

[5] A.I.C.P., "Constitution, Article X and XI," and "By-Laws, Article III and IV," printed *First Annual Report*, pp. 8–12, 19.

[6] A.I.C.P., *Third Annual Report for the Year 1846* (New York, 1846), pp. 16, 18, 21–22.

Each year the Association's workers were able to increase their efforts, to find their way into more and more slum apartments. In 1847, only three years after they had commenced their efforts, the visitors relieved some 5,500 families; this meant from five to six thousand visits a month. By 1853, the Association's *Tenth Annual Report* could note with pride that it had succeeded in organizing twenty-two districts with the help of 378 visitors. Clearly, the Association submitted, this growth attested to the dimension of the problems it hoped to solve and to the enthusiastic support tendered by charitable New Yorkers. Many, however, it admitted sadly, still remained outside their influence.[7]

As its name implied, the Association had aims more ambitious than the simple rationalization of outdoor relief distribution. Its managers and workers hoped by applying "scientific methods" of philanthropy to reform the moral character of the poor and thus permanently to reduce the amount of poverty in their city. They hoped by the same token to reduce proportionately the amount New Yorkers spent each year on charity. The "scientific" quality of the Association's endeavor lay not only in their hope of bringing order into the city's philanthropic world or in espousing as it did such pragmatic reforms as tenement-house legislation and medical dispensaries (though all were of recognized importance), but rested principally on the assumption that a moral reawakening of the poor might be guaranteed by a systematic and uncompromisingly realistic application of the methods prescribed by "modern philanthropy." Upon moral regeneration, the Association never doubted, all true economic and social reform must be based. Private and public funds, the

[7] A.I.C.P., *Fourth Annual Report for the Year 1847* (New York, 1847), p. 26; and *Tenth Annual Report for the Year 1853* (New York, 1853), p. 32.

Association asserted after several years' work, could never support all the city's needy. The only solution to unemployment and destitution lay in the moral elevation of the poor.[8]

Consistently enough, the Association emphasized this individualistic and moral approach to poverty in its first visitor's manual. The writer of these instructions was the Association's first agent, Robert M. Hartley, already an experienced leader in New York's charities. Their ultimate purpose, Hartley instructed the new volunteers, was "to induce persons to prefer a life of labor to dependence upon alms. . . . We are bound to relieve none, as a general rule whom we cannot elevate." [9] For this reason, the Association refused—at least formally—to help the elderly, the chronically ill, and the handicapped, as well as the morally irredeemable. Such unfortunates were the proper objects of the almshouse; they could never be made self-supporting, productive members of society. The purpose of the Association, Hartley instructed visitors time and again, was to elevate and morally reform the poor, not simply to aid the hungry or the sympathy-provoking. "The Constitution," he admonished in 1847, "allows relief only to those whose moral and physical condition will be improved by the *amount of attention and relief*, the visitor in the proper discharge of his duties will be able to bestow." [10]

[8] A.I.C.P., *Thirteenth Annual Report for the Year 1856* (New York, 1856), pp. 36–37, 39; *Seventh Annual Report for the Year 1850* (New York, 1850), pp. 16–17; *Eleventh Annual Report for the Year 1854* (New York, 1854), p. 18; *Twelfth Annual Report for the Year 1855* (New York, 1855), pp. 25–35, 37; and *Nineteenth Annual Report for the Year 1862* (New York, 1862), pp. 20–21.

[9] A.I.C.P., "Visitor's Manual, Article VIII," pp. 30–31.

[10] Robert M. Hartley, *An Abstract of the Secretary's Remarks at a Special Meeting of the Advisory Committees of Visitors of the Association for Improving the Condition of the Poor, New-York, March 3, 1847* (New York, 1847), pp. 2–3, 5; Hartley, *To the District Secretaries and Visitors of the New-York Association for Improving*

The decisions demanded by this policy could be made only by the knowing and sensitive. The visitor must be in effect a true friend of the needy family. If vice lay at the root of their misfortune, he must persuade them to reform through moral and religious instruction and by withholding aid. Indeed, the Board of Managers often warned visitors that the poor could in many cases only be helped by withholding temporal aid, or by using it as a reward for abandoning such "vicious habits" as drunkenness and gambling. Charity must be regarded as a stimulant, a means by which a temporary embarrassment might be overcome and a family enabled to join the ranks of the respectable and gainfully employed. If the destitute family, on the other hand, was the victim of sickness, the visitor was to obtain medical attention and, through the judicious provision of relief, keep the family above the level of pauperism until health and the possibility of employment returned. If want could be traced to lack of skills, the visitor was to seek jobs and training for his charges. The worst sin of all, visitors were warned, lay in allowing the aid they gave to undermine existing stores of self-reliance and morale. Financial aid should be regarded both by visitor and client as only a desperate and in a real sense degrading last

the *Condition of the Poor, May, 1850* (New York, 1850); Hartley, *To the District Secretaries and Visitors of the New-York Association for Improving the Condition of the Poor, January 15, 1855* (New York, 1855); Hartley, *To the District Secretaries and Visitors of the New-York Association for Improving the Condition of the Poor, February, 1857* (New York, 1857); Brown, *Confidential Instructions . . . December 1, 1855* (New York, 1855). All the above were printed circulars sent to visitors by the secretary or president of the Association; all are deposited in the Archives of the Community Service Society. Hartley's directives did not meet with universal compliance. Some visitors protested, arguing that if they did not care for the sick and the elderly, these dependents would starve; the city agencies were simply unable to care for all the genuinely needy and deserving.

resort. The Association would offer no quarter to the indolent, the intemperate, or the "sturdy vagabond," intent on
defrauding the charitable.[11]

In the intricate mixture of values and attitudes which motivated and justified the Association, the strain of would-be
efficiency, of "scientific philanthropy," played a significant
part. The Association did not limit its concern to the poor
and the vagrant. From Hartley's point of view, the city's
numerous and ill-coordinated charities were as much in need
of attention and reorientation as were the poor themselves.
Hartley and his colleagues sought to educate and reorganize
New York's charities in terms of what they felt to be the
three basic principles of a rational philanthropic practice:
detection, discrimination, visitation. New York, the Association reiterated in its early reports, possessed over forty charitable organizations, all actively distributing relief to the poor.
Besides these private groups, the city government supported
an almshouse, a juvenile reformatory, and a department of
outdoor relief. Yet each year the numbers of the poor increased and their condition seemed only to worsen. Unwilling
to see the cause of this destitution in the economic organization of the city, the Association sought it in the quality of
relief given and in the effect it had upon the poor.

Certainly, the Association felt, some of the problem lay in
the informal and "unscientific methods" of existing charities.
Many of New York's charities, Hartley argued, did not seek
to reform the poor, but simply to feed and clothe them.
The result was moral disintegration and inevitable pauperization. As an indispensable first step, the Association submitted,
the city's numerous charitable organizations should divide

[11] A.I.C.P., "Visitors Manual, Article VI," pp. 29–30; *First Annual
Report, passim; Eleventh Annual Report*, p. 39; and *Fourth Annual
Report*, p. 12.

the poor into categories reflecting the essential cause of their condition. Second, these organizations should take care not to duplicate efforts and thus subsidize the wily dissimulator. Last, aid should be given only in connection with systematic visitation and efforts to secure a moral reformation. Few of these organizations, the Association reported, thoroughly studied all the needs of their clients; comparatively few followed up their aid with constructive moral criticism, with religious instruction, with advice on child-rearing or efficient household management. Such admonitions were of far greater value to the poor themselves than a few pounds of coal or some castoff clothing.[12]

Characteristic of New Yorkers' indiscriminate charity was their traditional practice of giving alms to street beggars or food and clothing to those who begged from door to door. This charity neglected the needy whose self-respect would not allow them to accost strangers in the streets. Often, of course, these sturdy beggars were simply frauds. But in any case, such random and ill-considered giving was never accompanied by advice, sympathy, or pious encouragement. "Impulsive benevolence," Hartley wrote in 1848, "is selfish, indolent, indiscriminating, and generally produces evil."

To make want the sole measure of supply, without regard to character, conduct or consequences, is to subvert temperance, economy and industry, and to encourage pauperism with its attendant evils. . . . The chief cause of its [pauperism's] increase among us in the *injudicious dispensation of relief.*[13]

[12] A.I.C.P., *First Annual Report*, pp. 15–16; *Third Annual Report*, pp. 15–16; *Sixth Annual Report for the Year 1849* (New York, 1849), pp. 14–24; *Seventh Annual Report*, pp. 29–30; *Eighth Annual Report for the Year 1851* (New York, 1851), p. 25; and *Tenth Annual Report*, pp. 17–19, 21.

[13] A.I.C.P., *Fifth Annual Report for the Year 1848* (New York, 1848), p. 15; and "Minutes of the Board of Managers, November 11,

The Association's system of district visiting would completely eliminate street begging. An Association member, when approached by a beggar or asked for food or clothing at his home, would simply give the solicitor a ticket directing him to the visitor for the section in which he lived. The benevolent need never again have to deal directly with a stranger; the fraudulent beggar would be driven from the streets, the honest poor cared for in their homes and encouraged in their self-respect. And not least, available funds would go much farther. By just such judicious reforms the Association hoped ultimately to eliminate pauperism and reduce poverty itself to manageable dimensions.[14]

[2]

Organizations are sometimes, in truth, the lengthened shadow of one man. This was clearly the case with the Association for Improving the Condition of the Poor. For the first generation of its existence, the Association expressed with consistent faithfulness the ideas and leadership of Robert M. Hartley. In 1843, the executive officers of the New York City Tract Society hired Hartley as "agent" and executive secretary of their new Association, one of the first salaried executive positions in American philanthropy. For more than two decades Hartley was both key policy-maker and day-to-day administrator of the Association's work. He did not retire until 1876.

With remarkable fidelity, Hartley's career mirrors all of

1851"; Horatio Allen, *To the Visitors of the New-York Association for the Improvement of the Condition of the Poor, February, 1846, a* leaflet, n.p., n.d., Archives; A.I.C.P., *First Annual Report*, p. 17; *Third Annual Report*, pp. 16, 19; *Fourth Annual Report*, p. 17; and *Eleventh Annual Report*, p. 35.

[14] A.I.C.P., *First Annual Report*, pp. 17–18; *Third Annual Report*, pp. 16–19; and *Fourth Annual Report*, pp. 16–17.

the tendencies which we have sought to illustrate in preceding chapters: the transition from evangelical piety to secular moralism, from tract distribution to temporal meliorism, the growth of professionalization within the missions, the casual and intimate coexistence of spiritual and material concerns. The influences which shaped Hartley were the influences—disparate though they may seem in hindsight—which gave shape to the city mission movement generally. Hartley's ideas were not original; both in his activities and writings he mirrored the interests of many other Americans concerned with social reform in the 1830's and 1840's.[15]

Robert Hartley was born in England in 1796 and came to the United States in 1799 with his merchant father. Like his father, young Hartley went into business, beginning as a clerk in Schenectady, New York, then making a mercantile career of his own in New York City. But as was true of many of his fellow New Yorkers, the competitive urgings of commerce did not fill his life. As early as 1822, Hartley assumed leadership in his Presbyterian church's program of ward tract visiting, working closely with Harlan Page, one of the New York City Tract Society's most pious and influential members. Hartley soon joined several of the city's other benevolent societies and throughout the 1820's and 1830's played a leading role in the work of the New York City Tract Society. In 1829, he joined the newly organized New York State Temperance Society and in 1833 became its cor-

[15] For a discussion of Hartley and the public health movement, see Charles E. Rosenberg and Carroll S. Rosenberg, "Pietism and the Origins of the Public Health Movement: A Note on John H. Griscom and Robert M. Hartley." For evaluations of Hartley's place in the development of American social welfare, see Bremner, *From the Depths;* Watson, *The Charity Organization Movement,* esp. pp. 35–38; Lubove, *The Progressives and the Slums* (Pittsburgh, 1962), esp. Chap. I.

responding secretary and agent. Ten years later Hartley gave up his business career to become the full-time executive secretary of the Association for Improving the Condition of the Poor.[16]

Thus well before the Association's organization, Hartley had become familiar with New York's social problems and was committed to a number of institutional programs which were to influence strongly the newly formed Association. Hartley, for example, as chairman of his ward's temperance committee, had urged that the New York Temperance Society institute a program of systematic visitation, so as ultimately to contact every family in the ward. (This concept Hartley and Harlan Page had discussed even earlier as tract visitors for their Presbyterian church.) Hartley was convinced as well that the Temperance Society should work in close conjunction with the city's other charitable associations. Hartley soon became an advocate of that extreme social reform—total abstinence. Earlier than many of his pious associates, Hartley concluded that the sin of intemperance lay behind much of the nation's social disorder and individual misery;[17] this theme was to assert itself constantly during the Association's first half century of life.

Through his temperance work, Hartley became involved with public health problems even before the establishment of the Association. New York's dismayingly high infant mortality rate was a problem which concerned anyone who bothered even to glance at such statistics, and Hartley soon became aware of the role played by contaminated milk in

[16] *Memorial of Robert Milham Hartley. Edited by his Son, Isaac Smithson Hartley* (Utica, 1882), Chaps. I–X. This memorial is the basic biographical source for Hartley's life, containing as it does voluminous excerpts from his letters, diary, and other unpublished manuscripts.

[17] *Ibid.*, pp. 89–94, 98–104.

contributing to these alarming death rates. He was particularly shocked by the discovery that a good portion of the city's milk supply came from animals kept closely confined in filthy and poorly ventilated stalls and—worst of all—fed on distillery wastes. Hartley led reformers in a campaign against this swill-milk, a campaign culminating in an official State investigation in 1858.[18] It takes no great sophistication to discern the moralism, the temperance thrust, in this overtly pragmatic concern; and one could indeed make a good deal of the dramatic function played by images of pollution, of unnatural alcohol defiling God's pure milk.[19] The most significant point, however, is that such distinctions—between that which we regard as pragmatic environmentalism and that which we regard as pious or status-oriented moralism—are not very useful ones. Both styles of thought supplemented each other in the 1830's, 1840's, and 1850's, interacting to motivate and broaden Hartley's concern with the human problems of his city.

Nothing could be clearer from a reading of Hartley's personal diary. Through all these active years, Hartley remained intensely evangelical. His pietism inspired—was, indeed, in-

[18] *An Historical, Scientific and Practical Essay on Milk* (New York, 1842).

[19] For an important discussion of the background of such images of "infection" and the gradual and complex secularization of this concept, see Owsei Temkin, "An Historical Analysis of the Concept of Infection," in *Studies in Intellectual History* (Baltimore, 1953), pp. 123–147, esp. pp. 139–144. See also the discussion of the interaction between scientific thought and religious values provided by Lloyd Stevenson in two significant articles, "Science Down the Drain: On the Hostility of Certain Sanitarians to Animal Experimentation, Bacteriology and Immunology," *Bulletin of the History of Medicine*, XXIX (1955), 1–26, esp, pp. 3–4, and "Religious Elements in the Background of the British Anti-Vivisection Movement," *Yale Journal of Biology and Medicine*, XXIX (1956), 125–127.

separable from—his most "secular" and melioristic activities. Fortunately for the historian, Hartley kept a diary which demonstrates clearly the continuity of his spiritual commitment. The entry for March 19, 1856, for example, reads:

I am, on review, much dissatisfied with my labors to-day. I have done but little of that I designed to do. Truly I am an unprofitable servant; yet God mercifully forbears to punish. O for a higher wisdom than my own to direct the labors of my calling! At evening attended a sanitary lecture at the Cooper Institute. To-day my mind has been pervaded with a deep seriousness, and a desire to dwell on spiritual things.[20]

Not surprisingly, Hartley shared his generation's assumptions about the nature and origins of poverty. There were, he believed, essentially two classes among the needy, the victims and the vicious, the worthy and the unworthy. And, as we have seen in discussing the Association's visiting policies, an intelligent application of these standards was the logical basis for the Society's plan of organization. Overlying this rather pessimistic and static analysis of poverty was an ineradicable, if somewhat inconsistent, optimism; it was the heritage of Hartley's millennial piety.

No individual, he believed, need ever become or remain a pauper. Pauperism, for Hartley, was not a category in an analysis of income distribution, but a moral state. "The masses," he explained in the Association's *Annual Report* for 1856, "beginning with the individual, are improvable. And if the individual can be reclaimed, why not the masses?"

Until the feelings, opinions, and practices of the great mass are governed by sound principles and Christianity pervades and renovates the habits of social and civil life, there is no reliable foundation for prosperity.[21]

[20] *Memorial of Robert Milham Hartley*, p. 288.
[21] A.I.C.P., *Thirteenth Annual Report*, p. 39.

And the means through which this goal might be attained served as its own motivation: "The supernatural efficacy of Christianity is adequate to the work."

These were the strongest bonds of continuity between the city missions and the Association—the motivating optimism of Christian commitment coupled with the conviction that the only real solutions for pauperism were ultimately moral and religious. Hartley transmitted all of these attitudes to his new organization.

There existed still another assumption which united the evangelical philanthropists of the 1830's and their more pragmatically oriented successors of the 1840's and 1850's. This was the influence of a leading Scottish minister and political economist, Thomas Chalmers. Chalmers was a widely read theologian and a founder of the Scottish National Church; his works had long been popular with pietistic New Yorkers. But far more influential than his formal doctrinal studies were Chalmers' writings on the causes of and remedies for urban poverty. As pastor of city churches, first in Edinburgh and then in Glasgow, Chalmers had been required to assume certain administrative responsibilities in the distribution of poor-law funds. His experiences, combined with the memories of the simple social arrangements and unaffected morality of his first rural parish, convinced him that public charity given indiscriminately—and unaccompanied by human interest or concern—served only to debase the poor. Rather than assisting the destitute through impersonal municipal charities such as the almshouse and workhouse, Chalmers argued, the charitable should divide the city's poorer districts into small units and appoint a volunteer religious visitor for each. It would be the visitor's task to study the true cause of each family's poverty, encourage, admonish, and pray with that family, offering aid only when it was desperately needed.

The poor themselves, Chalmers argued, through their own industry and household management, by sacrificing such vicious habits as drinking and gambling, and by charitable assistance to each other, could transform themselves from paupers into self-respecting, church-going citizens. Ideally, Chalmers' geographic units would contain charity day schools, Sunday schools, libraries and industrial schools, all staffed by benevolent volunteers; such local institutions would be invaluable aids to the poor in their efforts at self-improvement.

In 1831 Chalmers published his massive and influential treatment of such problems, *On the Christian and Economic Polity of a Nation, More Especially with Reference to Its Large Towns*. But although charitable New Yorkers had begun to refer to his philanthropic writings in the 1820's, his influence upon New York's city missions was greatest in the 1840's and 1850's.[22] It was during these decades that New York's poverty first assumed the threatening dimensions traditionally associated with great European cities, and that city missions began systematically to consider means of alleviating such poverty. Chalmers' program provided direct inspiration for the Association for Improving the Condition of the Poor, with its districts, visitors, and its twin emphases on moral improvement and the dangers of indiscriminate almsgiving.

[22] Thomas Chalmers, *On the Christian and Economic Polity of a Nation, More Especially with Reference to Its Large Towns*, in *The Works of Thomas Chalmers* (25 vols.; Glasgow, 1836–1849). For standard biographies, see William Hanna, *Memoirs of the Life and Writings of Thomas Chalmers* (3 vols.; Edinburgh, 1852). For examples of Chalmers' American influence, see John Griscom, *Year in Europe*, II, Chap. XXXVII; Samuel Hanson Cox, *Interviews: Memorable and Useful; from Diary and Memory Reproduced* (New York, 1853), Chap. I. Cox was to be an ardent supporter of New York's city missions.

[3]

Although the Association assumed that individual moral failings were the most important single cause of poverty, its supporters did not limit their efforts to personal visiting and secular sermonizing.

Environmentalism had always coexisted with moral interpretations of want; and from its inception the Association played an active role in environmental reform. Hartley and the Association's managers believed that an intimate connection existed between the breakdown of living standards—a result of impersonal economic forces—and the deterioration of individual and family mores. Specifically, the Association concerned itself with programs to study and improve the health and housing of New York's poor. In part, these efforts reflected city mission workers' growing awareness of tenement conditions—an awareness based in large measure on experience and observation. These new melioristic programs reflected, as well, the influence of Edwin Chadwick, Southwood Smith, and other English public health reformers, an influence as pervasive in the 1850's, 1860's, and 1870's as that of Thomas Chalmers in the generation past.[23]

[23] It would be inappropriate to discuss the English public health movement here, for it has been the subject of a number of excellent studies. See, as but a few examples: W. M. Frazer, *A History of English Public Health 1834–1939* (London, 1950); R. A. Lewis, *Edwin Chadwick and the Public Health Movement 1832–1854* (London, 1952); S. E. Finer, *The Life and Times of Sir Edwin Chadwick* (London, 1952); Royston Lambert, *Sir John Simon, 1816–1904, and English Social Administration* (London, 1963); C. Fraser Brockington, *Public Health in the Nineteenth Century* (Edinburgh and London, 1965); M. W. Flinn, "Introduction," in Edwin Chadwick, *Report on the Sanitary Condition of the Laboring Population of Great Britain*, ed. by M. W. Flinn (Edinburgh, 1965). For the decisive impact of the English public health movement upon American reformers, see Rosen, *Public Health*, pp. 233–248.

The early 1840's marked indeed the first real quickening of awareness among New Yorkers generally concerning their city's slums and the effect of slum life on public health and morals. (Earlier moments of alarm were connected with the fear of epidemics—cholera in 1832 and yellow fever in 1822, for example—and were no longer-lived than the epidemic itself.) The tone of newspaper articles discussing such matters showed increasing alarm as knowledge of slum conditions became more widely diffused—and as epidemics and the rumor of epidemics dramatized the threat which such misery posed to every class in New York. In 1849, the two-year-old American Medical Association sponsored an investigation into health and housing accomodations in New York as part of a more general survey of American cities. That same year, Lemuel Shattuck completed his influential report as chairman of the Massachusetts Sanitary Commission; published in 1850, his *Report* emphasized the painful disparity between Boston's high mortality rate and that of Massachusetts' rural areas. The impact of the Shattuck *Report* was equally sharp in New York, for New York City's mortality rates were substantially higher than those of Boston.[24]

Few New Yorkers were more active than the City Tract Society's missionaries and managers in attempting to stimulate interest in the city's health conditions. By the early 1840's the City Tract Society's missionaries were recognized as being perhaps New York's most knowledgeable authorities on tenement life, and had begun to work with the city's public health officials, investigating and exposing tenement conditions. Quaker physician John H. Griscom was the most

[24] American Medical Association, *First Report of the Committee on Public Hygiene;* Lemuel Shattuck and Others, *Report of the Sanitary Commission of Massachusetts, 1850. With a Forward by Charles-Edward Amory Winslow* (Cambridge, Mass., 1948).

active and cooperative of city officials during his brief tenure as city inspector. Not surprisingly, Griscom was a member of the first executive committee of the Association and urged with unceasing conviction the moral benefits to be gained from public health reform.[25] I have already mentioned Griscom's historic analysis of New York's health problems in his 1842 report as City Inspector and his even more famous address on the "Sanitary Condition of the Laboring Population of New York" prepared two years later. Both reports were heavily dependent, as were other public health investigations of the 1850's and 1860's, upon the observations of Tract Society visitors. It is impossible to pinpoint the role of Griscom's work in precipitating the Tract Society's decision to inaugurate the Association, but it is certainly safe to argue that both were characteristic products of a period increasingly concerned with such matters as tenement construction, sanitation, and dispensary care.[26]

As early as 1846, only two years after the Association for Improving the Condition of the Poor had begun independent life, its directors voted to establish a committee to examine the housing of the poor. The next year, the committee issued its report; not surprisingly, their observations and conclusions paralleled those made by Griscom in New York and those which Chadwick, Southwood Smith, Neil Arnott, and their fellow public health workers had formed while studying England's new industrial slums. The city's tenements were utterly inadequate to the preservation of human life—much less

[25] A.I.C.P., *First Annual Report*, pp. 4–5.

[26] In ideas, in actions, in associations—Griscom consistently displayed the pietistic origin of his concern for public health. Indeed, in 1845, a reviewer of Griscom's *Sanitary Condition*, in the *New York Journal of Medicine*, actually suggested by way of conclusion that it be reprinted and distributed by the N.Y.C.T.S. *New York Journal of Medicine*, IV (1845), 30.

Christian morality. The Association's housing committee concluded by warning the Association firmly: if they hoped to reduce the amount of poverty in the city and improve the morals of the poor, they must first reform tenement conditions.

Great value should be attached to this much-desired reform, seeing it lies at the basis of other reforms; and as the health and morals of thousands are injured or destroyed by the influence of circumstances around them, an improvement of the circumstances in connection with other appropriate means, afford the only rational hope of effectually elevating their character and condition, and of relieving the city from numerous evils which now exist.[27]

Moral considerations were still an inextricable part of the concerns of even the most environmentally oriented. Indeed, this approach to housing contained elements even more simplistic and optimistic than its moral formulae for the relief of urban poverty. Housing abuses could be easily corrected—or so at least it seemed in 1847. They stemmed from the unethical practices of a group of marginal and unethical businessmen, the slum landlords. The solution was obvious. Substantial merchants, guided by traditional business ethics and Christian principles, must be drawn into the housing field. They, more even than the city missionary, would be the moral reformers of the poor.[28]

Decent housing for the poor, the Association's housing committee insisted, could be constructed and still bring a legitimate profit to the builder; six per cent could easily be realized on a sanitary and well-maintained multiunit dwelling. The housing committee drew up and printed model housing

[27] The committee's report was printed in the A.I.C.P.'s *Fourth Annual Report*, pp. 22–23.

[28] *Ibid.*, pp. 22–23.

plans which the Association's officers distributed widely among the city's business leaders in the hope of inspiring a new kind of tenement landlord. The success of a number of such projects in England and on the Continent provided encouragement.

But events in New York did not. Few substantial businessmen responded to the Association's housing report. Tenements built during the 1840's proved no better than the old reconstructed tenements in the city's lower wards.[29] The Association began to consider the construction of its own model tenements but was unable to raise the necessary funds. In 1853, it decided upon the need for a new and more vigorous program. Largely at the instigation of Hartley, the Board of Managers appointed a second housing committee and directed them to prepare a report on "the sanitary condition of the laboring classes and the practicality of devising measures for improving the comfort and healthiness of their habitations." [30]

The committee, able to call upon the observations and reports of their own visitors and the paid missionaries of the City Tract Society, presented a detailed ward-by-ward and section-by-section description of slum housing conditions in New York. They investigated in depth the largest and worst of the city's tenements and reported whole city blocks lined with ill-ventilated, filthy, and overcrowded buildings. The connection between such conditions and the city's high rate of crime and mortality seemed all too apparent. This report, a model of lucidity for its time, remained for decades a specific guide for American housing reformers and public health workers. The Association published an edition separate from

[29] See, for example, remarks in A.I.C.P., *Tenth Annual Report*, p. 27; and *Eleventh Annual Report*, pp. 20–21.

[30] A.I.C.P., "Minutes, Board of Managers, June 13 and October 10, 1853."

its 1854 *Annual Report*—where it had originally appeared—
and circulated the report widely among physicians, business
groups, and the press.

The poor, the committee argued with casual indifference
to the Association's still-dominant tone of moralism, "are
made filthy, reckless and vicious by the force of circumstance
over which in most cases they have no control." "Every
honest, sober and industrious resident," it concluded, "should
at least have it in his power to procure a decent and healthy
home for himself and family. This is now impossible to multitudes who dwell in this city." For the first time, New York
philanthropists were in a systematic way expressing the belief
that some of their citizens—no matter how pure their morals
and prudent their domestic management—would never live
in decent surroundings.[31]

The Association was, as we have already seen, chronically
—and perhaps necessarily—inconsistent in evaluating the roles
played by morality and environment in the causation of anti-
social behavior. Citations could easily be marshaled empha-
sizing either their continued moralism or their earnest environmentalism. (Indeed, in years of great unemployment—
1855, for example, or 1857—when the sheer numbers of the
importunate threatened its environmental programs, the Association tended to retreat in its rhetorical emphasis to a more
rigidly moralistic interpretation of poverty.) The point, of
course, is that the inconsistency was never a real one in the
minds of the Association's workers and leaders; common sense
seemed to endorse the validity and interrelationship of both.
If the reformer were to improve the poor morally, physically,
socially, or economically, the Association's officers stated in
their 1854 *Annual Report*, he must first destroy the slum.

[31] A.I.C.P., *First Report . . . Sanitary Condition*, pp. 3, 6-14, 20,
26-27.

While the poor remained in their accustomed tenement homes, they would turn to alcohol, have little interest in industry, economy, or cleanliness, be sickly, and die young. Children would inevitably follow in their parents' degraded footsteps. There could be no escape for succeeding generations until the housing conditions which bestialized the poor were remedied.[32]

To speed that day and to convince the city's landowners and merchants to enter the housing field, the Board of Managers voted in 1853 to begin the construction of a model tenement house for the poor.[33] Located between Mott and Elizabeth streets, just north of the Five Points, the building when completed in 1855 was rented exclusively to blacks. "The reason for selecting this class of tenants," the Association Managers explained, "is that they are usually forced into the worst kind of dwellings, and are deprived of most special privileges, and consequently were specially deserving commiseration." [34]

The Association attempted to correct all the abuses of the standard slum tenement. Water closets, while not in the apartment itself, were on the same floor and specifically assigned to each apartment. Each apartment had as well a supply of Croton water. The common halls were lit by gas; every apartment was assigned a storage area in the basement in which supplies of coal and food could be kept. The yard was to be kept exclusively for washing and drying. Each family had two bedrooms to preserve privacy; subletting was prohibited.[35]

---

[32] The A.I.C.P.'s *Eleventh Annual Report*, pp. 19–33, included a lengthy discussion of the environmental causes and social nature of poverty and urged immediate public health and tenement-house reform.

[33] A.I.C.P., "Minutes, Board of Managers, April 10, 1854."

[34] A.I.C.P., *Thirteenth Annual Report*, p. 46.

[35] The A.I.C.P. included in their *Thirteenth Annual Report* a detailed description of the Workingmen's Home including an artist's

Yet the apartments were pitifully small. The bedrooms each measured but eight feet by seven and a half feet, the living room fourteen by eleven. And except for end apartments, all rooms save the living room were dark and windowless. The Association felt that ventilating flues running between each room and the roof would eliminate the need for windows and thus allow an increased number of apartments on each floor. Yet as the history of the Workingmen's Home, as it was called, was to prove, the flues were no substitute for windows. A number of years would pass before New York builders devised a satisfactory blueprint for low-cost urban dwellings which would allow for both proper ventilation and a profitable number of apartments. The Association's more general expectations for its model home failed as well. Maintenance costs for a building housing 87 families were high, and tenants were not always cooperative. In 1867, it sold the building for $100,000 to the Five Points House to serve as a home for working women.[36]

As it became increasingly clear in the years after 1854 that private capital was not going to follow the Association's example and rebuild New York's tenements, the Association turned with increasing interest to the police and regulatory powers of both the municipal and state governments. In 1856 and 1858, the Association lobbied successfully in Albany to secure the appointment of special legislative committees to investigate health and housing in New York City.[37] Associa-

---

sketch and floor plans, pp. 45–51. For a modern discussion and analysis of the Home, see Robert H. Bremner, "The Big Flat: History of a New York Tenement House," *American Historical Review*, LXIV (October, 1958), 54–62.

[36] Bremner, "Big Flat," p. 56.

[37] The Association, its officers wrote in 1857, had worked for ten years to achieve housing improvements through the use of private capital and philanthropic appeals. But to no avail. Only the police powers of the state, they were now convinced, could change slum

tion members, city missionaries, and interested physicians all testified to the foul slum housing of the city and its baleful effects upon health. The legislative committees, convinced, recommended a radical series of regulatory housing laws, which fully accorded with the Association's demands and those of other public health advocates. Yet another decade was to pass, however, before the New York State legislature passed what was—for the times—a model tenement house code, the Housing Act of 1867.

The Association thus experimented with two solutions to the tenement house problem: private model dwellings and state regulation. Nearly a century would pass before Americans would turn to a third solution, government construction of low-income housing. The Association's experiments hold an important place in the housing and public health movement of the nineteenth century. Equally significant was its explicit recognition that poverty often resulted from, and was perpetuated by, conditions beyond the control of the poor. Poverty was a social as well as an individual dilemma— one justifying even the intervention of the state into private affairs.

The Association did not limit its meliorative efforts to matters of housing. No sooner had the Association been founded than it turned its attention to the health of the poor and the adequacy of the medical care available to them. In 1845, even before the appearance of its first annual report, the Association published "A Plan for the Better Distribution of Medical Attendance," a study of existing medical charities

---

conditions. They called for the state legislature to condemn defective buildings, establish regulations concerning the proper construction of new buildings, to require the city government to improve sewerage and drainage. A.I.C.P., *Fourteenth Annual Report for the Year 1857* (New York, 1857), pp. 17, 30, 36–37.

which pointed to the need for increased out-patient care for the poor. Within six years, the Association had established two new medical dispensaries (located in the new slums which ran north of Fourteenth Street along the East and Hudson rivers). Association visitors worked closely with dispensary physicians, bringing them to the sick poor and even distributing medicines from central depositories.[38]

Throughout the 1850's and 1860's, the Association continued to concern itself with the practical health needs of the poor. In 1852, the Association opened a Bath and Wash House, where for a minimal charge (imposed to prevent the pauperization of its users) the poor could bathe and wash their clothing. This was New York's first public bath.[39] In 1862, the Association established a Society for the Ruptured and Crippled which operated a hospital largely to aid laborers injured during work (a common and, the Association asserted, a clearly preventable cause of poverty).[40] And in 1862, as well, the Association at last won a state law regulating the production and sale of milk—a victory which came after two decades of lobbying and agitation by Robert M. Hartley.[41] During these same years the Association also supported (and gave a prominent place in its annual reports to) such general public health efforts as the movement to improve the city's sewer system, to regulate slaughtering houses

[38] A.I.C.P., *A Plan for the Better Distribution of Medical Attendance and Medicines for the Indigent Sick by the Public Dispensaries in the City of New York* (New York, October, 1845), Archives, Community Service Society; A.I.C.P., *Eighth Annual Report*, pp. 20–22; and *Ninth Annual Report for the Year 1852* (New York, 1852), pp. 38–39.

[39] A.I.C.P., *Ninth Annual Report*, pp. 39–40.

[40] A.I.C.P., *Nineteenth Annual Report*, pp. 38–43; *Memorial*, pp. 212–215.

[41] A.I.C.P., *Nineteenth Annual Report*, pp. 54–58.

and bone-boiling establishments, and to prevent farm animals from being stabled in tenement apartments. It fought with increasing urgency and final success to secure an effective and professionally staffed Metropolitan Board of Health.[42]

Its historians have, in recent years, tended to write off the Association for Improving the Condition of the Poor's leaders in somewhat disenchanted tones; the moralism and rigidity of the Association's expressed values have made it seem natural to interpret the organization's concern for the poor as a form of moral censure and social control. Yet at the same time it has seemed natural to praise the Association and its leader, Robert M. Hartley, for a pioneer involvement in such social problems as tenement house reform and public health legislation. The place of the Association and Hartley in the evolution of the social welfare case-work method and in the incipient professionalization of social work is also unquestionable.

There is, of course, no real irony here; the ambiguity is only apparent. Once we accept the pietistic orientation of the Association's leaders as valid and genuine, the seeming inconsistency disappears. Christian faith can be an idiom for the expression of social criticism as well as a motivation toward personal piety and evangelicalism; that those who chose to do good seem to us moralizing and socially conservative does not invalidate the genuineness of their commitment. (And it is, of course, hardly surprising that the brutal facts of tene-

[42] A.I.C.P., *Fifteenth Annual Report for the Year 1858* (New York, 1858), pp. 53–54; *Seventeenth Annual Report for the Year 1860* (New York, 1860), pp. 57–68; and *Nineteenth Annual Report*, pp. 16–18; Hartley, "Summary of the Accomplishments of My Tenure of Office," in Mr. Robert Hartley's File of Original Documents, Archives, Community Service Society. (From internal evidence it appears that this "Summary" was probably written in 1876.)

ment life made its victims and their styles of life repellent and menacing to the Association's middle-class supporters. More important is the strength and resilience of these reformers' commitment to helping their fellow New Yorkers—brutish though the objects of their charity may often have seemed.) And, it may well be argued that this particular mixture of seemingly inconsistent elements—of pious moralism and dedicated environmentalism—was the most characteristic aspect of both social welfare and public health reform in the decades between the Civil War and the twentieth century. This peculiar mixture of pragmatism, moral self-assurance, and pious commitment was a very American and not completely ignoble compound.

In the development of contemporary attitudes toward poverty and institutions for its amelioration, the city missions generally, and the Association for Improving the Condition of the Poor particularly, played a significant role. Many of their ambivalences and inconsistencies remain with us. More positive is their contribution in familiarizing Americans with urban poverty and their place as institutional vehicles for the gradual secularization of the activist reforming spirit of Jacksonian evangelicalism. Their spirit was unmistakably present in much later and even more self-consciously secular and rationalistic generations.

++++++++++ | Appendix
Bibliography
Index

On the Marginality
of Secular Benevolence

To test my assumption that philanthropic New Yorkers viewed the world in essentially religious—that is, evangelical Protestant—terms and that city missions were representative institutions of the times, I selected a random sample of twenty-four New York City and Brooklyn charities from the period 1830–1860, all with secular goals. The organizations chosen were concerned with the growing city's social problems: the care of the aged, medical aid to the poor, reform of juvenile delinquents, the care of vagrant children, the distribution of outdoor relief. Of the twenty-four, twenty-one seemed to me distinctly religious in character. Their annual reports demonstrate a casual yet intricate intermingling of secular and religious values, programs, and goals. They saw religion as a principal impetus toward reform in society and as an essential step on the path toward respectable self-sufficiency for the poor. Many offered regular Protestant religious services to the objects of their charities—even if they happened to be bedridden patients. Their annual reports are dotted with pleas for God's aid and reminders of His admonitions to help the less fortunate. It can, of course, be argued that such pious expressions are merely fund-raising rhetoric; but if the philanthropic vocabulary of the 1830's and 1840's is contrasted with that of the 1790's and 1800's, the shift in language and expression is sharp indeed. There was little place in the rhetoric of the earlier

organizations for the tone of pious exhortation which so domi-
nates the reports of their successors.

A number of these randomly selected institutions had strong
ties with New York's regular city missions, either through over-
lapping membership or close working relations. Two—the Northern Dispensary and the New York Juvenile Asylum—were
founded directly or indirectly by the New York City Tract
Society, and for years many of the same philanthropists served
on both boards of managers. Charles Loring Brace, founder and
long-time director of the Children's Aid Society, began his
philanthropic career as a volunteer missionary for the Five Points
House of Industry, an active and influential city mission, whose
director was later to encourage Brace in his efforts to found a
society for the benefit of vagrant children. The Five Points
House, the Children's Aid Society, the American Female Guardian Society, the Juvenile Asylum, the House of Refuge all
participated jointly in efforts to find rural Protestant homes for
neglected slum children. The New York Dispensary worked
closely with visitors from the Five Points House when distributing medical aid to the destitute inhabitants of the Five Points.
The Girls' Industrial School of Avenue D was eventually absorbed
by the American Female Guardian Society. Mrs. Anson Phelps,
whose husband had long been a manager of the New York City
Tract Society, was a manager of the Association for the Relief
of Respectable Aged Indigent Females as were Mrs. William
Vermilye, Mrs. Charles Minturn, Mrs. Theodore Dwight, all
wives of prominent male supporters of New York's city missions.

Of these twenty-one religiously oriented secular charities, fourteen compose what might be termed an inner core of the especially committed. (See list below for the names of these
institutions.) These fourteen institutions—devoted, it will be recalled, to ostensibly secular goals—not only shared in the general
pietistic expressions of the period but espoused, as well, decidedly
evangelical and missionary aims—aims identical to those which
characterized the city missions. These institutions considered the
spiritual rebirth of their beneficiaries to be one of their primary

goals. Most of the fourteen held regular Protestant Sunday services for the recipients of their aid, and frequently sponsored additional weekday or evening prayer meetings. Those dedicated to work with the "outdoor poor" regularly visited tenement homes, distributing tracts and Bibles, praying, and hopefully converting. Those institutions which organized industrial schools invariably included Bible reading and religious exercises in their regular curriculum, anticipating the conversion and hence both the spiritual and temporal salvation of their students. The efforts of the Girls Industrial School of Avenue D, of the Brooklyn Industrial School Association, of the Colored Home, to secure the salvation (and consequently the earthly happiness and economic stability) of their benevolent objects parallel exactly those of the New York City Tract Society distributors, the workers at the Five Points House, the teachers and visitors of the American Female Guardian Society. The managers of the Juvenile Asylum and of the Association for Colored Orphans carefully recorded and described the religious conversion of their inmates, conversions sought actively by the teachers and supervisors. Religion indeed emerges as the principal socializing tool employed by these benevolent organizations.

Annual reports for the institutions were studied for the years following 1828. They differ remarkably from the annual reports of the same or similar institutions of the late-eighteenth- and early nineteenth-century. The officers of these earlier organizations, while deeply pious in their personal life, had seemingly felt no need to make their private faith the basis for their organizations' specific activities. Nor did the charitable in those more orthodox days make the conversion and religious elevation of their charges the fundamental objective. The reason for this shift in general religious emphasis—and indeed the reason for the very development of the city missions themselves, as has already been argued, seems to lie in the Second Great Awakening and in particular in the culminating influence of Charles Grandison Finney's two great New York revivals in 1829 and 1831.

The following is a list of the institutions surveyed as examples of New York's formally nonreligious or secular charities. They span the period 1814 to 1870; principal emphasis, however, was placed on the years 1840–1870. Those marked with an "R" indicated religious orientation in their annual reports, those marked "R-E," an evangelical commitment, and those marked "N-R" seemed essentially secular or nonreligious in their motivation and goals.

Association for the Benefit of Colored Orphans (1837–1854) R-E

Association for the Relief of Respectable, Aged, Indigent Females (1844–1860)   R

Brooklyn Industrial School Association (1856–1860)   R-E

The Brooklyn Society for the Relief of Respectable, Aged, Indigent Females (1854–1870)   R

Children's Aid Society (1856–1860)   R-E

Eastern Dispensary (1838–1866)   N-R

Girls' Industrial School—Avenue D (1854)   R-E

Industrial School Association for German Girls (1859)   R-E

New-York Asylum for Lying-In Women (1840–1854)   R-E

New York Dispensary (1814–1869) R (indicating a steady increase in its religious orientation)

New York Infirmary for Indigent Women and Children (1857–1866)   N-R

New York Juvenile Asylum (1858–1871)   R-E

New York Juvenile Guardian Society (1868–1870)   R

New York Society for the Relief of Widows and Orphans of Medical Men   (1842)   N-R

Northern Dispensary (1852–1869)   R

Orphan Asylum of Brooklyn (1868–1870)   R-E

Prison Association of New York (1845–1869)   R

St. Luke's Hospital (1861–1868)   R-E

Society for the Reformation of Juvenile Delinquents (House of Refuge) (1828–1871)   R-E

Society for the Relief of Destitute Children of Seamen (1850) N-R

Society for the Relief of Worthy and Indigent Colored (1841)
 R-E
Society for the Support of the Colored Home (1844–1854)   R-E
Wilson Industrial School for Girls (1867)   R-E
Women's Hospital Association (1856)   R

++++++++++ | *Bibliography*

The following pages are by no means an exhaustive bibliography of sources consulted in preparing this dissertation; the notes to particular chapters provide a more detailed guide to relevant material. In this selective bibliography I have tried, first, to suggest those sources that have been most useful and influential in shaping an understanding of New York City and of American religion in the first half of the nineteenth century, and second, to present a brief description of the pertinent sources for each of the missions discussed in detail.

New York City

There is no good modern comprehensive history of nineteenth-century New York; there is not really even a bad one. Nor is there a complete and adequate bibliography of New York City history. Harry J. Carmen and Arthur W. Thompson in their *Guide to the Principal Sources for American Civilization, 1800–1900, in the City of New York* (New York, 1962), discuss some of the material available for the social and religious history of New York City, but their compilation is by no means exhaustive and should be used in conjunction with the bibliography and "Notes" in Isaac Newton Phelps Stokes, *Iconography of Manhattan Island* (6 vols.; New York, 1915–1928). Robert Ernst's *Immigrant Life in New York City, 1825–1863* (New York, 1949), besides providing an invaluable study of New York's immigrants, contains an excellent bibliography not only for immigrant sources, but for New York's social history generally. In addition, see: "Checklist of Works Relating to the Social History of the City of New York—Its Clubs, Charities, Hospitals, etc., in the New York Public Library," *Bulletin of the New York Public Library*, V (June, 1901), 261–293. The card catalogue of the New York Public Library and the New York Historical Society provide in some ways still the most comprehensive guide to New York City history.

Public documents have provided an extremely useful source of information. I have found the following publications most useful: New York City Almshouse, *Annual Reports of the Governors of the Almshouse, New York, for the Years 1850–1870* (New York, 1850–1870); New York City, City Inspector, *Annual Reports, 1835–1870* (New York, 1835–1870); New York City, Common Council, *Minutes of the Common Council, 1784–1831* (19 vols.; New York, 1917); David T. Valentine, *Manual of the Corporation of the City of New York, 1842–1866* (New York, 1842–1866).

Investigations and other special reports of state and city agencies often provided useful information. Some of the most illuminating were: New York State Assembly, *Report of the Select Committee Appointed to Investigate Frauds upon Emigrant Passengers Arriving in this State, December 6, 1847*, Assembly Document No. 46 (Albany, 1847); New York State Assembly, *Report of the Select Committee Appointed to Examine into the Condition of Tenant Houses in New York and Brooklyn, March 9, 1857*, Assembly Document No. 205 (Albany, 1857); New York State Senate, *Report of the Select Committee Appointed to Investigate the Health Department of the City of New York, February 3, 1859*, Senate Document No. 49 (Albany, 1859).

Much of New York's social history has of course to be sought in the personal documents—the diaries and letters—of contemporaries. There are many such published and unpublished writings by New Yorkers during the first half of the nineteenth century. I found three to be particularly revealing. One was the diary of Philip Hone in the Manuscript Division of the New-York Historical Society. There are two published versions of this diary, neither of which is complete: *The Diary of Philip Hone, 1828–1851*, ed. by Allan Nevins (New York, 1936), and *The Diary of Philip Hone, 1828–1851*, ed. by Bayard Tuckerman (2 vols.; New York, 1889). Of equal importance are the letters of John Pintard, chosen for publication from the Pintard manuscripts also at the New-York Historical Society's Manuscript Division: John Pintard, *Letters from John Pintard to His Daughter, Eliza Noel Pintard Davidson, 1816–1833*, ed. by Dorothy C. Barck (4 vols.; New York, 1940). For an extremely revealing diary covering the later period of this dissertation, see: George Templeton Strong, *The Diary of George Templeton Strong*, ed. by Allan Nevins and Milton Halsey Thomas (4 vols.; New York, 1952).

There are, of course, scores of books and memoirs which shed light on the social history of nineteenth-century New York City. The prints, maps, photographs, and charts printed in Stokes, *Iconography*, provide a basic source for the physical description of New York City. Another valuable source is the series of highly detailed street maps prepared by William Perris and his son beginning in the 1850's for use by the fire insurance companies of New York: William Perris, *Maps of the City of New York. Surveyed under the Direction of the Insurance Companies of Said City* (34 vols.; New York, 1852–1881). For an interesting insight into everyday life in New York, see Thomas Farrington DeVoe, *The Market Book Containing a Historical Account of the Public Markets in the Cities of New York, Boston, Philadelphia and Brooklyn* (New York, 1862). See as well DeVoe, *The Market Assistant* (New York, 1867). There are also an abundance of guide books, city directories, and travel accounts describing New York during the first half of the nineteenth century. Stokes, *Iconography*, and Ernst, *Immigrant Life*, in their bibliographies provide useful references. The New-York

Historical Society and the New York Public Library both have excellent collections of such accounts and descriptions.

While general histories of the city are disappointing, there are a number of useful studies of specific aspects of pre-bellum New York. For the commercial and mercantile development of the city, see Robert Greenhalgh Albion, *The Rise of the Port of New York, 1815–1860* (New York, 1939). For interesting comments upon population growth, see suggestions made during a recent conference by Everett S. Lee and Michael Lalli, "Population," in *The Growth of the Seaport Cities, 1790–1825,* ed. by David T. Gilchrist (Charlottesville, Va., 1967), pp. 25–37. Still valuable is Adna Ferrin Weber's *The Growth of Cities in the Nineteenth Century* (New York, 1897). Sidney Pomerantz discusses the early history of the city in his detailed study: *New York: An American City, 1783–1803. A Study of Urban Life* (New York, 1938). Douglas T. Miller's recent study of social class in Jacksonian New York City is, however, somewhat disappointing: *Jacksonian Aristocracy. Class and Democracy in New York, 1830–1860* (New York, 1967). For a modern study of the city's police force in the nineteenth century see James F. Richardson, *The New York Police, Colonial Times to 1901* (New York, 1970).

For a discussion of social problems, especially of immigration and of slums, see, in addition to Ernst's *Immigrant Life:* Robert W. DeForest and Lawrence Veiller, eds., *The Tenement House Problem Including the Report of the New York State Tenement House Commission of 1900* (2 vols.; New York, 1903), and David M. Schneider, *The History of Public Welfare in New York State* (2 vols.; Chicago, 1938). Robert S. Pickett describes the care of juvenile delinquents and vagrant children in his recent book, *House of Refuge: Origins of Juvenile Reform in New York State 1815–1857* (Syracuse, New York, 1969). Raymond A. Mohl in "Poverty, Public Relief, and Private Charity in New York City, 1784–1825" (doctoral dissertation, New York University, 1967), discusses charity in New York City at the end of the eighteenth and the beginning of the nineteenth century. Unfortunately, I was not aware of the study before the completion of this manuscript. John Duffy's *A History of Public Health in New York City 1625–1866* (New York, 1968), is a thorough study of public health and medicine in the city. The notes in Gert H. Brieger, "Sanitary Reform in New York City: Stephen Smith and the Passage of the Metropolitan Health Bill," *Bulletin of the History of Medicine,* XL (1966), 407–429, provide an excellent guide to relevant medical and public health literature. For a slightly different approach to the problems of public health, based on a comparative analysis, see Charles Rosenberg, *The Cholera Years* (Chicago, 1962). Charles E. and Carroll S. Rosenberg attempt to analyze the relation of pietism and public health reform in "Pietism and the Origins of the American Public Health Movement: A Note on John H. Griscom and Robert M. Hartley," *Journal of the History of Medicine and Allied Sciences,* XXIII (1968), 16–35. Appeals for the reform of public health conditions often provide social analysis and criticism as well as extremely graphic descriptive material. See, for example: John H. Griscom, *A History, Chronological and Circumstantial, of the Visitation of Yellow Fever at New York* (New York, 1858), Griscom, *The Sanitary Condition of the Laboring Population of New York with Suggestions for its Improvement* (New York, 1845), and the Citizens' Association of New York, *Report of the Council of Hygiene and Public Health of the Citizens' Association of New York upon the Sanitary Condition of the City* (New York, 1865). For a discussion of secular reform movements in New York see Walter Hugins, *Jacksonian Democracy and the Working Class* (Stanford, California, 1960). Two rather old and somewhat disappointing biographies of Fanny Wright exist: W. R. Waterman, *Frances Wright* (New York, 1924), and Alice J. Perkins, *Frances Wright, Free Enquirer* (New York, 1939). For two modern studies of the relation of church, state, and education in New York see: John Webb Pratt, *Religion, Politics and Diver-*

sity: The Church-State Theme in New York History (Ithaca, New York, 1967), and Vincent P. Lannie, *Public Money and Parochial Education, Bishop Hughes, Governor Seward and the New York School Controversy* (Cleveland, 1968). For an application of the social control thesis to education see Michael Katz, *The Irony of Early School Reform: Educational Innovation in Mid-Nineteenth Century Massachusetts* (Cambridge, Mass., 1968).

Religion

The historian of American religion has two valuable bibliographical tools with which to lighten his labors. For all sources up until 1961, Nelson R. Burr's excellent bibliography covers in detail every aspect of American religion: *A Critical Bibliography of Religion in America*, Vol. IV, *Religion in American Life*, ed. by James Ward Smith and A. Leland Jamison (4 vols.; Princeton, 1961). *Church History* publishes extensive book reviews and summaries of doctoral dissertations in the field of church history, which, in conjunction with Burr, provide a relatively complete and current bibliography of American religion. The *American Quarterly*'s annual bibliography of books and articles in the field contains a section for American religion. In addition, Gaylord Albaugh recently published an extremely useful guide to Presbyterian newspapers and magazines, "American Presbyterian Periodicals and Newspapers 1752–1830, with Library Locations," which appeared in four installments in the *Presbyterian Historical Society Quarterly* beginning in September, 1963. William Buell Sprague, *Annals of the American Pulpit; or, Commemorative Notices of Distinguished American Clergymen of Various Denominations from the Early Settlement of the Country to the Close of the Year Eighteen Hundred and Fifty-Five* (9 vols.; New York, 1857–1869), records an impressive number of biographical sketches and reminiscences of prominent American clergymen. Its inclusiveness made Sprague's *Annals* particularly useful for this study.

The volumes are organized by denomination and thoroughly indexed.

Secondary studies of American religious thought, 1775–1860, which have been particularly useful include Sidney Mead's excellent intellectual biography of *Nathaniel William Taylor, 1786–1858: A Connecticut Liberal* (Chicago, 1942); William McLoughlin's insightful study of Charles Finney in *Modern Revivalism. Charles Grandison Finney to Billy Graham* (New York, 1959); and his "Introduction" to Charles Grandison Finney's *Lectures on Revivals of Religion,* ed. by William G. McLoughlin (Cambridge, Mass., 1960). McLoughlin not only discusses Finney but comments perceptively upon developments in American theology during the 1820's and 1830's. H. Shelton Smith's *Changing Conceptions of Original Sin. A Study in American Theology since 1750* (New York, 1955), provides a useful perspective in which to place some of the theological developments of these enthusiastic years. Still essential is Joseph Haroutunian's *Piety Versus Moralism. The Passing of the New England Theology* (New York, 1932). Barbara Cross in her introduction to the new edition of *The Autobiography of Lyman Beecher,* ed. by Barbara Cross (2 vols.; Cambridge, Mass., 1961), and in her biography of Horace Bushnell, *Horace Bushnell, Minister to a Changing America* (Chicago, 1958), has given us two very suggestive studies of the significantly contrasting theology and lives of two of the leading Protestant theologians of the first half of the nineteenth century. Whitney Cross, in his now classic *Burned-Over District. The Social and Intellectual History of Enthusiastic Religion in Western New York, 1800–1850* (Ithaca, New York, 1950), has studied in depth the social aspects of revivalistic religion in one geographic area and at one comparatively limited period in time. William Russell Hoyt's recent doctoral dissertation on Gardiner Spring, a central figure in the early development of New York's city missions, has been most helpful: "The Religious Thought of Gardiner Spring with Particular Reference to his Doctrine of Sin and Salvation" (unpublished

Ph.D. dissertation, Duke University, 1962). William Speer's highly pietistic account of the *Great Revival of 1800* (Philadelphia, 1872), provides much valuable information about a seldom studied though quite important phase of the Second Great Awakening. E. H. Gillett in his *History of the Presbyterian Church in the United States of America* (2 vols.; Philadelphia, 1864), includes details not otherwise available concerning individual ministers and specific churches.

There are a number of studies of English evangelism during the early years of the nineteenth century, especially of the Clapham Set. I found the most comprehensive and detailed to be that by Ford K. Brown, *Fathers of the Victorians. The Age of Wilberforce* (Cambridge, England, 1961). The standard sources for the study of Thomas Chalmers are the biography by his son-in-law, William Hanna, *Memoirs of the Life and Writings of Thomas Chalmers* (3 vols.; Edinburgh, 1852), and Thomas Chalmers, *The Works of Thomas Chalmers* (25 vols.; Glasgow, 1836–1849). For Chalmers' writings specifically concerning the distribution and purpose of charity, see excerpts of his major writings in *Chalmers on Charity: A Selection of Passages and Scenes to Illustrate the Social Teachings and Practical Work of Thomas Chalmers*, arranged and ed. by N. Masterman (Westminster, 1900).

The following studies describing the social dimensions of American Protestantism have been useful: Aaron Abel, *Urban Impact on American Protestantism, 1865–1900* (Cambridge, Mass., 1943); Ray Allen Billington, *The Protestant Crusade, 1800–1860: A Study of the Origins of American Nativism* (New York, 1938); John Bodo, *Protestant Clergy and Social Issues, 1812–1848* (Princeton, 1954); Clifford E. Griffin, *Their Brothers' Keepers. Moral Stewardship in the United States, 1800–1865* (New Brunswick, New Jersey, 1960); Charles C. Cole, Jr., *The Social Ideas of Northern Evangelists, 1826–1860* (New York, 1954); Charles I. Foster, *Errand of Mercy. The Evangelical United Front, 1790–1837* (Chapel Hill, North Carolina, 1960); Timothy L.

Smith, *Revivalism and Social Reform in Mid-Nineteenth Century America* (New York, 1957).

The amount of sermon and biographical material shedding light on the theological and social aspects of American Protestantism during this period is overwhelming. A few of the representative and influential primary sources which have been most useful to me are: Charles Grandison Finney, *Memoirs of Charles Grandison Finney Written by Himself* (New York, 1876); Gardiner Spring, *Personal Reminiscences of the Life and Times of Gardiner Spring, Pastor of the Brick Presbyterian Church in the City of New York* (2 vols.; New York, 1866). Spring includes significant information concerning the early evangelical movement as well as his own opinions of such controversial religious leaders as Lyman Beecher and Finney. Joanna Graham Bethune's *The Power of Faith: Exemplified in the Life and Writings of the Late Mrs. Isabella Graham of New York* (New York, 1816), not only sheds light on conservative Calvinist thought at the turn of the nineteenth century, but contains information about many of the local charities with which Mrs. Graham was connected (in particular the Society for the Relief of Poor Widows with Small Children). Samuel Hanson Cox in his *Interviews: Memorable and Useful from Diary and Memory Reproduced* (New York, 1853), describes conversations with some of the leading religious figures of the first half of the nineteenth century, including Thomas Chalmers. An early New York evangelical, Cox was closely associated with several pioneer city missions. For a history of American Protestantism written by a minister who was a leader of the city mission movement, see Samuel B. Halliday and Gregory Daniel Seely, *The Church in America and Its Baptisms of Fire. Being an Account of the Progress of Religion in America in the Eighteenth and Nineteenth Centuries, as seen in the Great Revivals in the Christian Church, and in the Growth and Work of Various Religious Bodies* (New York, 1896). John S. Stone's pious *Memoirs of the Life of James Milnor, D.D. Late Rector of St. George's Church, New York* (New York, 1849), consisting basically of excerpts from Milnor's diary, is a valuable source for a study of the "Low-Church" faction among New York Episcopalians. The New York Public Library has a microfilm copy of Anson G. Phelps' manuscript Diary, 1806–1807, 1816–1853, which is valuable for any study of religion and philanthropy during the first half of the nineteenth century. Biographies of other religious and philanthropic leaders connected with particular missions are cited in the appropriate chapters.

The sermon and pamphlet literature related to the evangelical mission movement is sometimes difficult to locate. The libraries of Union Theological Seminary, New York Public Library, New-York Historical Society, Presbyterian Historical Society, and for Episcopal material, General Theological Seminary all possess excellent collections of such materials.

Church histories contain much interesting material for both social and theological history. Some of the most useful in preparing this study include: Morgan Dix, *A History of the Parish of Trinity Church in the City of New York; Compiled by Order of the Corporation, and Edited by Morgan Dix* (4 vols.; New York, 1898–1906); Shepherd Knapp, *A History of the Brick Presbyterian Church in the City of New York* (New York, 1909), which contains valuable institutional history as well as a useful biographical sketch of Gardiner Spring; William Rhinelander Stewart, *Grace Church and Old New York* (New York, 1924); two studies of the Broadway Tabernacle and the origins of the Congregational Church in New York City, Susan Hayes Ward, *The History of the Broadway Tabernacle Church from its Organization in 1840 to the close of 1900 Including Factors Influencing its Formulation* (New York, 1901), and L. Nelson Nichols, *History of the Broadway Tabernacle of New York City* (New Haven, 1940); Henry Anstice, *History of St. George's Church in the City of New York. 1752–1811–1911* (New York, 1911), which is a good source for the early history of the Episcopal Church in New York City, especially of the "Low-Church" faction; and finally, John P. Peters, *Annals of*

St. Michaels, Being the History of St. Michael's Protestant Episcopal Church, New York, for One Hundred Years, 1807–1907, Compiled by Order of the Vestry (New York, 1907), which is invaluable to a study of nineteenth-century Episcopal philanthropy.

Early New York Secular and Religious Charities

Beginning with the years immediately following the Revolution, New Yorkers founded a number of long-lived charities. Lists of these early charities can be found in any early guide book. Biographies exist for a number of New Yorkers most active in these charities. These include: John H. Griscom, *Memoir of John Griscom, with an Account of the New York High School, Society for the Prevention of Pauperism and Other Institutions Compiled from an Autobiography and Other Sources* (New York, 1859). This memoir is a valuable survey of early New York philanthropy. It is interestingly supplemented by John Griscom's own diary of his travels: *A Year in Europe Comprising a Journal of Conversations in England, Scotland, Ireland, France, Switzerland, the North of Italy, and Holland in 1818–1819* (2 vols.; New York, 1823). Samuel L. Knapp's *Life of Thomas Eddy, Comprising an Extensive Corrrespondence with Many of the Most Distinguished Philosophers and Philanthropists of this and Other Countries* (New York, 1834), consists essentially of excerpts from Eddy's diary and correspondence. It describes in detail the philanthropic career of an actively benevolent Quaker from the 1780's into the 1820's. Charles G. Sommers presents a very useful study of one of the most active of New York's early philanthropists in his *Memoir of the Rev. John Stanford, D.D. Late Chaplain to the Humane and Criminal Institutions in the City of New York* (New York, 1835). Sommers relies heavily upon Stanford's diary, which is deposited in the Manuscript Division of the New-York Historical Society. Charles H. Hunt in his opening chapters of *The Life of Edward Livingston* (New York, 1864), discusses the ideas and actions of this highly imaginative and socially conscious New York mayor.

A number of studies of the early charities exist. See, for example: Charles C. Andrews, *The History of the New York African Free Schools from their Establishment in 1787 to the Present Time* (New York, 1830); William Oland Bourne, *A History of the Public School Society of the City of New York* (New York, 1870); B. K. Pierce, *A Half Century with Juvenile Delinquents; or, The New York House of Refuge and its Times* (New York, 1869); Edwin W. Rice, *The Sunday School Movement 1780 to 1917, and the Sunday School Union 1817 to 1917* (Philadelphia, 1917).

The publications of the city missions discussed in this study are referred to in detail in footnotes of the chapters dealing with them. The New York Public Library, the New-York Historical Society, the Presbyterian Historical Society in Philadelphia, and the libraries of the Union Theological Seminary and General Theological Seminary (Protestant Episcopal Church), both in New York, contain virtually all the annual reports, journals, and other publications of these societies. The manuscript records of the societies remain on the other hand in the possession of the societies themselves. For a detailed listing of the printed and manuscript records see Rosenberg, "Evangelism and the Rise of the New City," unpublished Ph.D. thesis, Columbia University, 1968.

The New York Public Library, the New-York Historical Society, Union Theological Seminary, the Historical Society of Pennsylvania and the Presbyterian Historical Society all have excellent pamphlet collections which include the annual reports of a number of shorter lived urban philanthropies.

✦✦✦✦✦✦✦✦✦✦✦

Index

Religion and the Rise
of the American City

Designed by R. E. Rosenbaum.
Composed by Vail-Ballou Press, Inc.,
in 11 point linotype Janson, 3 points leaded,
with display lines in monotype Janson.
Printed letterpress from type by Vail-Ballou Press
on Warren's 1854 Text. 60 lb. basis
with the Cornell University Press watermark.
Bound by Vail-Ballou Press
in Interlaken ALP book cloth
and stamped in All Purpose foil.

17762

Rosenberg, Carroll
Smith.

BV
2805
N5
R68
1971

Religion and the
rise of the
American city

DATE			
DEC 20 '85			